T0157687

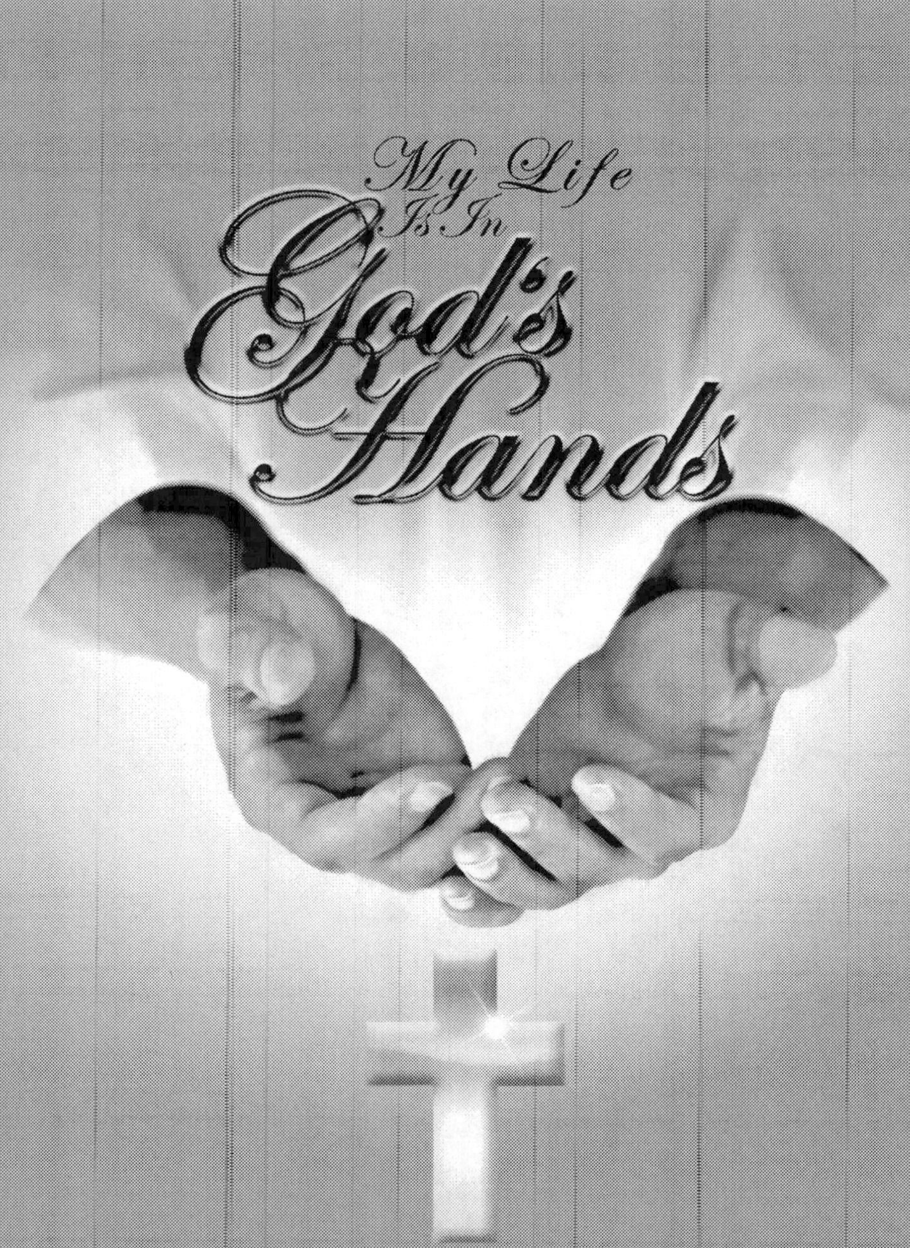
My Life
Is In
God's
Hands
The Autobiography of Shereice Garrett

Order this book online at www.trafford.com
or email orders@trafford.com

Most Trafford titles are also available at major online book retailers.

Printed in the United States of America.

ISBN: 978-1-4669-1532-9 (sc)
ISBN: 978-1-4669-1533-6 (e)

Trafford rev. 05/15/2012

www.trafford.com

North America & international
toll-free: 1 888 232 4444 (USA & Canada)
phone: 250 383 6864 • fax: 812 355 4082

Scripture quotations were also taken from www.biblegateway.com/passage

The excerpt taken from the poem "Footprints" was taken from "Footprints 3 versions" http://www.wowzone.com/fprints.htm

Medical information was taken from http://www.cigna.com/healthinfo/hard989.html

My Life Is In God's Hands: The Autobiography of Shereice Garrett

Table of Contents

Dedication ix
Introduction xi
Chapter 1: Early Years 1
Chapter 2: Maranatha Christian Academy 9
Chapter 3: Another Sister 13
Chapter 4: It's Time to Say Goodbye 19
Chapter 5: A Whole New World 24
Chapter 6: These Are the Things That Make Us Stronger 36
Chapter 7: A Change of Plans 54
Chapter 8: Tests and Trials 62
Chapter 9: A New Century, A New Beginning 71
Chapter 10: Miracles 93
Chapter 11: Another Answered Prayer 111
Chapter 12: New Beginnings 129
Chapter 13: A Step In The Right Direction 155
Chapter 14: My Life Is In God's Hands 170
Chapter 15: A Year to Love 176
Chapter 16: "Say What?" 187
Chapter 17: Precious Gifts 205
Chapter 18: One Year Old 217
Conclusion 221
Epilogue 225

Dedication

THIS BOOK IS DEDICATED TO THE LATE

DR. MARGARET T. G. BURROUGHS

THANK YOU FOR YOUR KIND WORDS, GUIDANCE AND INSPIRATION.
WITHOUT YOU, THIS BOOK WOULD NEVER HAVE BEEN COMPLETED.
THANK YOU FOR YOUR HONEST FEEDBACK.

THIS BOOK IS ALSO DEDICATED TO ONE OF MY SPIRITUAL MOTHERS,

MRS. DORIS J. MERRILL.

YOUR COUNTLESS HOURS OF EXPERTISE, IN AND OUT OF THE CLASSROOM, AND LOVE HELPED PUT THE FINISHING TOUCHES ON MY BOOK.
THANK YOU FOR EVERYTHING BEYOND THE PAGES OF THIS BOOK.

THIS BOOK IS ALSO DEDICATED TO ONE OF MY SISTERS IN SPIRIT,

MRS. DEIRDRE JACKSON JONES,

ALTHOUGH I HAVE ONLY KNOW YOU FOR OVER SEVEN YEARS, I FEEL LIKE I HAVE KNOWN YOU FOR A LIFETIME. THANK YOU FOR STANDING IN AGREEMENTWITH ME ON THE VISION. THANK YOU FOR NEVER BEING AFRAID TO

BE HONEST WITH ME. THANK YOU FOR EVERYTHING. I HAVEN'T FORGETTEN ABOUT THE ICE CREAM. ☺

THIS BOOK IS ALSO DEDICATED
TO MY PATERNAL GRANDMOTHER,

LORENER GARRETT.

WHO HAS ALWAYS BEEN A SOURCE OF STRENGTH FOR ME, I KNOW I COULD ALWAYS COME TO YOU ABOUT ANYTHING GRANNIE. I LOVE YOU. THANK YOU FOR YOUR HONESTY, NO MATTER HOW RAW. ☺

AND TO MY PARENTS,

REV. JOSEPH AND ROSA GARRETT

THANK YOU FOR NEVER GIVING UP, EVEN WHEN THE ROAD WAS ROUGH AND UNCERTAIN. I WILL ALWAYS LOVE YOU.

AND TO EVERY SISTER, BROTHER, AUNT, UNCLE, COUSIN, FRIEND, NEIGHBOR, SPIRITUAL ADVISOR, AND ANYONE ELSE I DID NOT NAME SPECIFICALLY, THERE IS NOT ENOUGH INK TO NAME EVERY INDIVIDUAL WHO HAVE BLESSED MY LIFE BUT DO KNOW YOUR ACTIONS AND LOVE NEVER WENT UNNOTICED. THANK YOU FROM THE BOTTOM OF MY HEART. I LOVE YOU ALL.

"For I know the plans I have for you, declares the Lord, 'plans to prosper you and not harm you, plans to give you hope and a future."

Jeremiah 29:11 (NIV)

Introduction

When one thinks about their life, many things come to mind. Family . . . friends . . . home . . . career goals . . . economic goals . . . other aspirations . . . and things to do for fun, just to name a few. Never does one think of pain, doctor's appointments, medications, diagnoses, death, numerous hospitalizations, surgeries or, counting the days one stays home, without getting sick or being hospitalized. Of course, that is, unless your name is Shereice Garrett. These are the things that have become the basis for what I call my life. However I am not upset, sad or even depressed about them. Why? I was taught a long time ago, as well as, reminded numerous times; these are the things that make us stronger. My faith in God plays a vital role in maintaining my sanity. I was taught a long time ago, God will never put more on us than we can bear. God gives us His holy word, the bible, for guidance. He also places people in our lives to balance us out. By this I mean, these people are a help to us but we may also be a help to them. Because God has blessed me with so many wonderful people in my life, my heart longs to make mention of all of you but some names have been purposely omitted and changed out of respect for their privacy because I will be forever grateful for their presence in my life.

"I can do all things through Christ who strengtheneth me."
Philippians 4:13 (KJV)

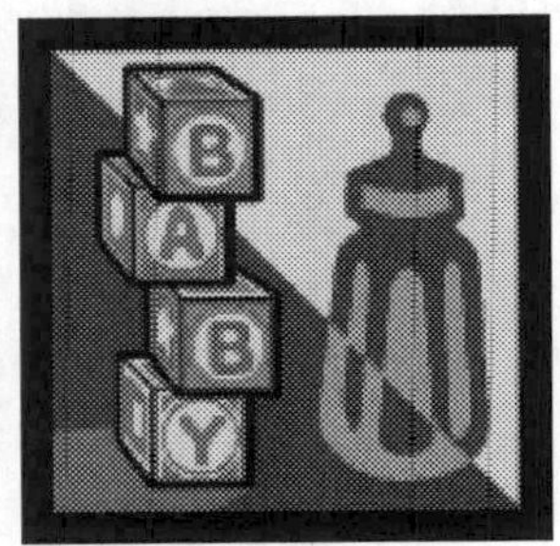

Chapter 1: Early Years

I was born on September 5, 1977 at Roseland Community Hospital in Chicago, Illinois. My father's name is Joseph Jr. He worked for Chicago Norwest Railroad as a technician, at the time. My mother's name is Rosa. She worked at Chicago Osteopathic Hospital, at the time. I was the youngest of three children, in my household, all of whom were girls. My oldest sister name is Netta. At the time of my birth, she was seven years old. My second oldest sister is Sha. She was six years old at the time of my birth.

At birth, I weighed six pounds, eleven ounces and had a head full of hair. Many people commented including family and friends, I had as much hair as an average two year old. At three months old, while on a routine doctor's visit, doctors felt there was something abnormal with the size of my head. I was referred to other specialists who confirmed the doctor's suspicion. Over the next ten months, I was admitted in and out of the hospital for a series of tests. Hospital stays ranged from three days to thirty days. Upon completion of these tests, I was diagnosed with an ***arachnoid cyst on the cerebellum with ventricular hydrocephalus.***

"Arachnoid cysts are fluid-filled sacs that occur on the arachnoid membrane that covers the brain (intracranial) and the spinal cord (spinal). There are 3 membranes covering these components on

the central nervous system: durra mater, arachnoid, and pia mater. Arachnoid cysts appear on the arachnoid membrane and they may also expand into the space between the pia mater and arachnoid membranes (subarachnoid space). The most common locations for intracranial arachnoid cyst are the middle fossa (near the temporal lobe), the supracellar region (near the third ventricle) and the posterior fossa, which contains the cerebellum, pons, and medulla oblongata.

. . . common symptoms are headaches, seizures and abdominal accumulation of excessive cerebrospinal fluid in the brain (hydrocephalus)."

http://www.cigna.com/healthinfo/hard989.html

It was decided that there was a need for surgery. During surgery doctors placed a VP (ventricular peritoneal) shunt in my head to drain the excess fluid from my brain. The surgery was successful. However, all of my hair had to be cut off for the surgery and I was reduced to being a bald head baby girl.

My earliest childhood memories are those of my uncle Mat and my very first school, Community Day Care Center. My uncle Mat was the youngest boy in a family of seven children, two girls and five boys, on my father's side of the family. During my early childhood years, my uncle Mat lived with my family. I loved him so much and it wasn't just because he spoiled me. Uncle Mat was a wonderful caterer who had a flair for fashion and hair. He loved dressing me up, making my hair pretty and, taking me places with him. He always protected me. In his eyes, I could do no wrong. When I wasn't with my parents, I felt safe with my uncle Mat.

The school, which began to set the foundation of my education and life, was Community Day Care Center, now called Community Learning Center on Chicago's south side. The director was Ms. Robinson, who everyone affectionately called Mommy Anna. My kindergarten teacher was Mrs.

Johnson, who everyone affectionately called Mommy Johnson. In addition to the developmental skills they taught me, they also showed me love and understanding regarding a childhood problem that plagued me. I dealt with heavy incontinence for all of my childhood. Instead of making a big issue of it, I can remember them being discreet about it when helping me get cleaned up, whenever it occurred. What these two women did for me, will have their memories ingrained in my heart and mind for as long as I live. As I graduated from kindergarten, I can remember feeling nervous and sad. These were the women who set the foundation for me. How would anyone measure up to them?

Throughout grammar school, my parents kept me in private school. They were still nervous about my health and felt that private school would do a better job of watching over me, as well as, provide me with a quality education. For the next three years, I attended Mount Calvary Christian Academy located 1257 West 111th Street on Chicago's south side. My God-sister, Ena, also attended Mount Calvary. We were two years apart in age and grade. The differences between us weren't important because we did a lot together. During this time, Ena practically lived with our family because she lived with her grandmother, who worked away from her home during the week. On weekends, she went home with her grandmother.

At the tender age of eight, I accepted Christ into my life and was baptized. Ena was six. She also accepted Christ in her life and was baptized. I became a member of True Right Missionary Baptist Church, located 311 East 95th Street on Chicago's south side. At the time, my pastor was Rev. Willie J. Murphy. I loved my church family. They were like my extended family. My best friend, Donyiel, at the time, attended this church as well. We sung in the Junior Choir together.

Sundays were special in our family. We got up early Sunday mornings and while we got ready for church, we listened to KKC. If for some reason we didn't listen to KKC, we listened to WGCI with Jackie Hasselrigg. I could remember my sister Sha loved Father Hayes and Cosmopolitan Church, "Jesus Can Work It Out." That was my sister's song. Sha would stop whatever she was doing and ". . . turned it over to the Lord and He worked it out . . ." She knew that song forwards and backwards. She always sung lead and Netta and I was always the choir. You didn't have a choice back then; everyone got up on Sunday mornings and went to church together. My father always quoted Joshua, placing emphasis on the last part of that scripture.

"And if it seems evil unto you to serve the LORD, choose you this day whom ye will serve; whether the gods which your fathers served that were on the other side of the flood, or the gods of the Amorites, in whose land ye dwell: BUT AS FOR ME AND MY HOUSE, WE WILL SERVE THE LORD."

Joshua 24:15 (KJV)

King James Version (**KJV**) Public Domain
www.biblegateway.com/passage

Just about my entire family was involved with activities at church. My father was in the Inspirational Mass Choir (he was also an ordained deacon until God called him further into the ministry and he became an ordained minister). He was a tenor. I have to admit, I enjoyed listening to my father sing. One of my favorite songs to hear him lead was "In My Veins." I also enjoyed listening to Daddy lead "Jesus Is Mine." My sister Netta also sung in the Mass Choir for a while. Sha was on the Junior Usher Board. The Inspirational Mass Choir had some wonderful voices in the choir. Willette, Daphne, Valerie, Momma Tucker, and my daddy, just to name a few. Then there was Emma Q. She came in the church praising God and left out the church praising God. She would dance from one end of the church to the other end and never fall, trip or miss a step.

Sunday dinners were usually full and plentiful. Momma sometimes began cooking Saturday night or early Sunday morning before we went to church, except those Sundays when there wasn't enough time for a big dinner because we were hurrying back to church for the afternoon musicals. Back then the Inspirational Mass Choir had monthly musicals that were held on the 2nd Sunday afternoon at 3:00pm. Those Sundays were full. My family and I would get up and go to morning service and come back home for dinner. Usually, because we were trying to hurry back to the musical, dinner was Kentucky Fried Chicken (thanks for the reminder Sha and Netta☺). We would then hurry back to church for the choir musicals. Those musicals were always spirit-filled and enjoyable.

One of the things I enjoyed growing up in True Right was "Homecoming Musical." The Inspirational Mass choir had "Homecoming Musical" every few years. Those musicals were awesome. Almost all of the old members, who moved on and were no longer members of the church, would come back for this special evening. Former members, as well as, current members of the choir would unite and sing together on this special Sunday. Junior Choir members also sung in the Homecoming choir. Rehearsals were usually held once a week, for several weeks, leading up to the big Sunday. On Homecoming Sunday, Rev. Murphy usually tried to get us out of morning service earlier than usual. We rushed home, ate a quick dinner and, hurried back to church. If you wanted a good seat, you had to be back at church at least one hour before the musical started. The parking lots were always packed to capacity on that Sunday. Attendees who weren't able to park in the parking lot usually parked somewhere on 95th Street or on the side streets parallel to the church. The sanctuary was packed. Folding chairs would have to be placed throughout the sanctuary to accommodate everyone, without being a fire hazard. Everyone enjoyed the Homecoming musicals so much; video tapes were made available of the service.

I enjoyed the activities I was involved in at church. When I was younger, I had a slight case of stage fright. Being a member of the choir helped calm that nervousness, although it would take several more years to be fully free of that fear. One of the reasons the junior choir worked so well was because of our director, Rev. Scott. She loved the Lord and it was evident when she spoke, played the piano and/or directed the choir. Rev. Scott often had us memorize bible verses because she believed although we were young, we still needed to understand what we were singing about. One of the first bible verses I memorized as a member of the choir was **Philippians 4:13.**

"I can do all things through Christ who strengtheneth me."
(KJV)

This scripture, I would later learn, would have a major impact on the thing I attempted and did accomplish in life.

Around this time, my best friend Donyiel, and I were practically inseparable. We did a lot of things together. Donyiel and her family was one of the few people whose house I visited and my parents didn't mind. At that time, I didn't ever think the bond we shared would ever be broken. Donyiel's parents treated me like one of their own. They were also very understanding of my bladder problem and didn't make a huge deal about the few occasions my incontinence was active. Donyiel's mother was like another mother to me. Over time I started calling her Momma.

Donyiel did as well, sometimes even better, than me in school. As I was coming to the end of the school year in third grade, I received some very good news. Donyiel, who was one year behind me in age and grade, would be allowed to skip a grade which meant we would both be in the fourth grade.

My parents were always concerned about my well-being. Whenever I became sick, it was their love and concern, along with the doctor's care, that speeded the recovery process. For example, my tonsils became swollen and infected. I was given the penicillin shot when my parents took me to the doctor. Unfortunately, by the next day, my neck and tonsils were twice the size they were when I went to the doctor. I was immediately hospitalized. Because I was only nine years old, I did not understand what was happening to me or why I had to stay in the hospital.

My mother made these times easier to cope with and understand. Throughout the duration of my hospitalization, my mother never left my side. She ate with me. She bathed me daily. When it was time to sleep, my mother made sure I was comfortable and proceeded to sleep upright in a very uncomfortable chair. To this day, I still do not understand how she did it the entire time I was in the hospital but, I am forever thankful to God and my mother that she chose to do it.

My parents felt they should get quality if they paid for quality. As a result, whenever my parents became unimpressed with the quality of the school I attended, they transferred me to another school. My parents transferred me to Richard Daniel Henton Academy when I entered fifth grade. By this time, Ena had started going through some changes which resulted in her grandmother transferring her into public school. These changes also caused friction in our relationship sometimes. However, I never gave up on Ena. She is my God-sister and I love her very much. I will always love her. I just prayed that God would continue to cover her with His precious blood.

Around this time we received another blessing and addition to our family. Ena has a younger sister name Whitney, like the singer. Whitney was lovable from the start. When she was first born, my family fell in love with her from the start. Over time, my parents made an arrangement with her mother that entailed my parents keeping Whitney on the weekends. Over time, Whitney and Ena's mother did a selfless act. When she realized she could not properly care for Whitney, my parents became Whitney's legal guardians. I was no longer the baby and everyone made sure I knew it. That is not to say I was being neglected, I just wasn't receiving the same attention I had become accustomed to receiving.

While attending Richard Daniel Henton Academy, my teacher was Ms. Calhoun. I will never forget this woman. She had spunk. She enjoyed teaching and it was exhibited in what she did. Another thing was Ms. Calhoun and I had two special things in common. We were both left-handed. We also loved the color purple. This came in handy because my daddy enjoyed making jokes about me being left-handed, a quality I inherited from my mother. I don't think he fully understood how much that irritated my nerves when he made those jokes. My father viewed left-handed people as being backwards. He told me this was a right-handed world and the only way to survive was to be right-handed. Ms. Calhoun always encouraged me. I can remember her teaching me that God made everyone unique and in His image. Just because I was left-handed didn't mean anything negative. She told me to ignore anyone who told me different. I worked very hard and it paid off. I didn't make the honor roll that year, as I had previous years, but my grades were still very good and I came very close.

For the most part, I got along well with my classmates at Henton. Among them was my friend Sharice. I will be forever grateful to Ms. Calhoun for introducing me to her. With the exception of the typical childhood disagreements, we got along very well. She was the first person who I met with the same name as me. It was ironic. There were three of us, with the same name, in the school, all with completely different ways of spelling our names. To differentiate between us, Ms. Calhoun, as well as many others, referred to us by our last names. There was also Kevin. He was very quiet and soft-spoken. He was also extremely pleasant when he spoke. There was also Timothy. We spoke to one another but it wasn't until my college years I realized how much of a blessing he was, and still is, in my life. This school year ran smoothly. Momma dropped me off, as well as, picked me up from school. Then she dropped Whitney off at Grannie's house, before proceeding to work. Back then, daddy had to be at work very early so he couldn't take me to school. Unfortunately, this school closed as the next school year began so I had to transfer to another school.

*"Train up a child in the way he should go:
and when he is old, he will not depart from it."*
Proverbs 22:6 (KJV)

Chapter 2:
Maranatha Christian Academy

My remaining three years of grammar school was spent at Maranatha Christian Academy located at 115 West 108th Street, also on Chicago's south side. This school was probably the smallest school I ever attended. This school also set the foundation for what I thought to be my future career plans. I was nervous when I first began attending classes. This school was definitely smaller than Henton. Another difference was beginning in the 4th grade, students switched classes. This was a new experience I would have to get accustomed to. I enjoyed all of my teachers except my 6th grade homeroom teacher. He did not know how to communicate with students unless he was hollering. I did not disrespect him. I just told my mother so she could talk to him.

Because I got dropped off early, I sat in the cafeteria (as everyone did) until the bell rang, indicating the start of classes. It was during this time I met Mrs. Love. Mrs. Love was in charge of the breakfast program, as well as, taught the kindergarten class. She had such a soft, Godly demeanor about her. Her love and faith in God was evident in all she did. One morning I asked Mrs. Love if I could assist her with the breakfast program. This began a wonderful relationship of mentor and mentee. As she taught me the ropes of the breakfast program, she also taught me many things about the bible. I first fully understood the significance of tithing from the teachings of Mrs. Love.

"Bring ye all the tithes into the storehouse, that there may be meat in mine house, and prove me now herewith, saith the Lord of hosts, if I will not open you the windows of heaven, and pour you out a blessing, that there should not be room enough to receive it"

Malachi 3:10 (KJV)

The preschool class was taught by Ms. Lee that year. I enjoyed watching Ms. Lee work with the children. I also assisted Ms. Lee by sitting with the children during prayer. The teachers began each school day by coming together and having prayer, prior to the start of classes. It was during that year that I decided that not only did I want to become a teacher, but I wanted to pursue a career in early childhood education. Ms. Lee and Mrs. Love made teaching 3-5 year olds look very enjoyable.

During this year, I continued to sing in the children's choir at church, as I did since the age of eight. The choir was now under a new director, Mrs. Anderson. She also loved God and worked well with the choir. During this time, the choir had regular skating parties. Daddy surprised me as he attended many of these parties. He knew how to skate pretty well. On one of the last skating parties I attended, Ena and one of our other friends came along. Everyone enjoyed themselves tremendously. I skated on the carpet because I didn't know how to skate very well, and was therefore, afraid to skate on the rink floor. All at once, I heard someone scream my name in caution. It was one of my friends and she was coming straight toward me, unable to stop. She grabbed my shoulders so she could stop. When she let go of me, I fell and hurt my ankle. By the end of the evening, my ankle was swollen.

My parents didn't attend that skating party so we rode the bus back to the church. When my mom saw me, she just shook her head. My mom took me to the emergency room. Needless to say, I had broken my ankle in two places. I had to wear a cast for two months. Fearing for my safety because of the balance problems I endured as a result of my diagnosis at birth, my mother kept me home for the majority of this time. In order not to fall behind in my classes my mother regularly went up to the school to turn in my work and pick up more. Towards the end of the year, my principal, offered me the opportunity to volunteer in the summer school program. I got permission from my mother.

For most of the time my principal asked me to assist the preschool teacher. This gave me a wonderful opportunity to learn more vital skills needed for teaching young children. I loved working with the children in her class. More importantly, I loved noticing the changes these children made from the beginning to the end of the program and knowing I had something to do with it. It was during this time, Whitney began attending Maranatha. She was also in the preschool class. I enjoyed watching the changes Whitney made over the summer.

It was during this summer school session I met Mrs. Harris. She taught the 1st grade class for the first half of the day and then left. I assisted the afternoon teacher with her students. Because I came up to her class almost one-half hour prior to her leaving, I got to know Mrs. Harris. I enjoyed being around her because she was a very pleasant person to be around. The more I talked to her, the more I learned from her.

Mrs. Harris was very young compared to some of the other teachers in the school, at the time. Mrs. Harris loved the Lord and her Christian attributes stuck out as she communicated with and taught her students. Because Mrs. Harris was pregnant, and her due date was rapidly approaching, she would not be returning to Maranatha the following school year. However, during our time together at Maranatha, we had become friends. Neither one of us wanted that friendship to end. Therefore we exchanged contact information so we could remain in touch with one another. At that time, I wouldn't have imagined the impact she would have on my life. I had gained another friend and her name was Michelle.

The year was 1989. On the home front, Netta had become pregnant with her first child. As a family we tried to make the best of the situation but it was very hard. She always wanted to be her own person and do whatever she wanted. Netta did not like to listen to what others tried to tell her. As a result, Netta was always in conflict with the family, especially my parents. My parents did what they could to make the best of the situation.

Christmas that year was stressful. Netta was past due and not even close to being in labor. My parents were taking her back and forth to the hospital. Finally after a very long and strenuous three-day ordeal, my sister gave birth to a handsome baby boy on December 26, 1989. Due to complications that arose from Netta being in labor so long, Lavare had to remain in the hospital for a while before he was allowed to come home.

During these times, I found myself praying and reading my bible for comfort. The one time I was allowed to visit Lavare in the hospital was very hard on me. He looked so precious. I hated seeing him connected to all those tubes and machines. I must admit I was somewhat mad at Netta because I felt that if she would have taken better care of herself, Lavare would not have been as sickly.

When Lavare was allowed to come home, he was very small and frail. Months passed before I was able to hold him. He was on numerous medications, some of which made him swell up. Natta's behavior worsened. She was dating a guy who did not appear to like Lavare.

These experiences only reiterated how I always felt about myself. As an adult, I planned to place God first in my life. I would then set priorities so I would not forget who or what was important in my life.

"The Lord is my shepherd. I shall not want.
He maketh me to lie down in green pastures;
He leadeth me besides the still waters.
He restoresth my soul; he leadeth me in the paths of righteousness for his name's sake.
Yea, though I walk through the valley of the shadow of death, I will fear no evil for thou art with me,
thy rod and thy staff they comfort me.
Thou prepareth a table before me
in the presence of mine enemies: thou anointest my head with oil; my cup runneth over.
Surely goodness and mercy shall follow me
all the days of my life.
I will dwell in the house of the Lord forever."

Psalms 23 (KJV)

Chapter 3: Another Sister

While growing up, my sisters always made remarks of me having another sister I didn't know. I never believed them because they only made these remarks when they were upset with Daddy. I eventually found a picture that proved they were telling the truth. I was never told any information about her. I had concluded I would just look for her when I became an adult and try to make some sense of the situation. As usual, God had another plan. Around the summer prior to the start of seventh grade, my father called my sisters and myself into the room together. It was at that time, he finally said we (or rather I) had another sister named LaKita. She is five years older than me.

On the evening I met LaKita, for the first time, she was home visiting her mother and sister. My brother Don was also visiting. He stayed with us during his visit. He lived in Indiana but I had met him some time ago when he became ill and we went to Indiana to visit him in the hospital. On the evening I met LaKita, we went out to dinner. Prior to dinner, we stopped by LaKita's mother house so she could get her older sister. When I first saw LaKita, I knew she was my sister. She looked just like me, or should I say, I looked just like her, since she is older than me. I was so overwhelmed. I thought I was going to be sick. The wheels in my head were beginning to turn. Some remarks my older sisters made whenever they got mad at my father in the past were turning out to be true.

LaKita is a beautiful woman of God. She has a beautiful singing voice. When she was younger, LaKita sang with the Soul Children of Chicago. Now she attended Hampton University in Hampton, Virginia. Before going home, after dinner, we exchanged contact information so we could keep in touch. Sha and Netta were not as enthusiastic as I was about keeping in touch with LaKita. It didn't matter to me, it had taken me too long to get hold of the truth and I was not about to let go now that she was standing in front of my face.

Truth be told, neither the intended participants nor the dinner went like it was suppose to. As a result, many hearts left that dinner happy and many hearts left that dinner hurt that night. It would take a very long time for those hearts that were hurt to heal, if those hearts that were hurt ever healed at all.

I couldn't wait to get home. I had to talk to someone. I needed to talk to someone. I needed to talk to my Grannie.

Thank God for my Grannie. She has always been a pillar of strength for me. She has always been someone I could talk to. She was the first person I called to gain some understanding and peace of mind about my day. She only remarked on the statements I made and gave me no additional information. I would find out the full truth a few months later. As mad as I was about how the truth was revealed to me, God always reminded me of Psalms 23, one of my favorite scriptures. I repetitively read that scripture for comfort. My journal I kept was on fire. I had to find a positive way of releasing my feelings. My journal became my outlet.

Before LaKita left to go back to school, she promised to keep in touch and she did. In the beginning communication between LaKita and I was slow. I found that LaKita didn't always answer my letters as quickly as I sent them. To make myself feel better about the situation I would often tell myself that her schedule prohibited her from writing as often as me. I also knew that I could not have a full course meal without doing something to make it happen. That is to say, I knew what I was getting myself into when I first started building a relationship with my sister. There were still many scars that had not healed completely. She was still hurt by my father's presence, or lack thereof, in her life.

Our relationship did eventually start to blossom. We grew to love one another very much. I began to find some peace of mind I needed. Thank you Lord. Over time I began calling her "KITA", for short. Each time she came home for break, we made it our point to get together. We also shared a special interest. We both loved Walt Disney movies. We started a tradition that entailed each time Kita returned home, we went to the theatre to see the new Disney movie playing. The first movie, which is also my favorite movie, we went to see together was "Beauty and the Beast."

Another common interest Kita and I shared was that we are both goal-oriented. Kita was in school to become a Speech-Language Pathologist. Kita loved her field. It was evident when she described what it entailed. Up until that point, I had never heard of that field. Now, because of Kita, I understood what it entailed. At that point, I did not realize how her field would be so important to my well being in the future. I always dreamed of becoming a preschool teacher. I wanted to specialize in working with children between the ages of 5 years old and younger. Helping Ms. Lee and Ms. Brown had a huge impact on my dreams. I will be forever grateful to my principal at Maranatha for giving me the opportunity. Mrs. Harris is another blessing from Maranatha that extends beyond the classroom.

When Kita came home for breaks I spent the night with her, at her mother's house. These times were very special to me. It was during these sleep-overs, I learned a lot about Kita. She has an eye for coordinating. She enjoyed reading some of the same type of literature as I enjoy reading. Her faith in God was strong. The only negative part was her feelings toward our daddy. He not having a continued presence in her life hurt her a lot.

Kita was not the only person affected. This also affected me. I was upset and hurt that my parents lied to me on the one occasion I was courageous enough to ask them about the truth of the matter, when I was younger. I needed to know the full truth. I knew one plus one always equaled two. Now I just needed it confirmed. During one of our sleep-overs, I asked Kita to confirm the truth regarding Netta and Sha. I must admit, by the time I got home I was upset with my parents. My mother had my father talk to me. Once again, he dealt with the issue by placing blame on someone else. I can't say I was surprised by his response. At that point however, I temporarily saw my daddy differently and I didn't like what I saw. I realize during earlier times, parents didn't divulge information to their children like they do in today's society. I understand that factor fully. It just felt like I was being slapped in the face when I learned the full truth of the situation. As I grew older and matured, I forgave my parents because just like when they took care of my medical needs, in this situation they were acting under their best judgment.

Once again Grannie was very supportive. She has always been someone I could rely on. She was the one support system that never altered herself. I love my Grannie very much. My good friends, and even some family members, laugh at me sometime because of my relationship with my grannie. When my daddy started commenting on my relationship with Grannie at church, some people at True Right embraced me even more. One unique thing about our relationship is that Grannie always seemed to know when I was ill or something was wrong before I or anyone else said anything to her about me.

There was (and still is) a lot of healing that need to take place. That is not to say I was or I am taking sides. How could I? I was not there to witness anything. Therefore it is not my place to say who is right and who is wrong. God know who is right and who is wrong. Now it is up to all the parties involved to be honest with themselves so some real forgiveness and healing can take place before it's too late.

In the later part of 1989, Sha and I were sitting around talking. My mother came in the room and without hesitation said, "I'm pregnant." Did I just hear her correctly? I immediately responded, before I could stop myself, "You're lying." Unfortunately and fortunately my mother was pregnant.

It seemed like immediately after she told us, things went downhill for my mother. My mother began having severe complications with her pregnancy. Regardless of how bad things got, she never thought about getting rid of her baby. She vomited frequently. My mother lost so much weight she was as small as Sha. Sha was always the smallest adult in the family. She stayed that way until she turned 40 years old and that's when she started gaining weight. My mother could not tolerate food and she was very weak. Seeing my mother like that frightened me greatly. I had never seen my mother so sickly in all my life. She was in and out of the hospital for a large duration of her pregnancy.

It was very hard for me to look at my mother when was home, in between hospitalizations. She couldn't work. She was sick and weak. She was on bed rest a lot. Momma even endured home nursing at one point during her pregnancy. My mother never let me stay in the room during those rare moments she cried from pain but, I always knew what was going on.

As a family we did the best we could in dealing with the situation. Daddy continued working. His attitude was even harder to cope with during this time. I think he was nervous about his wife's health but did not know how to express his true feelings. Sha often walked around like she had lost her best friend. There was a high point, Netta came back home, temporarily, to help care for momma. Whitney was scared. I just wanted my mom and her baby to be alright. I prayed the baby would not be born with any of the health issues I dealt with. Everyone prayed for a miracle. Thank you Lord for answering our prayers. On July 13, 1990, my mother gave birth to a beautiful baby girl named Nicole, whom everyone called Nikki for short. Although born one month premature, she endured no complications. With the birth of my baby sister, my nightmare ended. My mom began to improve almost immediately. She gained her weight back. My mother's skin began to glow again. She regained her strength. My mother was even laughing again. Thank you Lord for giving me my mother back.

"His anger lasts only a moment, his goodness for a lifetime. Tears may flow in the night, but joy comes in the morning."

Psalms 30:5 (GNT)

Chapter 4: It's Time to Say Goodbye

The summer of 1990 will forever remain engraved in my memories. This is the summer I learned that my Uncle Mat was very sick. What I didn't realize was how sick he really was. How could I have been so wrapped up in myself that I let that pass me by? My Uncle Mat was everything to me. I could always talk to him. He was my playmate when I was younger. We had even given one another play names. He was my protector. Oh God, please watch over my Uncle Mat.

The last time I saw my uncle Mat alive was a huge blow to my heart. My family went to see him at Grannies' house, where he was staying at the time. He looked so frail because he had lost so much weight. His face wasn't dancing and full of life as I remembered it. He tried very hard to perk up when we entered the room he was resting in. I knew something was wrong because he didn't greet me in his usual manner.

He couldn't even sit up very long. It was more than I could bear. *Oh Lord, please watch over my uncle ! ! !* When I got the opportunity to escape from my family, after returning home that evening, I cried.

September 5, 1990 was supposed to be a day to celebrate. It was my 13th birthday. It was the day I became a teenager. It was supposed to be a very special day. Once again, I was badly mistaken. The day started out boring. I decided to go outside with Ena and one of our other friends. I don't know why I had to go in the house at that precise moment but I did and will forever wish I hadn't. The telephone rang. My mom answered the phone. All of a sudden she got quiet. She hung up the phone. My dad and Sha were in the other room (kitchen, I think). I heard her tell them my Uncle Mat had just died at 3:00pm that afternoon. I knew I had heard wrong! I had to have heard wrong. My uncle could not be gone. A few moments later, my mom told me the news. At that moment I felt so overwhelmed. I went back outside without saying anything to my family. Up until the funeral, I refused to cry. I felt if I cried I was accepting the fact that Uncle Mat had died and I couldn't do that.

My Uncle Mat knew ahead of time that he did not have a long time to live. As a result, during his last few days in the hospital, he told my Grannie the details of how he wanted his memorial service to be carried out. My Grannie and my Uncle Mat's best friend, Roland, made sure the arrangements were carried out accordingly. The service was beautiful. He had the place decorated in his favorite colors, red and white. He had his favorite song by Patti LaBelle playing in the background. He had his best friend, Roland, officiating over the service. As I was sitting there, I tried to hold it together as long as possible. Finally, I couldn't hold it together anymore. My uncle was dead! I used Lavare as an excuse to go outside and get some air. Lavare was still an arm baby so no one said anything when I got up and left out for a minute carrying him. Whew! At the burial, as I watched his casket being lowered in the ground, I knew I would never see my Uncle Mat again. He wanted 33 balloons to be released at the burial site, in honor of his age, by his close family and friends. I released a balloon in his honor. It took me weeks to stop going into my private corner and crying but it got easier. I began concentrating on my final year (which had already begun) of grammar school at Maranatha.

During that year, I first began to understand some of the financial stresses put upon my parents. It would take a few more years for me to fully understand. By this time, my parents owned the building Grannie lived in. This meant they were financially responsible for the bills in our house, as well as, for that building. At one point, the bills became more than they could handle. As a result, I had to be taken out of school for about 2 weeks, I think, because my parents couldn't afford to pay my tuition. It hurt my parents having to take me out of school but they still refused to put me in public school. As soon as they were able to get caught up on my tuition, I returned to school to complete the school year. As bad as things got for them, I never heard them complain about it. I will admit some attitudes changed around the house but I would not find out about this financial dilemma until I was in my adulthood and my mother used this situation as an example while talking to me about something else.

My eighth grade year at Maranatha was a breeze. I stayed in touch with Kita and worked very hard so I could graduate. I continued working with Mrs. Love, during the mornings I was dropped off early. I also continued volunteering in the preschool class during the early part of the morning. That year the teacher was Ms. Brown. She always encouraged me. In fact, all my teachers were very encouraging. Mrs. Irwin was my Bible and Social Studies teacher. She had a knowledge and love for the Word of God that was apparent each time she taught. Mrs. Palmer was another piece of Richard D. Henton Academy that came over to Maranatha. Mr. Tate was the first teacher that helped me grasp a true understanding of Math, the subject I enjoyed the least.

My graduating class was very small. There were only six students in my graduating class, including me. Among them was Michael. Michael was a pest, at times, in my opinion. He had a crush on me for probably as long as we were in classes together at Maranatha. The negative part is sometimes

Michael didn't know what it meant to show a lady proper respect and he had an attitude problem. There was also Kevin, a classmate that also came from Richard D. Henton Academy. I had great respect for Kevin. He never seemed to allow the remarks being made about him annoy him. I must admit, I did hear some pretty mean things said about him. Instead of getting upset, most of the time, Kevin just ignored the person and continued whatever it was he was doing. Kevin loved to read. I never thought I would see anyone who loved to read as much as me. Kevin had me beat. There was also Benny, Lance and, Twana.

On the home front, my home was really starting to irritate me. I loved my family but they were driving me crazy with some of the things that occurred. One night I was awaken out of my sleep by loud voices. My mother and Netta was in the midst of a major argument. As I lay in my bed unable to sleep, I began to cry. Why was this happening to my family? Eventually, with police assistance, my mother kept Lavare, fearing for his well-being. Unable to take Lavare with her, Netta stormed out of the house, not to return for a visit for a long time. My parents became Lavare's legal guardians.

Netta isolated herself from the family for a very long time. I felt I was taking on more responsibility than I should. I had to baby-sit on a regular basis even when I didn't want to, getting paid very little, if at all. I wasn't able to do things kids my age normally did. Among other things, I washed dishes regularly, without help, although it was very apparent and highly visible that I had eczema and couldn't tolerate my hands in dish detergent. It seemed like all Sha did was follow my mother around, when my mother wasn't at the hospital with Lavare. Lavare's condition had my mother running back and forth to the hospital with him. Whitney was becoming a major behavior problem and a pain to baby-sit. Daddy's attitude was worse than usual. He had an attitude problem the size of Mount Rushmore. I think, or rather I pray, his attitude was due to everything happening to the family. I was beginning to hate living in my house. Don't get me wrong, I love my family very much. It was just getting to the point that it was hard to be around them. It was during these times, I continued to rely heavily on reading the Bible and prayer for comfort. My best friend, Donyiel and her mother was also very instrumental in helping me overcome these hurdles of my life. I often called and/or went over their house for solace.

The day I graduated from grammar school is a nightmare I am still trying to forget. My sisters, Netta and Sha, didn't even attend my graduation for which I was hurt for a long time. I do not remember why Sha did not attend. Netta was still alienating herself from the family. I guess it hurt so much because I could remember being at both of their grammar school and high school graduations, cheering for them. As I grew older and matured, I forgave them because I knew that anger could become a hindrance in our relationships and I didn't want that to happen. Thank God for whom He sends to stand in the gap. On the morning of my graduation, Daddy dropped me off and went back home to get ready (he and Momma spent the previous night at the hospital with Lavare). Thank God for Kita and Ms. Brown. They let me cry for a minute and let my frustrations out. Afterwards they helped me put everything aside literally and enjoy my day. I was dancing on the inside as Ms. Brown helped Kita pin my graduation cap to my head. My sister was there to help me. If only my mom would have been there. Thank you God for who you send to stand in the gap. Momma Merrill was also there to congratulate and encourage me. My parents, Nikki and Whitney made it back just as the ceremony was about to start. Although nervous, I performed my graduation speech, "The True Meaning of Graduation" very well. After the ceremony ended, I took pictures with LaKita, Whitney, Momma Merrill and my parents.

"Dear friends, do not be surprised at the painful trial you are suffering, as though something strange were happening to you.

But rejoice that you participate in the suffrage of Christ so that you may be overjoyed when your glory is revealed."

I Peter 4:12-13 (KJV)

Chapter 5: A Whole New World

High school was my first, and only, experience with the Chicago Public School system. This was a whole new world for me filled with people of other races, religion and ideals, just to name a few. My parents once again tried to place me in a private school for high school but, due to my parent's financial situation at the time, they were unable to. Therefore my mom searched and found what she believed to be one of the better high schools in Chicago.

I attended George Washington High School located 3535 East 114th Street on Chicago's southeast side. This was almost as far East as one could go before hitting Indiana. Washington taught me many things in addition to your typical high school subjects. I learned what it really meant to stand up for yourself and your ideals. I met many people. Some of these people did not like me and made it their point to ridicule me. There were also some who I hoped to remain friends with for a long time. My first year was very rough. I had to acclimate myself with my new surroundings. Each day began at 6 something in the morning. I had to be at the bus stop by 7, 7:15 at the latest, in order to get to school on time.

During my first year at Washington, I learned a lot about the person I was and wanted to be as a result of various experiences I endured. For example, I began riding the bus alone after a misunderstanding with some friends. Although the situation was resolved, I found it easier to just take the bus by myself. Another example occurred one morning when I boarded CTA's 106 bus and handed the bus driver my transfer as usual. I had never held a conversation with this man, nor had I indicated I liked the man. I only said "good morning," paid my fare and sat down. For reasons I still don't understand, one morning this bus driver handed me back my transfer with an explicit romance novel. When I realized what happened, I was stunned. Some may say I overreacted but I was a teenager and this was the first time something like that ever happened to me. By the time I got to school, I was scared. I went to the office and reported it to security. My mom was called and she immediately came to pick me up from school. Momma and Sha spent the day trying to cheer me up and get my mind off what occurred that morning. I don't think CTA did anything to rectify the situation because I saw the same bus driver several times during the remainder of the school year, driving the same bus route. I also saw him driving the same bus route during my remaining three years of high school.

My second, third and, fourth years at Washington were easier to endure. I had set the foundation of the person I wanted to be. I worked very hard to attain the goals I had set for my life. I was learning how to ignore people, whether they were in my home or at school, who meant to do me harm. I practiced turning the other cheek. The most important lesson I was constantly reminded of, was that God is with you always; you just have to call on Him. I don't think people realized I carried my bible with me. It gave me the peace of mind and assurance I needed to complete my day. There were times however, I allowed my human side to come out and respond in ways I am embarrassed to think about now.

During my sophomore year, I was diagnosed with asthma, as if I needed something else to deal with. God really watched over me during these times. I had some pretty severe attacks. I hated these times. My heart would race from the medication. I felt like the walls were caving in on me. It was at that time, I started going to the University of Chicago Hospitals for all my health care needs. I never realized the impact this hospital would have on my life. My pediatrician, at the time, decided that because I was having some pretty severe headaches, as well as, diagnosis at birth, I should be re-evaluated by a neurosurgeon to see if I needed to have a shunt revision. I had lived with the same shunt all my life, nearly 20 years, without having any revisions or problems. I definitely didn't need or want to deal with that during that time in my life. Thank God my prayers were answered once again. This neurosurgeon said everything looked great and in working condition. I didn't have to make another appointment for one year.

In high school I gave up trying to be close to my mother. She had held a yard stick between us for so long I was beginning to think it was bonded there permanently. I was tired of being literally slapped in the face each time I tried to get close to her. I love my mother more than anything in this world, with the exception of God. After all, this is the woman who gave birth to me. This is the woman who refused to give up on me when doctors said I may not live long. This is the woman who sacrificed her time and energy to run back and forth to doctor appointments and physical therapy appointments, when no one else would. I always knew she loved me deep down inside but she just would not show me outward physical affection. I would always see her showing affection to Sha, Netta, Ena, Whitney, and now, Nicole. She never seemed to be that way with me. I could never understand why. My daddy and I were always pretty close except, his attitude sometimes made it unbearable to be in his presence. Would my daddy ever learn patience and would my mother and I ever be close were issues I pondered for a long time.

Part of the way I dealt with things is by being involved with extracurricular activities in school. This gave me a chance to escape my house and become involved in some positive activities. Among the activities I was involved in was Student Council, Student Leadership, and Drama Club for my freshman year only. I was also an Attendance Office Aide, Teacher's Aide, and, The Sign Language Club. By being involved in extracurricular activities, I had less time to focus on the negative aspects of my life. I also learned leadership, teamwork and organizational skills. These organizations taught me things about myself I had not yet discovered. I learned many things I would later discover were important to my well-being.

I joined the Sign Language Club during my freshman year. This club was started by one of my friends that is hearing-impaired, while we were in high school. It was her dream to teach people how to sign so they could communicate with people that were/are hearing impaired or deaf. This club taught me how to sign. More importantly, this club taught me to be more understanding of others that are different from myself.

Among the other groups I joined in high school, I was a member of Student Leadership/Peer Helpers. Student Leadership/Peer Helpers gave me a different taste of reality I had never known. This group once a week and discussed various issues that affected many teenagers around Chicago, as well as, other parts of the world. This was a large group that was divided into 8 smaller focus groups. Among these groups were: 1. Video Previews, 2. Peer Pressure, 3. Teen Sexuality/Teen Pregnancy, 4. Verbal/Physical Abuse and 5. Alcoholism, just to name a few. During my first year, I was involved with the group Teen Sexuality/Teen Pregnancy. Although I practiced abstinence, I would later discover this group would give me information that would prove beneficial in my college years. For one year, I was also the leader of Verbal/Physical Abuse and Video Previews. Part of the reason this group was as successful as it was, was because of the faculty advisor.

During my sophomore year, I worked even harder in all my classes. This hard work paid off as I made the honor roll several times during the year. When I didn't make the honor roll, I was very close. I continued to work close with the youth of the church.

I didn't have a large amount of friends while I was in high school. The friendships I did establish, I hoped to maintain for a long time. Included in these friendships was Taliashia. I met Taliashia my first year at Washington. She was a year ahead of me. Taliashia had attitude and didn't take much from anyone. There was also David, who just happened to be in my division, so I saw him daily. He always made me laugh. I must admit, as time progressed, I started liking David. I just was scared to tell him so I kept it to myself. Besides, I was unsure if he felt the same way about me and I didn't want to risk the embarrassment. The other issue was David always seemed to have a girlfriend. As our friendship progressed, David sometimes asked my opinion of the girls he dated. I decided to keep my feelings to myself. If God intended for us to date one another, He would provide the opportunity.

My junior year of high school was when I was first made aware of the Golden Apple Scholars of Illinois Program. It was for students attending institutions of higher learning so they could pursue a career in teaching. I quickly found out everything I needed to know in order to apply for the program. At the same time my mother was encouraging me to pursue another career field that would pay better, as well as, offer better respect. I concluded that if I became a Golden Apple Scholar and got accepted to my first choice school, DePaul, my mother would see how serious I was about teaching and encourage me to continue. I was so nervous. I once again thanked God for my True Right family. Sis. Merrill, or should I say Momma Merrill, who was a teacher herself before she retired, was once again beneficial as she assisted me with my application, and reviewed it before I turned it in.

After I turned in my application, I learned that two other girls in my high school had applied. I was friends with both of them. I wished them well. The next stage was the interview and writing an essay. One of the girls interview was scheduled the same day as mine. We wound up seeing one another during the day. Following the interview, we were required to write an essay. The other young lady didn't think she did as well during this process. She was wrong. Unfortunately, I did not make it past being a finalist. I received a certificate for my status as a finalist. I went over in my mind several times the whole process so I could see what I did wrong. As I reminisced about that whole experience, I am very thankful to God because it turned out better in the end that I was not a Golden Apple Scholar.

Among the awards I received, within my high school, I also received two national recognitions. I was included in the 1994/1995 edition of "Who's Who Among American High School Students." I also received an award and was included in the 1994/1995 edition of the "United States National Leadership Merit Award" which is part of the United States Achievement Academy 1995 National Awards.

The year was 1995 and I had finally reached my Senior year. On the spiritual front, my church was going through some changes with our pastor (that no one spoke of publicly) that had me reexamining my faith. My senior year was the easiest of all four years in high school. I had completed all my graduation requirements, as well as, college entrance requirements. As a result, I had a relaxed schedule. I generally only had the classes I needed four years of to graduate. I joined the work-study program so I could make some extra money. Up until that point, the only jobs I had was baby-sitting for my siblings and mom, for which I was underpaid, if at all. I also helped my neighbor's child with homework. This would definitely be a new experience. My first real job was working retail at a clothing store in Evergreen Plaza in Evergreen Park, IL. It started out nice but as time progressed, I realized the drama one must deal with working retail and I did not like it.

Regardless of the changes I endured, I had many special people in my life as a result of my membership at True Right Missionary Baptist Church. Among them was a minister name Rev. Willie Mae Davis. Rev. Davis had been at True Right for a very long time. In fact, she was among the first members of True Right. I don't know how we got so close so quick, but I was thankful to God we did. My relationship with Rev. Davis blossomed as a result of the day I first visited her with Trouble. Trouble and her husband, Deacon Trouble (special nick name I gave them ☺), were visiting the sick and shut-in of the church, with some of the other deacons and deaconesses.

She had asked me to come with them. I didn't know what to expect but visiting the sick and shut-in that day showed me how much one act of kindness can uplift the heart of someone who was not feeling their best. I would experience that feeling personally for myself in the years to come. It got to the point I talked to Rev. Davis at least once a week. Unfortunately, or should I say, fortunately God took another one of His angels home as Rev. Willie Mae Davis departed this earth Monday, March 20, 1995.

During my employment at Evergreen Plaza, I became ill. As it turned out, it was my gallbladder. I dealt with it as long as I could. Finally, I couldn't endure the pain anymore and went to the doctor. It was discovered that I had large gallstones. I underwent surgery, March 25, 1995, to resolve the problem. This meant carrying a pillow on my stomach (anyone who ever endured the surgery knows exactly what I'm talking about) which is no laughing matter. This also meant time away from school and work. Under ordinary circumstances, this could have set me back in school. Thank God I had completed all of my graduation requirements so there was no need for me to be held back a year.

After healing from surgery, I returned to school and work. When the store I was employed at went under new management, I quit. I tried to find another job but was unsuccessful. This worked out because this gave me time to rest. During my senior year, I was Executive Assistant in Student Leadership, which meant I worked directly with the faculty advisor. After I quit my job, I used the time to assist the advisor, as well as, my work study teacher.

I also used the extra time to prepare for the road ahead of me. I learned that I was accepted to DePaul University as an Early Childhood Education major. Unfortunately, I received some not so great news; I was turned down for every scholarship I applied for. This meant I had to accept loans to make up the financial difference that was not covered by the financial aid grants I did receive. *"Lord if this is where I am supposed to be, why are things not working out financially?"* I had to remind myself of Philippians 4:13,

"I can do all things through Christ which strengtheneth me."
(KJV)

Secretly, I was beginning to wonder if my mother was correct in saying I should have chosen another career field to pursue. After all, I had been turned down for every scholarship I had applied for. The Lord reminded me that He has never left me alone. The Lord always take care of His children. I was reminded of the last part of the poem, "Footprints."

"The Lord replied, 'My precious, precious child;
I love you and I would never leave you. During your
Times of trial and suffering when you see only one
Set of footprints, it was then I carried you."
(Carolyn Carty, 1963)

http://www.wowzone.com/fprints.htm

I was then reminded of the scripture,

"For you have been called for this purpose, since Christ also suffered for you, leaving you an example for you to follow in His steps," ***I Peter 2:21 (NASB)***

New American Standard Bible NASB) Copyright © 1960, 1962, 1968, 1971, 1972, 1973, 1975, 1977, 1995 by The Lockman Foundation
www.biblegateway.com/passage

During this time, my headaches began to worsen. I was reminded of the information my mother taught me regarding the shunt and when there is a possible need to be concerned. Increased headaches that didn't improve were a sign of possible shunt problem. Changes in bowel and urine habits were another sign of possible shunt problems. The other sign to look for is to look for changes in sleeping patterns (I usually slept longer and harder when I am having shunt problems). I made an appointment to see my neurosurgeon. Once again, my neurosurgeon reassured me everything was fine. Secretly, I did not feel like everything was fine. That is not to say I wished anything bad on myself, because I would never do that. Therefore, I had to make the best of the situation by ignoring the pain and irritability, among other things, I felt when I got a headache. After all, I was about to reach all the main goals I had set for my life.

Preparing for DePaul was not easy. There were so many thoughts and concerns running through my mind. Would I really be able to live away from home? Would I really be able to attain a degree, something Sha or Netta had yet to do? That is not to say I was being negative. Could I have a successful career in teaching? The people in my church family were an encouragement to me. Among other things, my church provided me with the only scholarship I received. It was then God revealed His word to me again.

"For God gave us a spirit not of fear but of power and love and self-control." II Timothy 1:7 (ESV)

Part of the way I survived the craziness was through my cousin. She was employed by DePaul and was also a student, at the time. She assisted me with the application process. Following my acceptance, she encouraged me to enter the Bridge program. She misunderstood the program to be an honors program. I later found out the program was for students who either lacked the test scores or grade point average to attend DePaul but was given the opportunity to improve themselves over the summer. During the program, students would experience campus life, as they were required to live on campus. Students were enrolled in three courses:

Communication, English and Math (to be determined by placement exam). Upon completion of the summer program, students would take 12 credit hours during the Fall Quarter. If the students attained a 2.5, or better, grade point average at the end of the Fall Quarter, they would be full-fledged students at DePaul.

During my high school years, my family and I went through some changes with my oldest nephew, Lavare's health. Lavare was born with a very rare lung disease called Pulmonary Hemosiderosis. It was during my high school years that it was diagnosed. Because of the disease, my nephew spent the first few years of his life wearing a portable oxygen tank. My nephew was in and out of the hospital often during my high school years because doctors only knew how to treat the symptoms associated with the disease but have not found a cure. During these times I found myself worrying a lot about my nephew. My parents made these times somewhat easier to cope with by assuring me that even though the survival rate was low for children born with Pulmonary Hemosiderosis, they were confident Lavare would outgrow it, which he eventually did.

It was during this time I became aware of the Make-A-Wish Foundation. I love the idea of a foundation created to give terminally ill children a chance at happiness. Someone at the hospital, Lavare receives care at, recommended him to Make-A-Wish Foundation. His wish was granted. He spent a week in Walt Disney World with my parents and Nicole. Sha was not allowed to go because she was too old. Nicholas, her son, could have gone but at that time he was very attached to his mother. Everyone knew he would not cooperate being away from his mom for that long. Whitney and I could have gone but my parents would not let us miss school (they went during the winter to make it easier on Lavare). They all enjoyed themselves tremendously.

When I became overwhelmed because I was constantly worried about Lavare, I used my journal as my outlet for my emotions. I also relied heavily on the power of prayer, as well as, reading the word of God for comfort and direction. I felt that if my faith and prayers were strong enough, maybe God would watch over Lavare as God did me, all my life.

The remainder of my senior year was great. Earlier that year, I went to Homecoming Dance for the first time (my mom wouldn't let me go the other three years). I went alone but managed to have a decent time. Everyone talked about the highlights of our Senior year: the prom, the luncheon and the graduation. I always dreamed of going on prom but neither Sha nor Netta went on their prom. I was afraid of the response I would receive from my parents. My parents agreed as long as I had a date.

A fellow classmate and friend didn't want me to miss out on the excitement of prom night. She decided to assist in the process of getting me a prom date. She had been dating her boyfriend for several years. He had a younger brother that was one year younger than I. My friend asked her boyfriend's younger brother to go on prom with me. We should have left it as just an arranged prom date only. Unfortunately, we had some time (weeks, maybe months) to get to know one another before we went on prom. This is where things should have stopped. There is a saying, "opposites attract." That was true with the two of us. For the sake of privacy, I will just call him "Will." Will was not a Will Smith but he was enjoyable to be around, most of the time. Will and I decided to give a relationship a try. There was a major difference, between us, that caused major problems. I am a Christian and he was not. I had always held my Christian values dear but he tried to challenge this. On several occasions he tried to do things that went against what I stood for. Stupidly, I continued to date him.

Preparing for prom was fun. My mom and I shared financial responsibilities. We went shopping together and found a beautiful white dress with a lacy blue overlay. My Aunt Dessa, my mom's oldest sister, did the alterations on my dress. My Aunt Kathleen, my dad's baby sister volunteered to do my make-up. At that time, she did make-up at a major department store regularly. My Aunt Dorothy (Dot), my mom's sister-in-law, who was great when it came to hair styling, did my hair.

My daddy arranged the limousine transportation. You might say I kept it all in the family. ☺

On the day of the prom, of course I was running behind schedule trying to get the last minute arrangements taken care of. Donyiel, as well as, my cousin Neicy, came over to help me get ready. By 7:00pm, I felt like Cinderella going to the ball. When the limo arrived, I was putting on the final touches. We took countless pictures at my house. We then went to Will's house to take pictures. It was then off to the prom.

In general, I had fun at the prom. At one point, my date and his brother decided to ditch the prom, for a while. They disappeared for quite some time. Highly irritated, I decided to find some of my friends and enjoy the night. When he and his brother got back, I let him have it. We took pictures, danced a little while and left. My limo driver knew my daddy and was therefore very watchful of me, sometimes a little too watchful but it helped a lot. Every time Will decided to try something, the driver seemed to be watching. Will even tried to raise the divider for privacy but the driver let it right back down. This made my job so much easier. We walked around downtown Chicago for a little while and went home.

By the next day I was in a state of confusion. I knew I couldn't continue with Will in the manner we presently were. We were planning to spend the day together. I later realized this worked out perfectly. I think Will was still mad about the night before, or for whatever reason, he decided to break things off with me. Thank you Jesus! He made my job so much easier.

"Consider it pure joy, my brethren, whenever you face trials of many kinds, because you know the testing of your faith develops perseverance."

James 1:2-3 (NIV)

• •

"Even the youths shall faint and be weary,
and the young men shall utterly fall;
But they that wait upon the Lord shall renew their strength; they shall mount up with wings as eagles; they shall run, and not be weary, they shall walk, and not faint."

Isaiah 40:30-31 (KJV)

Chapter 6: These Are the Things That Make Us Stronger

After graduation, which was nothing to brag about, I had about one month to rest before I entered the Bridge Program. I used this time to rest and make the final preparations. Another program DePaul had was called "Premier DePaul." This was an over-night orientation for incoming freshmen and their parents. About a week before the program, I found out that neither my mother nor my father was attending with me.

I was a little upset. After all, this was going to be my first time on campus. Weren't they interested in the school I was attending?

After packing my bag and praying, I took the bus to the 95th Street "L" station. I took the "L" to the Fullerton station. During my train ride, I calmed down by reassuring myself that I would not be the only student without their parents. When I arrived at the registration, I realized how wrong I was. Literally everywhere I turned, there were students with their parents. To add insult to injury, the person I check in with asked if my parents were with me. There was about one-half hour of free time before the festivities began so I went to find a place to sit down. It was during this time I saw a young lady on the opposite side of the room who looked very familiar to me. She looked like one of my former principal's niece, Michelle. When she came on the side of the room I was seated on, I called out her name and realized it was her. She looked just like she did when we were in grammar school. Her mother was so sweet to me. Michelle and I got caught up, somewhat, on one another's lives. I was so relieved to have someone I knew attending that weekend.

The roommate situation was set up whereas, whomever you were next to in line, was your roommate for the night. My roommate was a girl I had met while waiting to register. She was nice to me. We were also in the same group. When the program began, we were divided up according to the school you were accepted in. Among the schools were Education, Liberal Arts and Sciences, School of Music, Theater School and Computer Science. The School of Education and Liberal Arts and Sciences combined for activities that evening.

All of the activities were fine except a game entitled, "Giants, Wizards and Elves." This game changed my life forever. Because of this game, I was accidentally knocked down and injured my left knee very badly. This game was a physical form of "Rock, Paper, Scissors." The teams were divided into two, one on each side of the room. You decided what you were, came to the center of the room, called it out (the other side did the same thing) and if you were IT, you tried to get back to your safety zone before being tagged out by the other team members. We were it. I turned to see someone behind me. I tried to get to my side. The person chasing me tripped, and fell on me. Immediately everyone laughed until they realized he landed on me. After helping me up, I tried to put my left foot down flat on the floor but as soon as I did, a sharp pain shot through me leg and stayed on my knee. My knee was bruised. I applied ice to it and sat out the rest of the activities. Later that evening, I wound up going to the emergency room because my knee was swollen and hurting very badly.

The Director of the orientation program really wanted me to go to the hospital. She assured me DePaul would accept full financial responsibility if I went to the hospital. I decided to go. DePaul Security took me to the emergency room. The Director went with me. Because I had one month before I was officially 18 years old, I had to call my mother to get permission to be treated. After my mother stopped laughing hysterically, she gave permission for me to be treated. I later learned this was laughter from stress rather than from my accident. At the same time, on different sides of the city, Lavare and Sha were also in the hospital. Sha was having complications with her pregnancy. Lavare was having more complications with his lung disease. After being x-rayed, put in a knee brace and, given a pair of crutches to get around with, I called my mother once more. Too stubborn to quit, I told my mother I felt well enough to return to campus for the duration of the program. By the next day, many people knew what happened and the jokes started. One good thing came out of the accident. Daddy gave me a ride home because I couldn't ride the train and bus on crutches, with my overnight bag. When my daddy saw me, he just shook his head and smiled. (Yeah right!)

I was referred to a Sports Injury doctor associated with the University of Chicago Hospitals for my knee. After being evaluated by the doctor, it was determined that I needed physical therapy for my left knee. The plan was for me to have physical therapy three times a week, for six weeks. I would then return to see the sports injury doctor. Depending upon the condition of my knee when I returned, I would be scheduled for surgery on my knee. Since I lived on the Lincoln Park campus for the duration of the Bridge Program, his nurse arranged for me to do my physical therapy at a facility down the street from the dorm I stayed in for the duration of the Bridge Program.

The Director of the Bridge Program was very helpful. As soon as I told her where the facility was I was having physical therapy, she told me that was too far for me to try and walk on crutches (it was actually several blocks down on Fullerton). She told me the company actually had another facility in the professional building located next door to the dorm I stayed in for the duration of the Bridge Program. She called their office and made arrangements for my physical therapy to be transferred to that facility. As far as dorm arrangements, I was assigned to a room on the TOP floor. This building had no public elevator for students to use. This meant I had to climb up and down all those stairs wearing my knee brace and on my crutches. Once again, the director was very beneficial. She spoke to the building engineers and arranged for me to get the elevator key they use. I only had to be buzzed in the outside door. This was extremely helpful as my first and only experience climbing up and down those stairs had me exhausted and gasping for air, from trying to keep my balance and not fall again, all the while hopping up and down those stairs. I thanked God for caring and understanding people like the Director of the Bridge Program who stood in the gap for me.

I had physical therapy at Accelerated Rehabilitation Center. The therapists at this facility were always very professional and nice to me. I was evaluated by Jillian. She was so small. When you first looked at her, you would not think she was the type of therapist she was. I must admit, whenever I worked with Jillian, I got quite a workout. She was my stand-in therapist when my regular therapist, Renee, who I nicknamed THE TORTURER, was unavailable. She was just as friendly as Jillian, but she often pushed me to my limit, if not beyond. I was happy to have the Torturer (and Jillian) as my therapist because I knew it was going to take hard work for me to get back to where I needed to be.

During the Bridge Program, I took three courses: English, Math (determined by placement exam) and Communication.

The Director of the Bridge Program taught the English course I was taking. My Communication course was taught by a very kind woman I will just call Whitney (I can just hear my sister Whitney cracking up at the idea of me having a teacher with the same name as her.☺) My day was busy as it was in high school, if not busier. I had to get up very early because I had physical therapy prior to the start of classes. By the end of the day, I was exhausted. I would often take a nap before doing my homework and studying. I would also try to spend some time with Marcus. I had met him shortly after moving on campus. There was an age difference between us but that didn't bother us. We got along very well.

Because the Bridge Program was organized like it was, there was a male and female mentor for each group. These mentors attended classes with us. They also helped us with homework and any other issues that arose that required assistance. The female mentor for my group was extremely nice. Her name was Olga. She always had a word of encouragement for me. She was available whenever I needed her. The male mentor was also nice. There was also another mentor in another group, Kimberly, who befriended me.

The main way I survived the Bridge Program was through my faith in God. When times got rough, and there were some times when I wanted to scream to the top of my lungs, I was comforted in knowing God watches over His children. I was reminded that God will never put more on me than I can bear. I do not know but I was often reminded of my diagnosis at birth and how long I lived with it, without having any complications or additional surgeries. I would conclude if I could live through this, I could make it through anything.

I did very well in the Bridge Program. Due to my knee not healing properly, the Sports Injury doctor decided to perform the knee surgery. The surgery was scheduled for one week before the Bridge Program officially ended, which meant I had to make arrangements to take all my final exams early. Thank God all my professors understood. My final for Communication class was an informal three minute speech. I decided to do my speech on my diagnosis, as well as, Lavare's diagnosis. The speech went very well. Before leaving, Whitney wished me well and asked me to call her to let her know how I was doing after surgery.

I healed from the knee surgery in just enough time to start the Fall Quarter of the 1995-1996 school year at DePaul. I also resumed taking physical therapy at Accelerated Rehabilitation Center. I took three classes, as well as, one clinical, which meant I observed for a few hours every week, in a school or a day care setting. I worked at St. Vincent DePaul Center for my clinical. The first half of the quarter I worked in the toddler classroom. For the second half of the quarter I worked in the infant classroom. I gained a lot more experience through my work here. I really enjoyed working with the toddlers, more so than the infants. This led me to believe I had chosen to focus on the right age group with the field I chose. Until I found a permanent position, I did several temporary jobs through DePaul's Human Resource Department. After all, I was in college and I still lived on campus, in Lincoln Park, one of the most expensive neighborhoods in Chicago, at the time. My final temporary position led to a permanent position with the Academic Affairs Office. As a result of my new job, I left my dorm early and didn't return until late evening. On the days I had classes early, I usually went to my classes first, then work, and physical therapy. On the days my classes were late, my schedule was reversed as I went to physical therapy first, then class and work.

The residence hall I lived in during the regular school year was University Hall. Because of the way the residence hall (dorm) was set up, I shared one full washroom with the room next to mine. The two girls occupying this room were nice, for the most part. Unfortunately, one of them kept a secret that blew up in her face one quiet weekend during the Fall Quarter. It seemed that one of the girls was pregnant but neglected to tell anyone, except her boyfriend. On one quiet weekend in October, my roommate (who had decided she didn't like DePaul and transferred), as well as, one of my suitemates, went home for the weekend. The suitemate that stayed had her boyfriend spend the weekend with her. They were enjoying themselves so much that they became very loud that night, as they played around with one another.

Prior to going to bed that night, I went over, asked them to quiet down and said good night. It was around 2 or 3 the next morning. I heard a lot of screaming coming from her room. I thought, "Oh Lord, will they ever shut up?"

Unfortunately, that time they were hollering for a reason. This was the time I wished I had ignored them a little longer and stayed in my room. This was the time I wish I had not heard her screaming. When I got to the room, my suitemate was on the floor screaming and crying while her boyfriend was on the phone. When I asked her what was wrong she said, "I'm pregnant and I'm losing my baby!" I was shocked and scared at the same time. There is nothing like the sight of a woman losing her baby. I stayed with her until the paramedics arrived. I returned to my room and tried to get some sleep. Of course, I was unsuccessful. When I left out for class later that morning some people, within my dorm, wanted to know what happened. I did not feel it was my place to tell anyone so I said she got sick and left it at that. We were all friends but she had become very close with my roommate and her roommate so I was even more surprised when they came back to school and I told them what happened but they didn't know she was pregnant. Thank God she was all right. Approximately two weeks later, she returned to school to complete the quarter. That is something I never wanted to witness again. My heart goes out to any woman who ever lost a child.

On Tuesday, November 7, 1995 at 12 noon, I left DePaul University's Lincoln Park campus to go to work at DePaul's Loop campus. I entered the Fullerton "L" station and paid my fare. During this time there was a ticket agent on duty who always made flirtatious remarks every time I came through the station. I ignored him, as I usually did and proceeded to the platform to catch the train. Because my knee hadn't totally healed, I still wore a knee brace and used one crutch.

The Fullerton "L" station had two sets of stairs one must climb to reach the platform. I had walked up (or rather, hopped up) the first set of stairs and went halfway up the second set of stairs when someone grabbed me from behind, causing me to partially lose my balance. My heart was racing. I felt like I was going to be sick. *Oh God, please let me be ok ! ! !* I turned my head and recognized the perpetrator as being the ticket agent on duty. When I found my voice I said, "You scared the !@#$% out of me! What if you made me fall?" He immediately responded, "that was the whole idea so I could catch you." I told him to let me go but he didn't. He held me for several minutes it seemed, all the while smiling, before letting go. The ticket agent then said, "I'll see you tomorrow, baby." He ran back down the stairs. Afraid of what he might have done if he saw me going back down the stairs, I proceeded to work.

By the time I got to work, I was so scared I could barely speak. When I regained some of my composure, I relayed the incident to my supervisor and co-workers. I then called my father, who was employed by CTA at that time. I spoke to daddy briefly. To say the least, he was not happy. He said he would call me right back. Someone from CTA called me but my supervisor was on the phone (during that time, the phone had not been connected at my desk so I shared my supervisor's phone). When I tried to call him back, he was out of the office. Due to phone problems on the LOOP campus that day, I was unable to speak to daddy for the remainder of my time at work that day. During the day, I prayed for my daddy. I did not know how he would react. I knew he was at work. I did not want him to do anything to lose his job. When he called my momma and told her what happened, she had one of his co-workers he was good friends with, put him in a room to calm down. I heard this later.

When I got to my dorm that evening, my roommate was concerned because my phone had been ringing all day, which was unusual for me. After talking to my roommate about what happened, she gave me some privacy so I could call my Daddy. He asked me if I had called the police and reported the incident to DePaul security. When I explained I was so scared I didn't know what to do, my daddy told me to go to the security office and report it immediately. He then wanted me to call him back and relay what they told me.

When I reported the incident to security, one officer asked me why I had waited so long to report the incident. I told him I didn't know what to do so I called my daddy who was an employee of CTA. However, there were phone problems on the LOOP campus that prevented me from speaking to him until I returned home this evening. The security officer then had me repeat what occurred. They called another security officer in the room, who was a former Chicago Police officer who once again had me repeat what happened that day. This officer said what he did is considered Simple Battery. He asked me if I wanted to press charges against the ticket agent. I told him I wanted to proceed. The police came and I once again relayed what happened that day. He told me a detective would be contacting me regarding a court date. I then asked Security to escort me back to my dorm (it was the evening time; there was an escort service in place, on campus that was offered beginning in the evening until early the next morning on a daily basis).

My roommate was waiting for me when I returned to my dorm. We talked for a brief moment. She then gave me some privacy so I could call my parents. I relayed everything to my Daddy. Daddy said he was coming to ride the "L" to work with me the next day. I knew he wanted to see the ticket agent but I didn't care. I was relieved that I didn't have to go in that station alone. I then called my mom, who was already at home, and talked about what happened. By this time, I couldn't compose myself and cried. After talking to my mom for a little while, I got off the phone and went to bed.

The next day, Wednesday, November 8, 1995, was extremely hard on me. I was petrified to enter the "L" station. Thank God when I spoke to my daddy, after I got back from Security the previous night, he said he was riding to work with me. I was thankful to God I didn't have to go in that station alone. When we entered the station, that ticket agent still made inappropriate remarks toward me as I paid my fare and went through the turnstile. Knowing how my daddy's temper was (and still is), I said a silent prayer that God would restrain my daddy. Thank you Jesus! My prayer was answered as he just protectively grabbed me and continued walking to the platform. Daddy assured me he would speak to someone when he got to work, now that he could identify the ticket agent, as well, to ensure he wouldn't bother me again. During the day, I was contacted by the manager of the Fullerton "L" station. I relayed the incident to him. He said he would get back in touch with me. While at work, I ran into my Communication Professor from the Bridge Program, Whitney. She was teaching a class on the LOOP campus that quarter. When I told her what happened, she was very understanding. She then surprised me as she offered to go to court with me. It made me feel much better knowing she was going to court with me.

Thursday, November 9, 1995, I was contacted by the Fullerton station manager because they were questioning the ticket agent. It was at that point, I learned that he was making it seem like he only touched my arm. I reiterated what happened and the manager promised to get back in touch with me. Even IF he only touched my arm, what gave him the right to do that? I didn't know him. I did not give him permission to put his hands on me. I had only seen him when I went to work. I couldn't believe this lie he was telling.

One week later, I was contacted by a detective from the police department. I once again relayed the incident. He told me I could press charges against the ticket agent. When he put his hands on me that was considered Simple Battery. When the detective asked me if I wanted the man arrested, and I consented, he explained the procedures I would need to follow. I would have to go to the police station and file a formal complaint. A date for us to appear in court would then be set.

I completed the Fall Quarter 1995 and went home for Winter Break. I had not heard from the detective handling the case. Concerned, I called the detective on Monday, November 20, 1995 to see what progress had been made regarding having the ticket agent arrested. I was told that CTA was saying that the ticket agent was on vacation. I told the detective that was untrue because I had just saw the ticket agent when I went to work that previous Friday. The detective promised to go back to the station and contact me.

Once they had the ticket agent in custody, the detective called me to ask me to come down to the station and identify him. He gave me directions on how to get to the Belmont Police Station. The detective went on to tell me if I arrived at the station at the same time as the ticket agent arrived, hang back and let him enter the station first. Thankfully, he said I could bring my father with me. My father took me to the police station. I identified the ticket agent. I signed the complaint. I was given a court date. My daddy took me home. As I lay in bed that night, I was reminded of my days in high school and that bus driver on the 106 bus. I wondered what happened to him. I prayed that he didn't bother anyone else.

In spite of the craziness, I continued to go to work. I completed Fall Quarter 1995 very well, if I do say so myself. I was now a full-fledged DePaul University student. DePaul had a very beneficial counseling service my cousin told me about when I told her what happened to me. My cousin also encouraged me to take the bus, versus the "L" until I became comfortable again since CTA still allowed that man to work the Fullerton station at the same time Monday thru Friday. I tried riding the bus temporarily but, had to resume taking the "L" as the buses made me behind schedule.

Wednesday, November 20, 1995 was my scheduled court date. I must admit that although I prayed and read my bible for comfort, I was still nervous. Thank God for

Whitney, my former Communications professor. She called me the night before to confirm that she was still coming and set up a meeting spot. We decided to meet in the lobby of the court building at 9:00am. On the morning of the court date, I was running late so I didn't arrive until 9:10am. Whitney was there as promised. I saw the ticket agent as he entered the building. Thank God for Whitney because she hugged me as my stomach started hurting as soon as I saw his face. We waited until approximately 9:20am for my daddy in the lobby. Whitney assured me he was coming and suggested we go find our seats so we wouldn't miss roll call.

Role call began. My daddy finally arrived. My case was called over an hour later. No public defender was called in this case, which meant the ticket agent had to find his own lawyer by the next court date. In the lobby, introductions were definitely in order. My daddy thanked Whitney for coming down to court with me. He then asked if everyone had transportation. I asked daddy to drop me back off on campus or at the "L" station. However, Whitney was heading in the same direction and offered to give me a ride. Daddy walked Whitney and I to her car.

Whitney and I headed to Lincoln Park to collect our things. We then headed to the LOOP campus. Thank you Lord for the people you place in my life to be a blessing to me. When I arrived at work, my co-workers were waiting on me. After talking about what occurred in court, they were very encouraging. When I got home that evening, I talked to my mom and then went to bed. That was a very long, exhausting day.

Christmas 1995 and New Year's 1996 was very nice. Marcus and I broke up shortly after the Fall Quarter ended so I spent the majority of my time at home with my family. Kita and I also spent time together. The more time we spent together, the more I loved Kita. The only negative aspect of the New Year was CTA, who apparently made no attempts to reassign or fire the ticket agent. Therefore I saw him every day I worked during Winter Break.

January 3-17, 1996

Since I went to court that ticket agent is still giving me dirty looks and acting stupid. I can't wait until this is all over so I can get some peace back in my life. Today that idiot ticket agent took the cake. I entered the station and paid my fare, ignoring the ticket agent as usual. However before he clicked me through the turnstile (or whatever they do to let you through the turnstile) he started hollering and smashing his face against the window at me. When he stopped hollering, he clicked me through and started laughing.

January 25, 1996 couldn't come fast enough. I needed some peace of mind. Once again, daddy went to court with me. He was in the lobby waiting for me when I arrived at the court building. Roll call began. When my case was called I approached the bench. The State's Attorney Office represented me. The ticket agent was responsible for obtaining his own attorney. He asked the judge for a continuance because he did not have the money to get an attorney because he just got paid. The State's Attorney representing me asked the judge if I could be excused from the next court date because that was my second court appearance in court and the ticket agent did not have an attorney. The judge agreed. Before I left, the State's Attorney said she would send me a letter in the mail informing me of the next time I had to appear in court. I never heard from anyone working in the State's Attorney Office again.

During that time, I started talking to and eventually dating this guy name Maurice. He started out very nice to me. We got along very well. We would often talk on the phone for hours at a time. Maurice was very understanding, most of the time, with regards to my health and the adventures I dealt with at the time. Unfortunately there was a dark side, a secretive side to Maurice that made me question the validity of our relationship. Lord, please guide me.

Despite the craziness that had begun erupting in my life, God allowed me to stay in the right frame of mind. DePaul had started making things difficult for me, with regards to the accident I had during Premier DePaul because they were not paying my doctor's bills as promised. My hectic schedule of classes, work and physical therapy was wearing away at my strength. My headaches were continuing to worsen (which I didn't always admit). I was tired. I am thankful to God that during this time I was blessed with some very good friends.

Among these people who blessed my life was Farrah. Although we were different in many ways, we got along very well. Among the programs I was involved in, I joined the Mentoring Program. Through this program, I met a wonderful woman. She was my mentor and a very good friend I could confide in. Whitney continued to be one in a million. There are not enough words in the English language to express my gratitude for what my mentor and Whitney did for me while I was a student at DePaul. I thanked God for their presence in my life. Surprisingly, my sister Sha was also very understanding and encouraging. At one point, I became overwhelmed by everything and thought about taking one quarter off from DePaul. She encouraged me to take the quarter off, saying I was not giving up by doing this. I was just thinking of myself. She told me she would talk to my parents about it, which she did. God gave me the strength I needed to complete my classes for the Winter and Spring Quarter classes for the 1995-1996 school year.

I spent my summer vacation working for DePaul, completing physical therapy and enjoying my time with my family. It was nice being home in the beginning then, everything resurfaced that made me want to move on campus. I love my family very much. It's just they have strange ways of responding to things that can get to be nerve wrecking at times. I counted down the days until the next quarter started. Ironically, my family was part of the reason I never gave up during all the craziness that erupted in my life since I became a student at DePaul.

Friday, October 15, 1996

What a day! I was really enjoying all of my classes. Thursday, I will be visiting a preschool. Actually I will be sitting in on a kindergarten class this teacher seems to be well-versed in her field of expertise, energetic and enjoy what she does. I met her through my RA for this year,— because she is her mother. I should say I will meet her because although we have spoken over the phone, we have never met face to face.

I joined DePaul's Gospel Choir. To God Be the Glory. We did our first concert, since I became a member, on Saturday it was nice. Afterwards, the choir went out and had dinner at Bennigan's. I saw Momma and Daddy Sunday I went to church and saw a miracle happen. My sister and her children came to church Sunday.

Thus far, I get along well with my roommate.

Around November 1996 I went for my yearly appointment with my neurosurgeon. I was somewhat nervous about this appointment because my primary care physician suggested I see him after we talked about how my headaches had worsened and increased. As I came closer to this appointment the nervousness disappeared. After all, this is the same doctor who gives me a clean bill of health each time I went for my yearly appointment to ensure the shunt was functioning properly and no problems had arose. On the day of the appointment things were hectic at the clinic because my neurosurgeon was leaving the hospital. As usual, he gave me a clean bill of health and referred me to another neurosurgeon, one who treats adults. When I went to this appointment I was fine until he decided to transfer me to another neurosurgeon, one who specialized in treating shunted patients. I had seen this neurosurgeon in the past so I could not understand why he was referring me to someone else.

I completed Fall Quarter of the 1996-1997 school year very well, in spite of the stress that had accumulated in my life. I was fired from DePaul University's Office of Academic Affairs because I was not meeting their expectations however I tend to disagree with the explanation. I think it was related to the legal issues I was dealing with, during that time. After all, I had been there for over a year. I had assisted with a very important project. I would think if I was not meeting their expectations, they would not have included me in this special project for which they recognized my work. I think if I was not meeting their expectations, I would have been fired a lot sooner instead of waiting almost two years to do it. I was planning to quit that job anyway because the Lord had blessed me with two better job offers. I was so thankful to God for bringing me through another year.

"The stone which the builders rejected has become the capstone; the Lord has done this, and it is marvelous in our eyes.
This is the day the Lord has made; let us rejoice and be glad in it.
Blessed is he who comes in the name of the Lord. From the house of the Lord we bless you. You are my God, and I will give you thanks; you are my God and I will exalt you. Give thanks to the Lord for he is good; his love endures forever."

Psalms 118:22-24, 26, 28-29 (NIV)

Winter Break was fabulous. On the day I was fired from DePaul, I was furious. Needing to calm down before going home, I decided to go to Evergreen Plaza and walk around. While riding the bus, I noticed a guy watching me. After a few moments of staring, he politely approached me and spoke. He made it his goal that day to cheer me up. I usually get offended by such things as what happened that day, but it was something about him. By the time I went home, I had calmed down. He was a perfect gentleman. He waited with me until my bus came. He gave me his phone number and asked me to call him. I eventually called him. Over time, we became friends. He always made time for me. My mother even got along with him. He cared about my well being. I remember one of my friends invited me to hang out with her one day because it had been a while since we saw one another. I was running late so we went to a later show and dinner. By the time I got home, my parents were worried and mad because I didn't call and tell them about my change of plans. Momma went a step further and said I needed to call my new friend because he was worried about me, as well. That had never happened; where my mother cared about what the guy I was dating thought.

"The LORD is my light and my salvation; whom shall I fear? the LORD is the strength of my life; of whom shall I be afraid?
When the wicked, even mine enemies and my foes, came upon me to eat up my flesh, they stumbled and fell.
Though an host should encamp against me, my heart shall not fear: though war should rise against me, in this will I be confident.
One thing have I desired of the LORD, that will I seek after; that I may dwell in the house of the LORD all the days of my life, to behold the beauty of the LORD, and to enquire in his temple.
For in the time of trouble he shall hide me in his pavilion: in the secret of his tabernacle shall he hide me; he shall set me up upon a rock.
And now shall mine head be lifted up above mine enemies round about me: therefore will I offer in his tabernacle sacrifices of joy; I will sing, yea, I will sing praises unto the LORD.
Hear, O LORD, when I cry with my voice: have mercy also upon me, and answer me.
When thou saidst, Seek ye my face; my heart said unto thee, Thy face, LORD, will I seek.
Hide not thy face far from me; put not thy servant away in anger: thou hast been my help; leave me not, neither forsake me, O God of my salvation.
When my father and my mother forsake me, then the LORD will take me up.
Teach me thy way, O LORD, and lead me in a plain path, because of mine enemies.

Deliver me not over unto the will of mine enemies: for false witnesses are risen up against me, and such as breathe out cruelty.
I had fainted, unless I had believed to see the goodness of the LORD in the land of the living.
Wait on the LORD: be of good courage, and he shall strengthen thine heart: wait, I say, on the LORD." *Psalms 27 (KJV)*

NOTE: THANK YOU MOMMA FOR SHARING YOUR FAVORITE SCRIPTURE WITH ME. I LOVE YOU. ☺

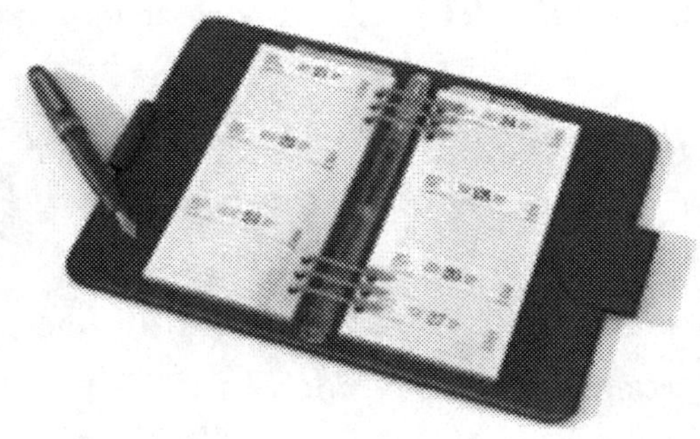

Chapter 7: A Change of Plans

January 2, 1997 is a day I will never forget. This day changed my life forever. This is the day I met my new neurosurgeon, Dr. David Frim. He was Chief of Pediatric Neurosurgery at the University of Chicago Hospitals, at the time. I must say, as I came closer to the day of my appointment, I became more nervous than I had ever been for an appointment of this nature.

When I arrived, I registered and sat down. The waiting room was filled with parents and children. I felt a little strange because I appeared to be the only adult seeing this neurosurgeon. After waiting for one hour, Dr. Firm's nurse came out to say he was running behind schedule. By the time my name was called, I was nervous, tired and irritated. After what seemed like forever

Dr. Frim's nurse returned to talk to me. Thank God for his nurse. She calmed my nerves and changed my whole attitude about the appointment as she told me about how she enjoyed working with him. My biggest surprise came when Dr. Frim walked in the room.

He was nothing like I imagined. In the past, my neurosurgeons have been older in age. Dr. Frim looked younger. When he spoke I was even more surprised as he repeated many things his nurse had previously said to me. He truly wanted to know how I felt. Dr. Frim had me tell him about myself. He asked me about my understanding of my diagnosis, as well as, the shunt. To make sure he truly listened to me, he tossed my chart aside which seemed to include many of momma's comments and a very few of mine, and asked me what I thought. Dr. Frim actually wanted my input of what made me think something was wrong. We talked for one hour before he did a neurological exam.

During this time, I learned that Dr. Frim specialized in treating patients with shunts. He even used a relatively new device called a telesensor. The telesensor is a device used to measure the shunt pressure, in order to determine whether or not the shunt is malfunctioning. Up until the use of the telesensor, doctors checked the shunt pressure by the CT scan, shunt series and/or the ever painful spinal tap. I thanked God because up until that point I had never had to go through the torture. I only heard the stories of people who endured the spinal tap. I was even more impressed by his concerns of what I expected of him as a physician.

Up until that point, most of my neurosurgeons seemed to concern themselves with what momma thought and had to say. Dr. Frim went a step further and asked what I expected of him. I knew immediately what I wanted. I wanted him to talk to me and not at me. I wanted to be a part of the decision-making process. Above all, I wanted Dr. Frim to believe me when I said something was not right, instead of just concluding it was just stress or in my head. This was my body and had been for 20 years, at that point, so I knew when something didn't feel right. Dr. Frim gained my respect at that very moment as I could see he was not only hearing me but he was also listening to every word I had to say. He made sure he understood me. He gave me his business card. Because I was in school and staying in Lincoln Park on campus, Dr. Frim gave me the option of emailing him for non-emergencies, although I could always call his office or page him. Thank you Lord for giving me some control over issues dealing with my health.

One of the symptoms I had endured was night time incontinence, a problem I dealt with all my life. Unfortunately, as my headaches worsened, so did my incontinence. Dr. Frim asked permission to examine my back, something none of my neurosurgeons in the past had done. While examining my back he noticed a distinctive mark on my lower back. Dr. Frim asked permission to run some tests to check my back, the shunt, and the cyst. I consented. Dr. Frim said if it was the shunt, I may need to have it replaced, which of course meant surgery. At that time, I wasn't worried because God had brought me 20 years without having any complications or problems with the shunt.

To keep me from having to run back and forth to the hospital, Dr. Frim had his nurse arrange for me to have all the tests done that day. He also promised to contact me within three days with the tests results. I ended up spending the entire day at the hospital because the MRI department was running behind schedule. I called momma to tell her what was occurring. When I got back to my dorm that evening, I called momma so we could talk in detail.

In the beginning, momma seemed to have been quite upset when I told her about my appointment. She would tell me nothing was wrong with the shunt so no one was touching it. As the days passed, she calmed down. I was on pins and needles as I waited to hear back from Dr. Frim. During this time, I also had to figure out a way to tell my new friend. He cared about me very much. I knew he would be worried so I waited until I spoke to Dr. Frim to tell him. On day three, I got up and went to classes assuming my neurosurgeon was not going to keep his word. Later that afternoon, my daddy called me with a message from Dr. Frim's office. He wanted me to come in for an appointment.

On my return appointment, I was extremely nervous. While sitting in the waiting area, time seemed to have stood still. By the time I was called, I was asking God to just allow me to receive some answers. As with my initial appointment, Dr. Frim's nurse came in to talk to me before he did. When she left out it seemed like eternity before Dr. Frim came in to say he was running behind schedule. He then surprised me as he handed me the tests results to look over while he finished up with the patient before me.

When Dr. Frim returned, he asked me what I thought of my test results. Unsure of what some of the test results were, I asked him to explain what I was looking at. He started with my spine. The lower part of my spine had somehow grown attached to my bladder. There was no way of telling whether it had been like that all my life or whether it had grown that way over the last few years. Dr. Frim said I would need surgery to correct it. He then moved to the shunt. At the time, it was unclear whether the shunt was fully functioning or not. Therefore, he wanted to concentrate on correcting my back before looking at the shunt. Dr. Frim went on to say because the surgery was not urgent, I could have it done at the completion of the quarter I was completing at DePaul. Later, when I showed my momma the test results, she immediately became concerned because it showed I have scoliosis or curvature of the spine. My spine is shaped like the letter "C." Momma wondered how I was able to stand and walk without difficulty. She was still concerned about the surgery. After speaking to Dr. Frim herself, my mom became more comfortable about the surgery and agreed with my decision. This is also when momma got her first nickname, "the weapon."

During the Winter Quarter, being a member of DePaul Gospel Choir proved beneficial. Rehearsal alone uplifted my spirit so I knew the choir was for me. as a result of my membership in the choir, I established several new friendships. The choir also provided me with the spiritual balance I needed. I must admit, it was becoming a little hectic with all the doctor appointments, physical therapy, college work and the stress that was accumulating because DePaul was not keeping their word about the accident. I refused to complain. God had brought me too far and through too many hurdles in my life to complain or give up. Besides I couldn't return home and face my family if I did.

Among the things I experienced as a member of the gospel choir was the joy of going to gospel concerts. Various choir members enjoyed going to gospel concerts. Among them was my friend Tonya. Tonya made plans to go to Fred Hammond's "Pages of Life" concert with another choir member. When she found out I loved Fred Hammond's music, she invited me to go with them. She blessed me further by purchasing my ticket. It was truly a blessed experience. Thank you Tonya. ☺

I completed Winter Quarter of the 1996-1997 school year with no problem. The back surgery was scheduled for Tuesday, March 25, 1997, which is also Whitney's birthday. Whitney was very nervous about me having surgery. Since I knew I was going to be at the hospital on her birthday, and to cheer her up, I bought her a cookie cake from the Original Cookie Co. in Evergreen Plaza. Just as I hoped it would do, the cake cheered her up and helped Whitney be less nervous about my surgery. Because this was my first surgery with Dr. Frim, I had to go see the anesthesia doctor. During this appointment, blood was drawn, and I was told what medicine I could take before the surgery. On the morning of the surgery, momma and daddy took me to the hospital. Shortly after I arrived at the hospital, I was called back so I could be prepped for surgery. Daddy sat in the waiting room while momma came back with me until I was taken into the operating room. The surgery was successful. Thank you Jesus! The only thing connecting my bladder to my spine was tissue. I stayed in the hospital for several days to recover from the surgery. I had to use a quad cane until I healed from the surgery.

One week later, I went for my post-op appointment. Dr. Frim said my back was healing well from the surgery. Now I had to work on regaining my strength so he referred me to physical therapy. I had physical therapy 2-3 times per week at the hospital. During this time, momma sacrificed her time, going to work late each day I had therapy to drive me back and forth. During this time, I also began taking medical notes of my surgeries.

1. VP Shunt Placement–5 months old
2. Hernia Repair–1 year old
3. Gallbladder Removal–March 1995

4. Knee Laproscopy, Meniscus and Cartiliage Repair (left knee)–August 1995
5. Meniscus, Cartilage and ACL Repair (left knee)–March 1996
6. Unteather Spinal Cord – March 25, 1997

Although I didn't take classes Spring Quarter 1996-1997 school year, my true friends I made at DePaul called and visited regularly to make sure I was feeling better. When I became stronger, I returned to work for Vicki. She was always understanding of my health. I thanked God for working for such an understanding person. During the later part of the Spring Quarter 1997, I returned to see Dr. Frim. My back healed very well from the surgery, although my headaches and incontinence continued. He prescribed me some medication to alleviate the pain from the headaches. On the spiritual front, my church family was becoming somewhat divided regarding our pastor. To maintain my relationship with Christ, I relied heavily on the power of prayer and reading the word of God to get me through this somewhat challenging chapter of my life.

During the summer of 1997, I continued working for Vicki. Vicki was a great person to work with. She was very understanding of my health. She had a business partner who worked out of her home, majority of the time. In addition to Vicki and myself, there was also Jenny, who worked in the office and assisted with the field work. Jenny was preparing to enjoy motherhood for the first time.

One month prior to the start of the Fall Quarter for the 1997-1998 school year, I met my new roommate, Kymmie. In August, we met in person for the first time. There was one other person who was assigned to the apartment however, I did not meet her until the day we moved in. On the day we moved in, the other roommate moved out. I try not to be judgmental but I believe the other roommate moved out because of race. I'm sad to say that but her parents got a strange look on their faces when they saw Kymmie and I. Oh well. I had the bedroom to myself temporarily. Kymmie had moved in one month early because she was a member of DePaul's track team and had chosen the single room. Initially, Kymmie and I got along very well.

As the school year progressed, the roommate who didn't care for me the previous year became my roommate again. Within a few days, literally, of her moving in, I could see things were not going to be much different that year. We were once again members of the DePaul Gospel Choir but that did not make a difference. I prayed things would improve between us. During times when things were most irritating I often visited my friend Farrah. I could always talk to her. There was also a pair of twin RA's (resident advisors—they monitored and assisted the residents of the building they were assigned to) in the building, as well as, a nearby building. Their names were Linda and Glinda. They were very good friends who looked out for my well-being. On the few occasions I missed classes due to my health, they were very helpful. They made sure my professors were made aware of the situation and turned in my work so I wouldn't fall behind in my classes. My headaches, as well as, my incontinence, was worsening and had started interrupting my life.

During this time, I also continued having problems with DePaul regarding the accident I had during Premier DePaul. Although DePaul accepted full financial responsibility, when the bills started coming in, the people put in charge of the bills was not paying as promised. It worsened when someone else was put in that position to handle my bills. He was very rude and unprofessional. As a result, this led to more aggravation in my life because daddy's insurance company was being billed. He often called me complaining because he thought I was not handling my affairs properly. During this time, I found solace in my mentor who also became my friend. In the end, I wound up seeking legal counsel to deal with the issue with DePaul. My mentor was especially helpful during these times. She encouraged me not to give up on my dreams, in spite of everything that had occurred. I also found solace in reading my bible and praying regularly. Although the situations arising in my life were becoming more hectic, as I continued at DePaul, I could not give up. I was just too stubborn to allow that to happen.

However, God know all and is in control of it all. He gave me the strength I needed to complete the Fall Quarter of the 1997-1998 school year.

"I waited patiently on the Lord: he inclined unto me, and heard my cry.
He brought me up also out of a horrible pit, and out of the miry clay, and set my feet upon a rock, and established my goings.
And he hath put a new song in my mouth, even praise unto our God: many shall see it, and fear, and shall trust in the Lord.
Blessed is that man that maketh the Lord his trust, and respected not the proud, nor such as turn aside to lies.
Many, O Lord my God, are thy wonderful works which thou hast done, and thy thoughts which are to us-ward: they cannot be reckoned up in order unto thee: if I would declare and speak of them, they are more than can be numbered."

Psalms 40:1-5 (KJV)

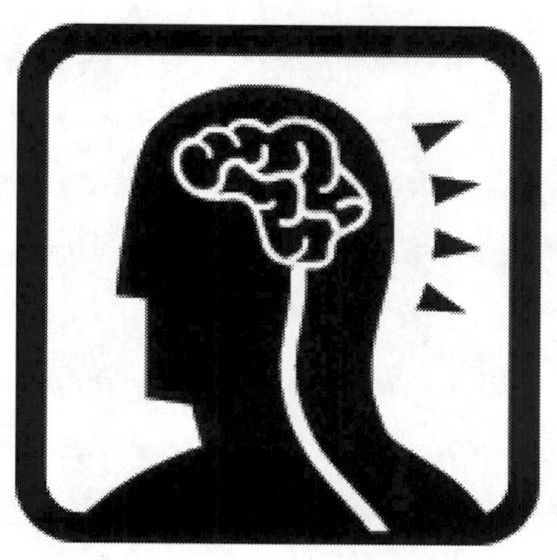

Chapter 8: Tests and Trials

When I returned home for Winter Break of the 1997-1998 school year, Dr. Frim was still concerned about my headaches and incontinence. I returned to see him the Tuesday prior to Christmas. He decided to do an exploratory surgery to examine the shunt. IF the shunt was functioning properly, he would do nothing but clean it up and add a telesensor to monitor the shunt pressure. IF the shunt was malfunctioning, the shunt would be replaced, in addition to Dr. Frim adding the telesensor.

The Sunday prior to the scheduled surgery, I got up and went to church with my parents. I told Momma Tucker and the rest of the family of the upcoming surgery. I also told Momma Merrill. During service, Momma Merrill told Rev. Murphy of the upcoming surgery. Rev. Murphy asked one of our evangelists, Evangelist Roscoe, to pray for me. It was during that time, reality truly set in of what was getting ready to occur in my life. Thank you Lord for my parents, who have always been there for me through the storms, such as with regards to my health. My mother always seemed to be more hands on when it came to the decision making and talking to the doctors. It would take years for me to truly understand why.

On the morning of the surgery, December 29, 1997, both of my parents accompanied me to the hospital. The surgery was believed to be successful, initially. God is truly a miracle worker. As a result of the surgery, we found out that the shunt had become blocked at one end. There was also a whole in the side of the tubing. This meant the shunt was not functioning at all, for God only knows how long. The shunt was replaced and the telesensor was added to the new shunt, as Dr. Frim had discussed with me during my initial appointment. I was in a lot of pain from the surgery. Prior to being released, Momma became concerned about my ability to properly rest at home, due to the noise level in the house from the children. She asked me if I wanted to go stay with Grannie so I could rest and heal from surgery. As much as I love my Grannie, I definitely had no problem with staying with her for a while to heal from surgery.

When I was released from the hospital, one week later, I went to Grannie's place. On that first night, Grannie made sure I was all right and resting as comfortable as possible before she went to bed. During the night, I suddenly woke up in agonizing pain that brought me to tears. I had a headache and it was hurting really bad. My head felt so heavy. My head felt like the percussion section of the orchestra was playing in my head. My head felt so much pressure that it felt like someone was squeezing the left and right sides of my head together. The pain had my throat on fire. I needed help quickly. I tried to call Grannie but she didn't hear me. I went to get up and fell back down in the bed from dizziness. I finally made it into the living room, where she was lying down, and with all the strength I could muster called her name. it even hurt to talk to my Grannie. Grannie immediately knew something was wrong and helped me back to bed. She turned on the lamp beside her bed and I screamed. The light made my eyes feel like they were on fire. She turned the light back off and called daddy. After asking me if I wanted to go back to the hospital (daddy hated to see me in the hospital), he came to get me. Grannie stayed by my bed until my daddy came to get me.

At the hospital, I was readmitted. For one week, doctors ran additional tests. Dr. Frim decided to do another shunt revision.

He was very supportive and you could tell he hated to see me in this pain. The surgery was scheduled around January 9, 1998. Two days prior to this, I experienced the ever-painful spinal tap for the first time. Daddy was visiting me so they let him stay by my side during the spinal tap. I had another shunt revision approximately one week later. During this surgery, an additional VP shunt was added to the one Dr. Frim changed when I was readmitted to the hospital. I stayed in the hospital, several more days after this surgery. My healing was slow. I noticed various family members that hardly ever visited me, started visiting me but never understood why. I had another painful spinal tap one week after the second surgery. About one week later, I was released.

7. VP Shunt Revision–December 29, 1997
8. VP Shunt Revision–January 9, 1998
9. VP Shunt Revision–January 16, 2008

I must admit, at that point, that was the scariest experience I endured in my life (I would later discover this was nothing compared to what was to come). While I was in the hospital, the room remained dark because light burned my eyes badly. I was constantly running a fever and hot so the fan had to be kept on in my room (might I remind you this was Chicago during the Winter) all the time.

I had such a low tolerance for noise, my chart and door (I'm told) warned that I was sensitive to sound. I had to muffle the sound of the tv (my only light source) when I had it on. Finally after twenty-one days (21) days of being in the hospital, I was allowed to go home. Everyone was very nervous as I still endured great pain from my headaches. It was during this time, it was believed I might not make it through the year. These people forgot there is an almighty doctor bigger than any surgeon in the world. GOD ! ! !

When I was finally released from the hospital, I went to stay with Grannie again. She took great care of me. on my follow-up, Dr. Frim said I was slowly improving. When I became well enough to leave Grannie's place, as I could tolerated light and sound better, I returned home. Shortly after returning home, Vicki, my boss from Historic Certification Consultants, called to check on me. During our conversation, she volunteered to tell the lady in the choir who introduced me to her initially (no one at DePaul knew what happened because I didn't get a chance to tell anyone).

The lady Vicki spoke to was the president of the choir. She told the members of the choir what happened. As large as the choir grew to be, only about ten members called to check on me. When I returned to school Spring Quarter 1997-1998, much to the dismay of Momma and Dr. Frim, they were constantly checking on me.

My summer vacation was nice, despite the changes that had arisen in my life. I had started forgetting things like what day of the week it was or the current date. On several occasions I could not remember where I put things, like my money, and thus lost it. My family accused me of repeating myself. At that time, I didn't see a problem and just thought my family was playing a cruel joke on me.

I'M VERY SORRY MOMMA, DADDY, SHA, LAVARE, NICOLE, BRI and NICK FOR THINKING YOU WERE PLAYING A CRUEL JOKE ON ME WHEN YOU WERE NOT. PLEASE FORGIVE ME. On my follow-up appointment with Dr. Frim, Momma accompanied me so she could make sure he understood how bad my short-term memory had become. My long-term memory appeared to be intact as I could remember things from my days at Community Day Care Center. If you said something to me and asked me to repeat it five minutes later, I was unable to repeat it.

When I went back to DePaul for the Fall Quarter 1998-1999 school year things were quite different. Kymmie, one of my roommates from the previous school year, was my roommate again. I did not perform as well in my classes because of my memory worsening. One of my professors, during that quarter, suggested I go see Karen, Director of the PLUS Program. This program was designed for students with learning disabilities, primarily. Although mine was physical, Karen and her staff was able to get me the assistance I needed. Over time, Karen and I became good friends. She encouraged me by the way she spoke of the things I endured, with regards to my health, but did not give up. I often told Karen that it was because of my faith in God that I was able to endure what I had endured in my life. Karen also encouraged me as I often saw her racing across campus (she uses a wheelchair) with no problem.

Reality set in for me during Spring Quarter of the 1998-1999 school year when I got lost while traveling on CTA's "L" on a route that should have been familiar to me. By the time I realized I was lost, I was so far north I had to call Daddy to come and get me. As luck would have it, he was working on the opposite side of the city so it would take him a while to get to me. As a result, he gave me specific directions to get me back to my dorm. When he got off the phone with me, daddy went a step further and notified the station I was leaving from. Just as the train was about to pull off, it stopped. I saw two CTA employees looking from car to car. When they got to the car I was on, they asked me my name. When they realized I was the person they were looking for, they had me switch cars to get on the car with the conductor, so he could help me get back to the campus. I was so embarrassed! I couldn't tell anyone about this.

Prior to the start of finals, I had a scheduled doctor's appointment at the University of Chicago Hospitals. Since I needed to run some errands while I was in Hyde Park, I took the bus to the "L" station, following my appointment. As I waited to cross the street to enter the correct side of the "L" station, a car pulled up and stopped in front of me. Not thinking anything of it because the traffic light was red, I continued standing where I was. Suddenly, the front and back passenger side windows came down and out came a Super Soaker. Everything happened so fast. The boys in the car wasted no time. They sprayed me from head to toe until I was soaked. When they drove off I was afraid to open my eyes or mouth because I was not sure if it was water or something else and my eyes were stinging. Some passersby helped me get dried off as much as possible, once it was determined I was sprayed with water. By the time I got back to my dorm, I had developed a cough but thought nothing of it. Two days later, I woke up having a very bad asthma attack. I called my parents house to tell them what happened. Sha answered the phone and immediately knew I was having an asthma attack.

She paged daddy to come and get me but it would have taken him too long to get to me. I called DePaul Security to see if they would take me to the hospital. They called paramedics and two security officers came and waited with me until the paramedics arrived. During this time, Kymmie who was asleep in her room, got up and volunteered to notify my professor (we took one class together that quarter) so I could make up my final.

Once I got to the nearby emergency room, I informed the doctor and nurses attending to my care that I have a hard time with breathing treatments. I get extremely jittery and my heart rate accelerate (yes, this is the general side effects but it does me a lot worse). They proceeded to give me THREE (3) breathing treatments, without pausing, to get my breathing back to normal. My heart felt like it was jumping out of my chest. I was so jittery, I couldn't see straight. I felt miserable. Just as I was given the third treatment, Momma and Sha walked in (Momma later said, if she knew that was my third treatment, she would not have let them give it to me). After several hours of observation, I was released from the hospital, although my breathing was still problematic. The breathing treatments still had my heart racing and feeling like it was jumping out of my chest. I was still so jittery. Momma had to hold my hand so I could sign my release papers. Momma didn't trust me staying on campus so we went to my apartment, collected some of my things and went back to my parent's house. Later that night, just as my mom had feared, I woke up having another asthma attack. It was so bad I had to use a bat to knock on the floor because I couldn't talk or make it down the stairs to my parent's bedroom. This time, daddy took me straight to the University of Chicago Hospitals.

In the emergency room of the University of Chicago Hospitals, doctors determined I was indeed having another asthma attack but I had also been overdosed at the other hospital. My heart was still racing and feeling like it was jumping out of my chest. I was still extremely jittery. I had to be put on a heart monitor temporarily because my heart rate was very high. I was so overdosed, in the beginning the doctors could only treat me with oxygen until they got the other medicine out of my system. The doctors and nurses were very upset. They made me promise never to allow myself to be put in that type of predicament again. They reminded me that I always have the right to question and refuse treatment if something doesn't feel right to me. I wound up staying in the hospital for two weeks. When I got home, I called Karen and she arranged for me to make up all my final exams, after I went for my follow-up appointment.

During the summer, Momma did everything she could to keep me from returning to DePaul for the 1999-2000 school year. She was concerned because my short-term memory was continuing to worsen (in her eyes), not to mention the adventures with my health. I still continued to have headaches. My incontinence worsened to the point I was losing control of my bladder during the day. Dr. Frim referred me to an Urologist to see if he could offer me an option that had not been tried. He started me on new medication.

I decided to share an apartment, on campus, for the 1999-2000 school year. I often spent time with my friends during the summer prior to the start of the new school year. During August 1999, I returned to see the Urologist at the University of Chicago Hospitals because unfortunately the medication he prescribed was having no positive effect on my incontinence. During this time, he told me about another device, INTERSTIM, that was being surgically implanted to treat incontinence. To ensure the device worked properly so I wouldn't have to undergo any unnecessary surgery, the doctor took me through a trial period. During the trial, the device was partially implanted to hang outside my back. I dropped all my Fall Quarter 1999 classes and made arrangements with DePaul's Housing department so I wouldn't lose my apartment (students lose their housing if they take the quarter off).

On the home front, momma was becoming more concerned about my health (because it seemed to be worsening) and my ability to work. After many conversations, she finally convinced me to apply for Disability. She also suggested I apply for a medical card because of the mounting medical bills my parents were incurring on my behalf. I was working part time at a place that paid more than Vicki but because I had to take so much time off work for my health, I never saw the difference. The Interstim was unsuccessful so it was removed. Thank God for the test stage. I would have hated to undergo the surgery and it was unsuccessful. My Urologist decided to try another medication that was also unsuccessful.

10. Interstim Continence Control Therapy (TEST)– September 28, 1999

Prior to my follow-up appointment, Momma Tucker and I discussed what had been happening recently. As a result, Momma Tucker went with me to my follow-up appointment. During this appointment, my Urologist told me about another surgical option to help with my incontinence. During this surgery, my bladder would be rebuilt, or rather made larger, using part of my large intestines. That sounded weird at first. Thank God Momma Tucker was with me because she helped asked questions that I had not thought to ask. Unfortunately, the decision for the surgery was not made until the end of December 1999. As a result, the surgery was scheduled for January 2000 which meant I now had to take the Winter Quarter of the 1999-2000 school year off from DePaul.

....

Sunday, December 23, 1999

3:10am – I am unable to sleep again. I can't get the upcoming surgery out of my head. Nothing bad ever happens. This time I dreamed about the preparation for the surgery. I already know I have to clean my bowels out prior to the surgery because they have to take part of my large intestines for the surgery. Everyone is there. Momma and Daddy are sitting in the waiting room. Surprisingly, Sha even came to the hospital. I don't know where the kids are. After the surgery, I am in a lot of pain. Daddy finds Kita and she comes to the hospital.

Wednesday, December 26, 1999

4:30am – I am sick of going to the bathroom every hour on the hour! I am sick of having accident after accident! I can't wait for January 19th to get here. Lord Jesus please let this surgery work so I could get some relief. Oh well, let me try to go back to sleep.

• •

Wednesday, December 29, 1999

I am feeling better since I started journaling again. I feel like a weight is being lifted off my shoulders. Today was very good. The kids were good. I didn't have any disagreements with anyone. Thank God! Well, I'm getting tired. My quiet times are getting longer since I have been journaling them. I feel like I am getting more out of my quiet times too. Thank you Lord!!!

• •

The funny part is that I was dealing with my health so much, I didn't have time to think about the so-called "MILLENIUM BUG" that was getting ready to take over the world supposedly. I felt sorry for the people who ran out and spent all their money on those so-called MILLENIUM SURVIVAL PACKS because the world was supposed to go haywire at midnight as a result of computer systems, or whatever, not understanding 2000and thinking of it as 000, or whatever the experts said would happen. I forget why I had to go to the store near December 31st but when I went down the aisles that held such things as WATER, PAPER PRODUCTS and BATTERIES, all of the aisles were practically empty. I knew I had heard on the news about it, as well as, read in the newspaper articles concerning it but at that very moment, I realized how many people took that warning seriously. I just couldn't bring myself to believe the hype. God had brought me through so many things worse than this MILLENIUM BUG. If God could bring me through everything I had went through so far, I knew he could bring me through this so-called MILLENIUM BUG.

"And we know that all things work together
for the good to them that love God,
to them who are called according to his purpose."
Romans 8:28 (KJV)

Chapter 9: A New Century, A New Beginning

10 . . . 9 . . . 8 . . . 7 . . . 6 . . . 5 . . . 4 . . . 3 . . . 2 . . . 1 . . . HAPPY NEW YEAR ! ! !! Well it was after 12 midnight so it was officially January 1, 2000. I didn't see any signs of the millennium bug. None of the negative things that were broadcast across various media, over the last few months leading up to the New Year, had occurred. I can happily say I was not surprised. That is why I didn't go out to the stores and spend all that money buying things to prepare me for the millennium bug. God is the one who has total control over the world. He has the final say.

. . . .

January 3, 2000–Thank God for an awesome day. All went well. Daddy is in New York but only for one week instead of the usual two. I talked to him today. It was pretty much quiet today although Bri Bri stayed home with me because her school was closed. That was fine except, she continuously cried because she could not wear the outfit she wanted to wear. Tomorrow is Sha's birthday. I had an awesome quiet time today. Thank you Lord! Well I'm getting tired. Momma Tucker has been on my mind all day today. I don't know why. I will call her tomorrow.

....

As I approached the scheduled date of my bladder surgery, anxiety was very high. It wasn't that I was scared. I just wondered of the surgery would be successful, since none of the other medications did me any good. After all, the Stem was also unsuccessful. On the day prior to the scheduled surgery date, January 18, 2000, I woke up early for a doctor's appointment I had scheduled for my medical card appeal (my original application was denied). When I woke up, I had an extremely bad headache that covered my face. I told Momma as a precaution, prior to us leaving for the appointment.

After parking her car, Momma and I caught the bus to the 95th Street train station. We got on the middle "L" car and sat down. (During this time I always sat in the middle car because that was usually the car the person who called out the stops was on). My head was pounding as the train left out of the station. The last thing I remembered was two uniformed CTA employees boarding the train at 79th Street. When I first partially regained consciousness, I was in what appeared to be an ambulance. The second and complete time I regained consciousness, I was in the emergency room of a hospital I had never received care at before. I knew this because nothing looked familiar to me.

I felt hands on me. When I turned my head to my left, there was a nurse checking my vitals. On my right, was my momma. I had never seen Momma look so frightened or surprised, whichever the case was, as she looked at me and told me I had a seizure on the train. She said an army officer was on the train at the time and intervened. Momma said the seizure caused me to swallow my tongue. Momma told me I was at Northwestern Hospital. After running some tests and observing me for several hours, doctors decided to admit me to the hospital. Due to my medical history, as well as, the distance between the hospital and my parent's house, my mother asked them to transfer me to the University of Chicago

Hospitals. She asked me if I wanted her to call Dea. Edgerton since Daddy was in New York (his job had him working 2 week out of the month in New York), so he could come over to the hospital. I told her yes.

When we arrived at the University of Chicago Hospitals, Momma called Dea. Edgerton to come over to the hospital with us. He came over immediately. I was admitted to the hospital for additional tests and observations. I had two MRI's and an EEG to add to the x-ray and CT scan that was done at Northwestern Hospital. Because my heart rate had become elevated, doctors also ordered an EKG. The seizure was caused by some activity on the left side of my brain, which was considered active. I would have to start taking anti-seizure medication again. In the past, I was prescribed anti-seizure medication to get some control over my headaches. Because my bladder surgery wasn't considered urgent, it was postponed. I went home on medication to control my seizures.

When I was released from the hospital, Momma did not let me out of her sight until my follow-up appointment with my neurologist. When Daddy got home from New York, he was also very watchful of me. During this time, I learned a little more about the gentleman who saved my life. He was currently in the army program at DePaul. How ironic, right? His name was—. Momma was able to get his contact information so I could call him personally when I was able to. Unfortunately, I misplaced the information so I went in search of a spy. ☺My friend Karen's office was located next to his at DePaul. She happily got the information for me. When we finally spoke, I was so overwhelmed, I said "thank you" and forgot everything else I wanted to say to him. I will be forever grateful to him for intervening and not just sitting back and doing nothing. Unfortunately, I have lost touch with him but my prayer is that God will continue to bless and keep His arms of protection around him. Who knows? Maybe one day God will allow our paths to cross once more. Until then, God bless you.

I am forever grateful to my mother as well. She and I haven't always been as close as I wanted us to be however, when it came to my health and well-being, she always looked out for me. Dr. Frim had it right when he first nicknamed her "the weapon." Then as time went on, he changed her nickname to "the boss." Up until that time, I don't think anything happened to me that ever surprised Momma like that seizure. She later told me the seizure began by me turning my head toward her in a deep stare. I then began making this strange noise. Momma thought I was joking and told me to stop playing because that was not funny. It was at that point, the army officer politely said, "excuse me" and intervened. I am so thankful to God for that army officer being on that train. I knew Momma's lack of response was out of shock. After all, this is the same woman who had worked in the medical profession since before I was even born.

....

January 31, 2000

The last two weeks have been very challenging, both physically and mentally. I'll begin the last time I wrote in my journal. It was about two days before the scheduled bladder surgery. Anxiety was high and I had to keep reminding myself what God has for me, it is for me. I woke up the morning before the day of surgery "kind of" early because I had that doctor's appointment for my medical card appeal. I had a very bad headache over my face. I told Momma and we left for the appointment. After parking her car, we caught the bus to the 95th Street Station. We got on the middle car and sat down. My head was still pounding. The last thing I remember is 2 conductors getting on the train. When I first came to I was in an ambulance. The 2nd and complete time, I am in the emergency room I never received care at. I know this because nothing looked familiar to me. I am scared and in pain. Momma told me I had a seizure on the train and some guy saved my life. I was transferred to the University of Chicago Hospitals, a place I am more familiar with. Dea. Edgerton met us there. I was admitted and stay in there for 6 days, during which time I had 2 MRI's and an EEG to add to the x-rays and CT scan the other hospital did. The seizure was caused by some activity on the left side of my brain that is still active. The surgery was postponed. I am now on medicine to control my seizures and I have been on house arrest for the past week. My Momma, the weapon, will not let me out of her sight. I go see my neurologist Tuesday to see what's up. I just want momma to go back to work and stop worrying about me and, have my bladder surgery so I can have some relief.

God is so awesome!!

• •

On my follow-up appointment, I was very surprised as my neurologist said he was not made aware of me being in the hospital for a seizure until the day I was released. Of course, that didn't make my Momma or myself feel any better about the situation. Due to complications I had with abdominal pain and an inability to keep food down, my momma took me back to the emergency room where I was readmitted on February 3, 2000. This time I remain hospitalized for 18 days. Eventually I improved enough to reschedule the bladder surgery for February 22, 2000. I had a short break from the hospital as the insurance company put pressure on the hospital so I was released to go home February 20, 2000.

• •

Saturday February 19, 2000

Today I witnessed something I never want to see again. I saw a hardworking woman, a nurse, disrespected and ridiculed for something that was not her fault. It hurt me because she is a very sweet nurse and what occurred could have been avoided. Well . . .

• •

Sunday, February 20, 2000

11:00am—I'm going home! Thank you Jesus!

It's hard to pretend you don't want something to happen when you really do. I always wanted to go home, if only for 1 day—so be it. Now I have the opportunity. My parents want me to stay until Tuesday but, the insurance company (or hospital, whichever is responsible for the decision) won't let me. These things are so weird. I just hate being an inconvenience to Momma. She has been through so much for me. I love and appreciate her so much. Countdown time: 2 Days until Tuesday. Hallelujah!!!

It felt good to get out of the hospital, even if it was for just 1 ½ days. While at home, I spoke to the Edgertons regarding my surgery. They wanted to accompany me to the hospital. After getting permission from my parents, the Edgertons agreed to meet my parents and myself at the house the morning of the surgery. On the morning of the surgery, when the Edgertons arrived at the house, they had a surprise for me. I had been talking about Richard Smallwood's newest CD because it had a song on it entitled, "Healing" that truly spoke to my spirit. Of course, I had to hear that song before I went to the hospital. I begged Momma and Daddy to let me listen to it. Momma agreed as long as I hurried up so I wouldn't be late getting to the hospital.

11. Bladder Augmentation–February 22, 2000

At the hospital, when my name was called, Momma let Mrs. Edgerton (Trouble) sit with me while I was being prepped for surgery (Hospital rules allow one person to be with you while you are being prepped for surgery).

Thursday, February 24, 2000—University of Chicago Hospitals

5:00pm—What's to come is better than what's been. Celebrate a new beginning. Please don't pass me by.

This is definitely a new experience in itself. My life is in God's hands. I don't know what to make of it. I will not and cannot give up on the vision, regardless of what happens. I have been blessed with beautiful parents who have always been willing to go to bat for me, with regards to my health. My mom truly understands and believes the vision God has given me for my life. It is very reassuring when you go through something to know someone is in your corner who believes in you. In my case, I have two people.

10:30pm—I cannot seem to get these songs out of my head: "Healing" by Richard Smallwood, "Write the Vision" and "What's to Come Is Better Than What's Been."

As I continue to live through these situations, I am reminded I will make it. Thank you Jesus! I have been blessed with two very beautiful parents. In the past, and probably future, we have not always agreed, nor have we maintained the relationship I hoped for. Thank you Jesus for change. My momma understands, much more than daddy (surprisingly), the vision God has for my life. She has been very supportive of me since I've been in the hospital. She tells me she is even journaling now. ☺

. . . .

As I continued this hospital adventure, God began to open my eyes. The more God opened my eyes and heart, the more I was comforted and the less I concentrated on the pain I endured. I began being a blessing to others in ways I still do not completely understand. For instance, one of the lab techs who regularly drew my blood always encouraged me and uplifted my spirit as she said God's presence was evident in my life. She encouraged me to remain faithful to God because he would never leave me nor forsake me. I had a beautiful 86 year old roommate, at that time, named Ms Wolnak. Ms. Wolnak was never satisfied unless she got a hug from me every day. She would tell her family and friends I was "her angel from God." This still brings tears to my eyes when I think of her. I love you Ms. Wolnak.

The main person I expected to hear from never called or visited. True Right had a new pastor because Rev. Murphy died tragically of a heart attack while fishing. This accident took place during my last days at DePaul. The newly appointed/elected pastor never called or visited me. Momma Merrill continued to read the announcements and she always included the Sick and Shut-In when she read the announcements. Even more importantly, Daddy was still an active minister of the church. By then I was no longer singing in the choir but I was still active as I continued doing the announcements on Youth Sunday. I was a Teacher's Aide and helped out with Vacation Bible School during the summer, as well as, participated in the youth activities. I know he was busy with his pastoral obligations but I had been a member nearly 20 years. Would it have hurt him to call me ONE TTIME and just ask how I was doing? He could have even just said "God bless you" and hung up.

When I was released from the hospital on March 14, 2000, things were different. I went home on numerous medications. I was on more medications than I have ever been on in my life. My Urologist referred me to a Gastroenterologist (GI) because I had begun having trouble with my stomach that caused me to be nauseated and vomit frequently. When I went home, things seemed to have worsened to the point I could barely eat because each time I did, whatever I had just eaten came back out, either through my mouth or the other end.

By the time I returned to the hospital for my follow-up appointment, my momma was very concerned and wanted me to be readmitted to the hospital. On March 20, 2000, I had two scheduled doctor's appointments. My first appointment was with the Gastroenterologist (GI) doctor. As soon as she saw me slumped over the table, she knew something was wrong and immediately admitted me to the hospital. Momma immediately gave me that "I told you so" look.

During this hospitalization, as with the previous hospitalizations, Momma took a lot of time off work to stay at the hospital with me. She only went home intermittently, to check on Nicole and Lavare and, freshen herself up. Thank God she worked for the same doctor all my life, which at that point, meant at least 23 years. I know she would have lost her job if she was anywhere else. At this time, many tests were ordered. I also experienced a feeding tube for the first time as doctors placed a NG[1] tube in my nose to feed me through. The NG tube was temporary because I sneezed it out within the first 24 hours. When the tube cannot be placed in the nose or when tube feedings will be required for more than 6 weeks, a surgically created opening is made either through the esophagus (esophagostomy), the stomach (gastrostomy), or the intestines (jejunostomy).

Because she was not satisfied with the outcome of that feeding tube anyway, my GI doctor ordered another test. After reviewing the results of that test, she decided to place another type of feeding tube, called a gastrostomy tube or G-tube, in my stomach during the later part of March 2000. This was definitely a new experience for me. Through this tube, I was fed four times a day. The only uncomfortable part was the feedings, through the tube. I had to take in a certain amount of water, in addition to the feedings through the tube. The feedings and water made me very full and uncomfortable as I had lost my appetite so I was always full. Because I was being sent home with this feeding tube, my mom (who would help me at home) and I had to learn how to properly care for the feeding tube and the machine it was connected to. This involved learning how to flush my feeding tube so the feedings wouldn't get backed up in the tube and cause additional problems.

• •

---

1 Nasogastric tube: it is inserted through the nose and runs into the stomach or small intestines.

Sunday, April 1, 2000

It has been a long time since I have had time to record my thoughts. Things are a little crazy however I know things will work out for the good of them who love the Lord.

I was released from the hospital almost one week ago. What an adventure! It began with my bladder surgery. The surgery itself, I am told went well. Unfortunately, there were a few complications. I developed a cyst and an abscess. The cyst was removed and the abscess was drained. Unfortunately it came back.

The doctors thought I was suffering from depression because I preferred to keep to myself in my room. It took Momma talking to the doctors for them to back off. To add to this, I became more nauseated and completely lost my appetite. In fact, for a while I was vomiting. The greatest part of this adventure has been my parents.

My parents have always been there for me, with regards to my health. Momma took off work. She even spent the night with me on several occasions at the hospital. The first time, I was put back in the hospital. Daddy cut his trip to New York short so he could come home and see about me.

I love my Momma and Daddy. Momma has held up well. She is an important source of strength for me. of course, God is the supreme source of strength. I don't know if I could have made it through this without God and Momma.

"I can do all things through Christ who strengthens me."

Monday, April 2, 2000

What an adventure 2000 has turned out to be. I have spent most of the year in the hospital. Momma and Daddy joke that I have made the hospital my home and my home have become just a place to visit. In reality, that seems to be true. I can count how many days I have been home. Momma, Daddy and Sha have been wonderful. They always try to cheer me up on those rare moments when the craziness gets to me. Today I listened to the Richard Smallwood CD the Edgertons bought me. I was reminded of God's word where he says, "I will never leave you nor forsake you." I was also reminded that there is healing in the name of Jesus!

Upon my discharge from the hospital, my GI doctor set it up so I could have in-home nursing. The nurse kept calling to schedule but never showed up on the scheduled day. Finally, he showed up in just enough time for me to be readmitted to the hospital on April 3, 2000 for a blocked G-tube.

As with the previous hospitalizations, I endured numerous tests and doctors as they tried to figure out what happened to me. My friends were wonderful. Among them was Sarah, who was one in a million. There was also Lisette, who at the time was attending medical school at University of Chicago so I saw her almost every day, when her schedule permitted. I had met her through my friend John some time ago. On the occasions she didn't get to visit, she made it her point to call and check on me. Over time, many doctors and nurses began to think we were blood sisters.

Thursday, April 6, 2000–University of Chicago Hospitals

"This is the day the Lord has made. I will rejoice and be glad in it."

Today is a beautiful day. The sun is shining bright. I know with God's guidance the doctors will find out what's wrong with me, instead of just saying nothing or calling me depressed.

1:40PM – I just came back from Urology a short time ago. As usual, his exam showed nothing. I might go home today or tomorrow. It all depends on the meeting the Gastroenterologist (GI) scheduled with Momma and myself this evening. When I spoke to Momma a short time ago, she said she said she could bring me home tomorrow. For some reason whenever I am in a state of uncertainty, God always send someone to shine some light. Today, for instance, God used some people in the hospital to show me. I ran into another hospital employee who said they remembered me because I blessed them with my smile. This has occurred several times each time I am hospitalized.

8:15PM – I'm going home tomorrow. Thank you Jesus!!!

....

After this discharge from the hospital, some of my friends called to say they wanted to visit and spend the day with me. On the day of their visit, I received another surprise as another member of the choir asked to come with them. This was great except my home nurse scheduled her visit on the same day and was running late. Of course, she arrived the same time as my friends. I then received an added bonus, as the Edgertons came to visit me, as well. I wound up going from one room to another.

When my nurse, as well as, the Edgertons left my friends and I had the remainder of the day to ourselves. I had so much fun with them. That is not to say I did not enjoy seeing the Edgertons. It just felt good to hang out with my friends as I had not spent time with them in a very long time unless you count the times my friends visited me in the hospital. I had to hold back tears of joy. We reminisced about some of the good times we shared. The thing that really struck my heart was the card from the DePaul Gospel Choir that included personalized messages from the members of the choir. Secondly, the choir brought me a "thank you" balloon because they said I encouraged them. To say the least I was surprised and speechless. I knew I had endured a lot but I did not realize how much of an impact I was having on other people's lives.

Around this time, Momma felt confident about me staying home alone again, so she returned to work. During these times, I had the house to myself. During these times I did my quiet times during the day as I knew I could do them uninterrupted. I began to focus on and study the book of Job. It is amazing how God works. I was allowing my human side to come out and starting to worry about my health situations (although I wouldn't allow my family and friends to know). I had just begun to study the book of Lamentations when for some reason; God led me to the book of Job.

Job was a man of God as I am a woman of God. He went through numerous trials and tribulations in his live, as well. He lost everything. He was at, what many would consider to be, his lowest point. However, Job remained faithful to God in his daily life as I have been trying to do. He even reprimanded his own wife and friends when they didn't understand and tried to get Job to turn away from God. Job reminded me God knows how much we can bear and as a result, God will never put more on us than we can bear. Our only role is to be submissive to God always, when times are good or bad, knowing that God always takes care of His children. We must always remember to put our lives in God's hands.

Wednesday, April 13, 2000

Today was a trying day. I vomited twice and was nauseated all day. I rested most of the day, while trying to find some relief. My male nurse finally showed up today.

One of True Right's deacons called once again to say True Right's New Pastor was coming to visit me today but never showed up. Oh well. I talked to my Grannie today. I always enjoy talking to my Grannie.

The person who did my phone interview for the medical card was very rude. I called to tell June but she is on vacation this week.

The Ct scan for my stomach and pelvis has been scheduled for Saturday. I pray I get some answers as I have been miserable all day. I still have no appetite and must force food down when I eat. I hate having to do that.

I miss Kita. I will probably ask Momma if I can call her tomorrow. I pray all is going well with her. I am so thankful for the good things happening to her. Kita has been hurting for so long. I am happy she is beginning to find a little peace in her life.

God's presence is evident in my life. I know this because I know I would not survive without having God in my life.

....

I guess I had been at home for too long. I had actually got to stay home for eight days that time before I was readmitted to the hospital on April 14, 2000. On the day I was admitted, I woke feeling sick and remained sick all day. All my tube feedings kept coming back up. I called Momma and she told me to page my GI doctor. Of course, I did not want to go back to the hospital so I put it off as long as possible. Eventually, I paged her and she in turn, readmitted me to the hospital. The doctors continued running tests. Momma and Daddy visited me regularly. I had them call my close friends and Mack (the minister who worked with DePaul Gospel Choir) to let them know I had been readmitted to the hospital. Tonya, Sara, as well as, many others continued to call and keep me lifted up in prayer. Lisette was wonderful, as always, sacrificing her free time to come keep me company and keeping me lifted in prayer. She had become a dear friend and sister who I prayed would remain in my life.

Mack was always supportive. He came to visit me regularly. Each time he visited, he always had a scripture to uplift my spirit. Over time, because he visited me so much many of the hospital staff started to think he was my pastor.

Friday, April 21, 2000 – University of Chicago Hospitals

10:30am – "This is the day that the Lord has made: let us rejoice and be glad in it." Psalms 118:24 (KJV)

I am going to come out of the hospital with a strong experience to use in the ministry God has given me. The test I was originally scheduled to have Friday has been rescheduled because I still have too much barium in my system, from the other test. I don't know who was more upset when I got back to my room, the resident or me. I can't wait to see what my GI doctor has to say about all this.

I spoke to Kymmie, my former roommate, last night. She is still the same. I don't think she will ever change when it comes to caring about people. She was very upset and fussed about me being in and out of the hospital for the past few months. I also talked to Grannie yesterday. I miss her so much. I must go see her when I get out of the hospital.

4:00pm – Mack White surprised me and came to visit me. To say the least, I needed the visit. My GI doctor just left. She said this weekend will be just like last night. I will have to have that liquid infused through my G-tube. At least, I don't have to drink it by mouth. Yuck!!!

I almost forgot these are the scriptures Mack blessed me with today:

"You who bring good news to Zion, go up on a high mountain. You who bring good news to Jerusalem, lift up your voice with a shout,

lift it up, do not be afraid; say to the towns of Judah, "Here is your God!"

See, the Sovereign LORD comes with power, and he rules with a mighty arm. See, his reward is with him, and his recompense accompanies him." Isaiah 40:9-10 (NIV)

"Even youths grow tired and weary, and young men stumble and fall; but those who hope in the LORD will renew their strength.

They will soar on wings like eagles; they will run and not grow weary, they will walk and not be faint." Isaiah 40:30-31 (NIV)

"For I know the plans I have for you," declares the LORD, "plans to prosper you and not to harm you, plans to give you hope and a future." Jeremiah 29:11 (NIV)

....

Several days later, I underwent another procedure as my GI doctor decided to try another feeding tube. This tube would be placed in my chest, in that main vein that runs to the heart. The doctors placed a single-lumen central line on April 26, 2000. During this time, several nurses, headed by three nurses I always called "Momma" (because they acted just like my momma) in the hospital, decided to cheer me up. When my hospital stays first started getting longer, Momma bought me a small radio to listen to music in my room. Whenever they came to do my vitals, the nurses joked about the size of it. Since all the nurses knew I enjoyed listening to gospel music, several nurses joined with all my mommas and bought me a bigger radio, a boom box with a CD player on it, so I may listen to my gospel music. They also took a large sheet of paper and made a large happy face on it. As the day progressed, many nurses, and even some doctors, signed the happy face. At the end of the day, my nurses took the happy face and hung it under the TV in my room. Now I could look at it regularly. Yes, it did cheer me up. ☺ A day or two later, my GI doctor and her team discovered I had a small bowel obstruction. This of course, meant more surgery. The surgery was performed May 3, 2000.

12. Small Bowel Obstruction – May 3, 2000

Around this time, my sister Netta and one of my cousins, Neicy, came to visit me in the hospital. I was very surprised to see them. They bought me a card and a book to read. To this day, that book still sits on the headboard of my bed. As usual, Momma kept up with me constantly, sleeping at the hospital with me for a few days then returning home to make sure everything was in order, before she came back to the hospital with me again. At one point, my blood count dropped extremely low. As a result I received my first blood transfusion on May 9, 2000. Daddy kept me company that evening while I received the blood. It stung a little as it went in. Daddy kept my mind off that by talking to me. Days later, as a result of the central line insertion, my GI doctor began a different type of feeding that also provided me with the nutrition I needed. The new feeding was called TPN, total parenteral nutrition. In addition to containing the vitamins and nutrients I needed, it contained lipids so I could maintain a healthy weight. I had lost so much weight over those last few months; my GI doctor was trying to get me back up to a healthy weight.

• •

Friday, May 12, 2000 – University of Chicago Hospitals

12:10am – Another day in the hospital. Latest news is that I may be going home soon. I will still have to be on TPN but only for 16 hours out of the day.

The church blessed me with a love offering to help with my bills and expenses. That's exactly what it was used for. It was supposed to be a surprise but Trouble accidentally told me. Momma had planned to surprise me and use the money to get my bills caught up, that I had fallen behind on, and then surprise me with the statements showing the bill was paid. She was then going to tell me where the money came from.

Momma said the Sunday before the offering was collected, Rev. Wilson, True Right's new pastor, told the congregation so they could bring a special love offering the Sunday the offering was collected. I love my True Right Family!!!

Momma has been wonderful through all of this. We have grown much closer. I only hope and pray we remain that way.

God is doing something tremendous in my life. Thank you Jesus!!!

....

Once again Momma and I, received training and instruction on how to care for the central line and the feedings, prior to me being discharged from the hospital to go home. I had to be connected to the feeding tube sixteen hours out of the day. The good part was I decided when I did the feedings during the day. I was also provided with a travel-convenient pump and carrying case so if I chose to go out during my feeding, I would be able to do so without any problems. Momma and I was a team again. Momma and I had an arrangement. Momma always changed the dressing over the line because I was afraid to do it. I didn't mind hooking myself up and unhooking myself when the feedings ended. We both flushed the line, when it needed to be flushed. Momma prepped the bag to make sure all the air bubbles were cleared before I was hooked up. Sha wouldn't even look when Momma and I did those things so asking her for assistance was definitely out of the question. She always hated needles, although this system was needleless, she still wanted no part of it. Daddy is a very strong man but even this was too much for him to handle and I was beginning to understand why.

Shortly thereafter, I began a clear liquid diet and tolerated it which moved me even closer to being discharged. I still endured TPN but the amount was lowered. Unfortunately, I was not discharged in time for Mother's Day 2000. Because of this Momma had to, or rather chose to, spend part of her special day at the hospital with me. She got up that morning and went to church with Daddy, Nicole and LaVare. Everyone then came to visit me and keep me company for a little while. I loved seeing everyone but I hated the idea of Momma having to spend part of her special day in the hospital because of me. thank you Jesus another chapter ended as I was discharged from the hospital on May 17, 2000, only 10 days before Momma's birthday.

I was so happy to be home but, it felt so strange, as I had not been home in over one month. When I got home, Sha teased me about how much weight I had lost. Sha hated hospitals, doctors and especially, shots. The idea of seeing all that stuff I went through made her cringe so she never visited me (except for two special days that had not arrived yet). After I got home, someone even joked I looked as small as Sha. Oh Lord. I did lose weight if I am as small as Sha (at that point, Sha was the smallest adult in the family). My appetite was gone so I had a hard time eating. Momma and Daddy did everything they could think of to help bring my appetite but nothing they tried brought my appetite back. On my follow-up, my GI doctor warned me if I didn't improve my eating habits, I would have to be put back in the hospital. I did somehow manage with God's help, to remain out of the hospital for a few months. I only had to go to the emergency room once in May when I got an extremely painful headache and Dr. Frim wanted to make sure it wasn't the shunt. Thank God the shunt was functioning fine.

I developed a routine which I continued for a long time. I saw my nurse once a week for labs and check-up. I did my TPN 16 hours a day. I followed a liquid diet at first. Then I upgraded to a soft diet. Things had started to look up. I started hanging out with my friends again. During the summer, June 3, 2000, I was able to witness my friend Donyiel, marry her sweetheart, Terrence. I was so happy for her. My little sister looked so beautiful. Donyiel will always have a special place in my heart, regardless of the changes life may bring upon us. I am so thankful to God that Daddy said he would take me to the wedding, which was held at True Right. It was beautiful. Donyiel was beautiful.

As the summer progressed, I was able to spend time with some of my friends. Lisette and I hung out a lot when she wasn't working. In August, Sara and I even went to a gospel concert together. I was looking forward to my birthday that year.

As I came closer to my birthday, my GI doctor became concerned again as I was not doing as well as she had hoped. She ordered some tests which was unfortunately, scheduled right before my birthday. Four friends, I nicknamed "my favorite schemers" had something up their sleeves. At the time I didn't think anything of it. Sara, Lisette, and John stopped calling me and answering my messages and I didn't have the slightest clue as to why. I got up as usual, finished and disconnected my TPN. I got ready for my day. I suddenly got a phone call from a friend. She said she wanted me to meet one of her family members. I didn't think anything of it. Just as I was putting the finishing touches on, the doorbell rang.

Sha opened the door and said it was Lisette. Something wasn't right. My closest friends were like family. As a result, it was not abnormal for them to come in my parent's house and come find me. Sha called me out to see Lisette. When I got into the dining room, the front hallway door was left open, which was also unusual. Sha was adamant about me closing the door. I then found out why. When I got to the door, Sara jumped out and hollered, "Surprise!" Everyone was laughing so hard. Lisette and Sarah had come to take me out to celebrate my birthday. We went downtown where we were joined by John. We went to the movies and out to eat. It was at that point I was elated as they forgot I couldn't eat solid food and accidentally took me to a nice restaurant but stopped short when they realized what they did. I was not offended. In fact, I was thankful to God that they were not concentrating on my health, per se, but on taking me out to have fun. We then found another restaurant where I could get a cup of soup and they could get a nice bite to eat. I really enjoyed myself that day with my friends.

As September 2000 came to a close, I found out that my legal battle with DePaul was coming to a head. I must admit, I was very happy. I just wanted DePaul to keep the promise they made me. I just wanted Daddy to get off my back about his insurance company being billed for the accident. I just wanted some peace of mind about the accident. Finally I did my first deposition during that time. I had the pleasure of meeting

DePaul's attorney. All I could say is there are some people who need little prayer and there are some people who needs a lot of prayer. I knew she was only doing her job but what happened to character and decorum?

October 3, 2000 gave me a great scare. I work up and disconnected my line, as I finished my TPN. All of a sudden blood began to squirt all over me from the central line. Horrified, I called Momma. She immediately called paramedics but they could only take me to the neighborhood hospital, a place Momma nor myself cared for. The paramedic helped Momma put me in her car, assuring her I would be fine. She then took me to the emergency room at the University of Chicago Hospitals, of course. The emergency room doctor attending to my care said it was only a urinary tract infection and sent me home on antibiotics. Of course, my Momma and I were both surprised and a little upset. Why would a urinary tract infection have a central line shooting out blood, when the line was in my chest? That question was answered the next day by my GI doctor.

That following day, October 4, 2000, my GI doctor called me very concerned. She asked me, "Shereice was the blood drawn for your labs yesterday taken from your arm or the central line?" Without thinking, I responded, "my arm." Before I got a chance to say anything else, she said, "Are you sure?" I said, "No, I'm sorry. It was taken from my central line because I didn't feel like being poked more than once."

My GI doctor continued. "You have an infection in your central line. I am arranging a room for you right now. You need to be admitted immediately." Wonderful, I thought. Here we go again. I told Momma what she said. Of course, Momma took me straight to the hospital. I was put back on the 5th floor, in a room that had become like a second home to me because it seemed like each time I was admitted that year I wound up in one of the same rooms each time. I stayed in the hospital six days. During that time I was given IV antibiotics to clear up the infection. Unfortunately, I did not know I was allergic to Vancomycin, which was the first antibiotic they administered through IV. Almost immediately after the nurse started the IV and left out of the room, I started itching ALL OVER MY BODY ! ! ! I was itching from head to toe. My head, my face, my eyes, my lips, my tongue, my hands, my arms, my stomach, my back, my legs, my feet, the inside of my mouth, even my throat itched. I buzzed for the nurse and asked her to come quickly because something was wrong. I told her I was irritated all over. I was in a ball scratching because I was itching so badly. She immediately paged the doctor on call. When he came into my room, he took one look and me and immediately knew what was wrong. He ordered the antibiotic stopped immediately. He then had the nurse run a plain bag of saline to flush all the medicine out of my system. The doctor also ordered Benadryl to give me some relief. He said I had an allergic reaction to the Vancomycin. Another antibiotic was later given, through the IV, in its place.

Friday, October 6, 2000–University of Chicago Hospitals

11:45am–Thank you Jesus for allowing me to see another day. The last couple of hours have been very interesting. Despite the infection in my central line and what is happening to me as a result, the residents were talking about sending me home. However, I voiced my concern to the nurse taking care of me who in turn, spoke to my doctor. It was determined I needed to be in the hospital for treatment.

2:15pm–Mack White just left from visiting me. it was wonderful seeing him again. He is such a blessing to me. God knew what he was doing (as always) when He allowed me to meet Mack.

I did not enjoy being in the hospital. I much rather been at home. What I enjoyed the least however was being a weight on my parents' shoulders. Momma was great through everything. During that time, she started experiencing sympathy pain. ☺ I believe that's how she knew something was wrong, even before I called for help the day I was admitted to the hospital. Daddy was a trooper. He hated seeing me in the hospital but he tried so hard to hide it when he visited me. My friends continued to call and visit me regularly.

"So he said to me, 'This is the word of the Lord To Zerubbabel: 'Not by might, nor by power, but by my Spirit,' says the Lord Almighty."

Zechariah 4:6 (NIV)

• •

"At the same time God added his witness to theirs by doing signs of power, wonders, and many kinds of miracles. He also distributed the gifts of the Holy Spirit according to his will."

Hebrews 2:4 (GW)

Chapter 10: Miracles

On October 30, 2000 I was lying down resting in my room, at my parent's house. Momma was in the other room keeping busy when I got up feeling really sick. Momma took me to the hospital where I was readmitted. During this hospitalization, my care was managed by another doctor, who was covering for my GI doctor as she was going out of town for a conference. Momma took me to the hospital and confirmed I had a room before leaving because it was very late in the evening. As usual, I was taken up to the 5th floor. On this particular evening, Momma Percy was my nurse as my other two mommas had the evening off. She did my admission paperwork and took my vitals. She then called my parents before saying "goodnight" and leaving my room. The last thing I remember is saying "goodnight" to Momma and Daddy.

"Momma you look so beautiful ! ! !"

"I have never seen you look so beautiful!
Your hair is so long and beautiful!"

"Look at your dress. It is so beautiful.
Yes momma, hold my hand and don't let go."
Momma held my hand as we watched something.
No. Wait a minute.
We were watching someone.
WAIT A MINUTE! That someone was ME!
I was in the hospital. Doctors were working on me. Momma held my hand.
I felt comfort as she held me. Suddenly her grasp loosened as she let go of me. "Where are you going? . . . Wait a minute! . . . Wait a minute! . . . Don't leave me! . . ."
[Up until that point, Momma never let go of my hand.
Momma comforted me as she let go of my hand and disappeared into a beautiful light that surrounded her.
Momma assured me everything would be alright through her gestures, never saying a word.
The light was so bright and beautiful.
It was something the human eye could not fathom.]

I opened my eyes to hear, "She's back . . . Ms. Garrett can you hear me . . . Do you know where you are at . . ." There a slight pause and silence as the person who was speaking awaited a response. Bewildered, I shook my head. There was another slight pause. Someone then said, "You are at the University of Chicago Hospitals. You are going to be fine." I felt so tired and weak. All I wanted to do was sleep. I was then encouraged to try and rest as they waited for a room in the

ICU for me (at that time, that last statement went right over my head).

October 31, 2000 I woke up in a lot of pain and very confused as I looked around my room, trying to figure out where I was. At that point, I remembered nothing from the previous day or night. The first person who came to see me was my nurse, a lady who appeared very nice but one I had never received care from.

After she took my vitals, she asked me three questions: did I know where I was, did I know what happened to me and, did I want to know what happened to me. Yes. Maybe. No and yes.

This was how she explained it to me. I had drifted off to sleep and had a seizure. During the seizure, I went into a crisis. Huh, what? Anyway, after getting me stabilized I had to be taken down to the emergency room so I could be monitored more closely while they waited for a room in the ICU. ICU ! ! ! I'm in the ICU! Later that morning, Momma and Daddy came to visit me for a while. Daddy looked awful. Momma tried to be strong as she asked me how I was feeling.

The next day was no better that the first. I woke up in a lot of pain. Momma came over early that day to see me. As my nurse went to give me my medicine through my feeding tube (I couldn't have anything by mouth), I vomited everywhere. I also woke up having some breathing problems. It was at that point my crazy (in a good way) ICU doctor implemented three rules which he put in writing, I had to follow while I was in the ICU. ☺ 1. NO vomiting, 2. I must breath at all times and 3. My heart must beat at all times. Once my doctor left, my nurse cleaned me up. During this time, I discovered my central line had been moved from my chest to the last place I imagined. As my nurse finished cleaning me up, she went to write the notes in my chart and started laughing. My ICU doctor had actually written the rules in my chart.

After making sure I didn't mind, Momma called some of my closest friends, as well as, some family members to tell them what happened. Now Momma has always been private when it came to telling people's business so she used discretion when calling people. Lisette immediately came to see me when she came back to work. In fact, she came to see me regularly during her breaks and when she was not working. Lisette even had her best friend, Collette, who lived in Florida, concerned and praying for me. I began seeing family members, including Grannie, who didn't like coming to see me in the hospital.

I stayed in the ICU 1-2 weeks before I was well enough to be transferred back down to the 5th floor. For the first few days, Momma Percy avoided me. I knew why and I didn't mind. In fact, I hated that she had to be working when it happened. My other two mommas came to see me. They were both happy to see me doing much better. It took Momma Percy several days to come and see me. The person I was scared, literally, to see even more was my GI doctor who was still out of town (only because she cared about my well-being so I knew she would have quite a bit to say). Momma would often say she prayed she was not in the hospital when my GI doctor returned because she didn't to see or hear her.

Momma spent many days and nights with me. it was during that time we inadvertently argued about Momma's whereabouts that fateful night. Momma kept saying, "I was at home."

I told her, "No you was at the hospital with me."

Momma would then say, "No I wasn't. I sent your daddy to the hospital because they would never tell us what was wrong. They just kept saying someone needed to come to the hospital immediately."

I would then say, "No, you were at the hospital with me, holding my hand."

Momma then said, "No, I stayed home with Samella (one of momma's good friends) and cried."

I then said, "No, you were at the hospital holding my hand."

We went back and forth like that for several days.

When my GI doctor returned, everyone, including the doctor covering for her, gave me the heads up. Momma went home early because she did not want to see the look on my doctor's face. The evening my GI doctor came to see me, the doctor covering for her, accompanied her. When she first came in the room, all she gave me was THE LOOK. Imagine for a moment you are a child and have done something to get yourself in a lot of trouble. Your momma, or whomever, don't say anything but they just stare you down, giving you THE LOOK. With this look, you knew you were in a lot of trouble. That was the look my GI doctor gave me. She stared me down, with her arms folded, for a few moments. All I could do was apologize and laugh. My GI doctor then went down the list of messages she received and that was waiting for her when she got back to the hospital, with regards to me. We then got serious and talked about my future. Something had to be done to keep this from happening again.

In the days that followed, my GI doctor and I began discussing the possibility of me being transferred to another hospital for treatment options that had not been thought of at the University of Chicago Hospitals. She mentioned three hospitals I could possibly be transferred to for other treatment options. After discussing it with Momma, we decided on Mayo. Later that evening, my GI doctor came back with the option for me to be transferred to Mayo. She had even spoken to a physician at Mayo. The only problem was with the insurance company. The insurance company didn't want to approve me being transferred to Mayo. My GI doctor had my central line placed back in my chest. Three days later, just as my GI doctor came close to discharging me home, the insurance company finally approved my transfer to Mayo. Now all my problems were resolved, right? I wish. The insurance company didn't cover transportation costs for me to be transferred. This meant it had to be paid out of pocket.

Momma called me to see if I had enough money to cover the transportation costs. Unfortunately, I did not. We needed this money and we needed it quickly. Who could I call? I thought about Mack. Unfortunately, he was not home when I called. One of the members of True Right who was very close to my family explained the situation to the new pastor but he refused to help. God bless him. After all the confusion happening at True Right under his leadership, I had already decided to find me a new church home, when I got back on my feet.

After several hours of praying and searching, Daddy was able to borrow the money from a mutual friend and co-worker. THANK YOU. Because it was so late in the evening when we finally got the money, the transportation company arranged to pick me up the next morning, which was Friday, from my hospital room. For the rest of the evening, I spoke to a few friends and rested. Mack called me back to make sure I had everything I needed. Lisette kept me company for a while and promised to come see me before I left the next morning.

I woke up early that Friday, November 11, 2000 morning so the nurse could help me get ready. Lisette came to sit with me, as promised until I left. She bought me a nice book to read called "Chicaken Soup for the Christian Soul." My parents arrived just as the transportation company arrived to take me to the airport. Momma was going to stay with me in Minnesota so I wouldn't be up there alone. Thank God. This was one battle I did not want to fight alone. My Momma was the perfect person to go with me because she specialized in making sure the doctors stayed on top of things and did everything they were supposed to do.

Lisette bid me well as the medics put me on the stretcher and in the ambulance. Momma rode in the ambulance with me. Daddy followed the ambulance in his truck, to the airport. I was taken to Midway Airport where the medic-copter was waiting to take me to Minnesota. There were nurses on the plane to make sure I was ok during the flight. I slept the entire flight. I felt sorry for Momma. Her seat was in what looked like an awkward position on the plane so I knew she was not too comfortable, although she said nothing about it. When we arrived at the airport in Minnesota, it was very cold. I was wrapped in covers but I only had on a hospital gown so I felt the coldness. There was another ambulance waiting to take me to St. Joseph's Hospital, which is a part of Mayo. The transportation company was excellent. They were very efficient and did everything they promised my parents they would do, providing me with bed to bed transportation (from Chicago to Minnesota).

Upon my arrival, I was placed in a room with a roommate. The nurse then took my vitals, changed my hospital gown and completed my hospital admission papers. Doctors wasted no time. Just after my admission papers were completed, doctors ordered x-rays of the shunts, my central line, and the areas where the other feeding tubes had been previously. When I returned to my room, my roommate said my room had been changed. I now had a room to myself. Thank you Jesus! It's not that I didn't like having a roommate, I just needed to fight this battle without the distractions of a roommate.

Momma spent most of the evening with me, until it began getting dark. As this was her first time in Minnesota, she was unfamiliar with the area and she didn't want to travel alone at night. My nurse was very helpful during this time. When she found out the hotel Momma had reservations in, she told Momma that was too far for her to travel and helped her get a room in a hotel much closer to the hospital. In actuality, it was much closer. It was so close, I could look out the window in my hospital room and see it.

My first full day at Mayo was nice and quiet, as it was Saturday, the weekend. The doctors had told Momma and I of some tests that had been planned for the following week. Momma spent most of the day with me, keeping me smiling as much as possible. I also spent the day reading the book Lisette bout me. I knew I would finish it within a few days which I did. My Uncle Howard also called and kept me company for over an hour, by way of the telephone. He had always encouraged me. I thanked God for his presence in my life. I thanked God for all of Daddy's crazy brothers. I also thanked God for all the ones on Momma's side of the family. ☺

Monday, November 13, 2000 was a tiresome, yet somewhat busy day for me at Mayo. I had a test that took up a large portion of the day. Momma came over to the hospital early and spent most of the day with me. Her presence helped a lot, although I spent most of the day sleeping when I wasn't at the test the doctors had scheduled that day. Thus far, the situation caused me to remain faithful to my heavenly Father, my Lord and Saviour Jesus Christ and know that everything works out for the good of them who love the Lord. Momma Tucker called to check on Momma and myself while I was at Mayo. She is one of the people I prayed would remain a permanent fixture in my life.

The remainder of the week modeled that previous Monday. Momma usually came over to the hospital early in the morning and stayed late into the evening. I usually had some type of test that took up a large portion of the day. In the evening, or when I wasn't at the test, Momma and I usually rested, watched movies and talked.

It was during this time I developed a deeper respect, admiration and love for my Momma as she told me why she treated me in the manner she treated me while I was growing up. Momma told me she always loved me. She treated me like she did because that was the only way she knew to make me stronger. She knew I would have a harder road to travel than Sha, Netta or Nicole. Momma knew because of my diagnosis at birth I needed strength to endure. Without this strength, I would not have lived through all I had survived in my life. Wow! My momma really did love me. My momma was proud of me because through it all, I never gave up.

I then went back to the night of October 30-31, 2000. I asked Momma to tell me everything that happened and don't leave anything out. She started talking about how I got sick at home and Momma took me to the emergency room. As it turned out, I had another infection in my central line. Momma made sure I had a room first, then she left and went back home. I remembered being taken up to my room and momma Percy came in to complete my admission papers and take my vitals. I remember momma Percy saying, "goodnight." Momma explained the rest. During the night, she said, I had a very bad seizure. Someone from the hospital called my parent's house and told my parents that someone needed to come to the hospital immediately. The person on the phone wouldn't give them any information over the phone. Momma said she knew something was wrong and sent Daddy to the hospital while she stayed home. Momma said she called one of her good friends, Samella, over to the house. They stayed at the house and cried. Daddy went to the hospital and stayed by my side until I was taken to the ICU.

It was at that point, I began having flashbacks of that night. I definitely remembered seeing Momma very clearly, but not Daddy. That was so weird to me since Momma said he stayed by my side all night. I peeled my memories of that night thoroughly. My momma was with me holding my hand. Why didn't I remember Daddy? WAIT A MINUTE ! ! ! That night my momma's hair was very long, but that was impossible because my momma had cut her hair some time ago and she had started wearing her hair short. She was wearing a long dress with heels and that also wasn't my momma style. She was skinnier. It was at that point, God turned on a light, per se, as I began remembering the stories I was told while growing up about my maternal grandmother. I asked Momma, "didn't you say your mother look just like you?" My momma looked at me and replied, "Yes. Why?" All I could say was, "Oh my God!" I remembered being surrounded by the most beautiful light the human eye could fathom. There were no concrete items around us, just that light. I then remembered something else. I remembered her holding my hand as we watched doctors working on someone. WAIT A MINUTE! That someone was me. She [my maternal grandmother] assured me through her gestures, never saying a word, I would be fine. Moments later, she began separating herself from me as she faded into the light. There was a slight resistance as we separated as it seemed, she didn't want to let go and I didn't want to let go. She faded into the light. I then woke up in the hospital to hear someone say, "she's back!" That wasn't Momma after all. That was my maternal grandmother. She was my guardian angel. I told Momma.

It was at that point Momma said, "oh my God!" as she realized the same thing. My guardian angel was Mrs. Idonia Royal. Momma smiled. I smiled, thinking to myself, maybe I am doing something right after all. I know I serve an Awesome God. I just never thought of myself at that spiritual level. It's funny how that realization brought me closer to Momma. More importantly, it encouraged me. It seemed like that realization brought Momma even closer to her siblings because they seemed to talk more after that. This also reaffirmed my faith that God was/is in control of everything happening to me.

Toward the end of that first week, doctors decided on a different type of feeding tube, the J-tube, to treat me. Doctors believed the jejunostomy tube, or J-tube, would improve my symptoms because the position it was placed, bypassed the problem area in my stomach. To ensure the feeding tube benefited me and functioned properly, the doctors tested it by placing an NG tube, first. It was anything but comfortable. The doctors started me on a different type of nutritional feeding. Because they had the feeding running at such a high rate, I was very uncomfortable, having a hard time breathing and moving around. Momma noticed my distress and decided to talk to the doctors. As a result, I received a short break from the feedings so that the portion I had already taken in could digest properly.

On Monday, November 20, 2000 Momma and I had a meeting with the doctors attending to my care at Mayo. My Momma and I was concerned because they were talking about sending me home with the J-tube, still in my nose. What if the feeding tube fell out of my nose, like the very first nasal feeding tube I had at the University of Chicago Hospitals? I was not willing to take that risk and neither was my mother. By the end of the meeting, the doctors understood our concerns and decided to move the tube to my stomach, prior to my discharge. Later that day, we were told the NG tube would be moved the following day. This meant more surgery as the J-tube was place the following day, November 21, 2000.

That evening, Momma and I talked about Thanksgiving, which was that upcoming Thursday. Daddy had planned to drive up to Minnesota with Nicole and Lavare for the holiday. Since they hadn't seen one another in a while, I was going to have the kids at the hospital with me, while Momma and Daddy spent some time together.

Tuesday, November 21, 2000~St. Joseph (Mayo)~ Minnesota

The J-tube was moved to my intestines today. Momma came over before the procedure and stayed in my room for most of the day. They put me to sleep for the surgery. Thank God. I woke up in great pain. Later, the doctor told me they had to cut through a lot of scar tissue to place the tube properly.

....

Wednesday, November 22, 2000~St. Joseph's (Mayo)~Minnesota

Word is I'm going home tomorrow. Daddy and the kids arrived late this evening.

....

HAPPY THANKSGIVING 2000 ! ! ! Momma came over to the hospital early so we could have what turned out to be, our last meeting with the doctors. As previously done, some of the doctors avoided eye contact with me, when discussing my present and future health. In the beginning, the doctors didn't feel that moving the tube was the best thing to do. Suddenly, their opinion changed as they felt Momma and I made the right decision having the tube moved. The doctors went on to say everything should be better in one month. I didn't doubt God's miracle working power but I seriously considered calling their bluff on that one. As far as the tube feedings, the doctors sent me home on a very high rate, despite how full and uncomfortable the feedings made me at that rate. Doctors then added table food back to my diet, in addition to the feedings. I couldn't wait to see my GI physician so we could discuss things out thoroughly.

After saying our goodbyes, we packed up and left. Momma and Daddy decided to leave immediately, rather than later. The road trip back to Chicago was rough. The pain medicine I was given in the hospital, wore off. I felt every whole, bump, rock and anything else that wasn't smooth. My parents wound up pulling off the road into a gas station, so my parents could get me something so I could take some more pain medicine.

When we finally got back to our home in Chicago, my family was hungry. After making sure I was comfortable, my parents, Nicole and Lavare went to Aunt Kat's house for Thanksgiving dinner. My sisters, Netta and Sha, were already there with their children. During the evening, Momma and Daddy called to check up on me. This also gave me a chance to greet my family as everyone hollered through the phone, "HAPPY THANKSGIVING SHEREICE ! ! !"

That following Friday was nice and quiet. It felt good to be home instead of laid up in the hospital. I had to talk to some of my friends. Lisette and I talked during her break. She was so happy I was home. We had planned to get together before she went home to her family for the holiday. I also spoke to Lisette's best friend, Collette, who I had yet to meet face to face. The funny part is Lisette talked to each of us so much about the other one, that by the time we did meet, we felt like old friends.

Monday, November 27, 2000

Today was as normal as it will get for me. I had a doctor's appointment with my GI physician today. She was surprised to see me back in Chicago already. We talked about my experience at St. Joseph's Hospital (Mayo). I showed her my copy of my discharge report from the hospital. She agreed with what the physician's at Mayo said. She said this was the response she was looking for. I am still somewhat baffled. Both of them say I should be better with 1-3 years however; neither of them want to remove the central line, just in case it has to be used again. Go figure. If everyone is so sure the J-tube will work, why do they want to keep the central line? My wonderful, dear mother got me in trouble today (as usual☺). Not really trouble, she just told on me. The conclusion reached: I have lost a few pounds and I am not taking as much fluid in as I should. If I lose any more weight, my GI doctor said they might have to use the central line again. I am having such a wonderful year.

I spoke to Lisette today but we missed one another while I was at the University of Chicago Hospitals for my appointment. The true friends I do have.

Surprisingly, I think December 2000 was the quietest month out of the entire year. Yes, I still had to do the tube feedings several hours a day and I had many painful days but at least, I wasn't in the hospital. Thank you Lord. I said it once and I will say it again. God blessed me with some wonderful friends. My friend Timothy, who was one of my classmates at Henton but when it closed I neither saw nor talked to him again until my college days at DePaul) always has an encouraging word for me, once we got past the joking. ☺ My true friends make me get tearful when I think about everything they did for me. They are the epitome of true sacrifice, besides my parents, of course.

I received confirmation approximately one week after returning home from Mayo. Momma and I were sitting down talking in the dining room. She got up and brought back her personal photo album. She turned to the page which contained her mother's picture and showed it to me. "Oh my God! That's her!" I cried. I now had the confirmation I needed. My guardian angel was Mrs. Idonia Royal. Momma embraced me and we just stayed frozen in the moment. Thank you God!

That trip to Mayo really blessed my relationship with my momma. It seemed like after we were honest with one another, we got along so much better. We became so much closer. I understood Momma now more than I ever have in my life. Momma showed me tough love growing up to make me stronger and equip me with the tools I needed to be an independent Black woman, capable of making wise decisions. She knew that was the only way I would survive my condition and everything I had to deal with in regards to it. I just wish she would have told me sooner because it hard thinking your mother love you but just don't like you. Now I know she did everything she did because Momma truly love me. Momma likes me. We talked. We laughed. We even had heart to heart conversations unlike any we ever had.

As I came closer to the end of the year, I began to pray for many things. I prayed that God would continue to bless and strengthen all of my dear friends. As I came closer to Christmas, I really became excited. Lisette was going home for the holidays so unfortunately, I wouldn't see her until after the beginning of the new year. John was with his family. Sara's family didn't celebrate Christmas.

Lisette came to see me before she went home for Christmas. We had fun. The highlight of my day was when I gave Lisette her Christmas present. It will be a long time before I forget the expression on her face. She liked her gift. Thank you Momma for helping me pick out Lisette's gift. I missed her when she went home.

It was during this time I received a card from my future brother-in-law. Sometimes people say things and don't realize how offensive their words are until after the words roll off their tongue. In his previous letter, my future brother-in-law said some things about my whole experience with my health that was really harsh. It really hurt my feelings. I got so hurt, I told my momma, which is something I don't normally do. In his card, he apologized and said he was only trying to be sarcastic. At the time, I wasn't in the mood for sarcasm of that magnitude. Besides, there are some topics that should not be addressed sarcastically, if at all.

A few days before Christmas, I received another surprise. I spoke to Donyiel. It was wonderful hearing from her again. Now that she was married and working, she didn't have the free time to talk to me as she used to growing up. It was nice having that time to share. Around this time, I also got to see Kita. I cherished every moment I saw her because she had moved to another state by then, so it was not as easy to see her anymore.

Christmas was the first major holiday, for the year 2000, I got to spend with my family. The other holidays I was either in the hospital or recuperating at home because I had just recently been released from the hospital. Everyone planned to go to one of Daddy's first cousin's house for dinner. Everyone that is, except Grannie. I did everything I could to convince her to come out but she still refused. I was a little nervous about going to the dinner myself because I still used the J-tube for feedings and couldn't eat solid food. Daddy promised Momma and myself that he had told his cousin of my dietary needs so they would have something I could eat. Of course, it was soup.

When we arrived, I was so happy to be able to spend my first major holiday with my family. Within minutes after everyone arrived, long standing family jokes, laughs and memories filled the air as the Garretts, Turners and Rayfords got together. I was hooked up to my machine but no one made a big deal about it. Thank you Jesus! My crazy cousin even took a picture of it and he kept making jokes about me hiding something other than what was supposed to be there, in the feeding bag. Everyone laughed. More importantly, I laughed. I felt more at ease that day, being around a large portion of my family than I had felt all year. Happy Birthday King Jesus!

I had my annual appointment with Dr. Frim the following week. He was satisfied with my shunt levels. Thank you Lord. The rest of the year was pretty quiet. I found myself thinking about my dreams of becoming a teacher. I wondered if I would have excelled at being a teacher if all those issues hadn't arisen with my health.

Monday, January 1, 2001

Happy New Year!!!!

12:01am – Praise the Lord! Thank you Jesus!!! God has allowed me to see another day, another year. Hallelujah!!!

I cried in the new year and lost $0.25 in the process. How? Nicole and I made a deal if I cried the new year in; I would give her $0.25. That's quite all right. I am overjoyed. God brought me through so much in 2000. I had to be happy. Well, now I am getting tired. Until later. I almost forgot, gave Momma a great big hug and kiss. Then my Daddy. I then gave everyone a hug.

Toward the end of January 2001, my dear friend Timothy sent me an email forward. The first time I read this story, it brought tears to my eyes and filled my heart with joy because the story was so beautiful. The story is entitled, "One Last Wish"

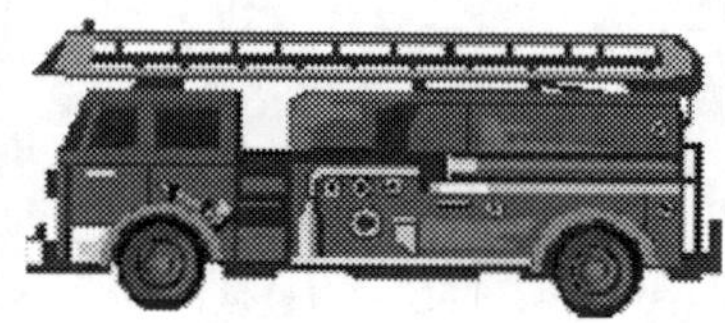

One Last Wish

The 26 year old mother stared down at her son who was dying of terminal Leukemia. Although her heart was filled with sadness, she also had a strong feeling of determination. Like any parent she wanted her son to grow up and fulfill all his dreams. Now that was no longer possible. The leukemia would see to that. But she still wanted her son's dreams to come true. She took her son's hand and asked,

"Billy, did you ever think about what you wanted to be once you grew up? Did you ever dream and wish what you would do with your life?"

"Mommy, I always wanted to be a fireman when I grew up."

Mommy smiled back and said, "Let's see if I can make your wish come true."

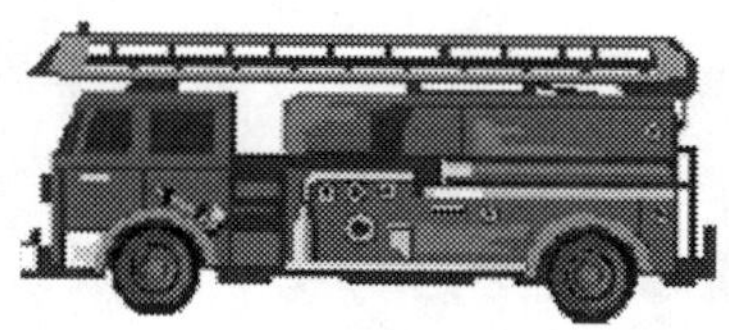

Later that day she went to her local fire department in Phoenix, Arizona, where she met fireman B, who had a heart as big as Phoenix. She explained her son's final wish and asked if it might be possible to give her six-year-old son a ride around the block in the fire engine. Fireman B said, "Look we can do better than that. If you'll have your son ready at seven o'clock

Wednesday morning, we'll make him an honorary fireman for the whole day. He can come down to the fire station, eat with us, go out on all the fire calls, the whole nine yards!" "And if you'll give us his sizes, we'll get a real fire uniform for him, with a real fire hat—not a toy one—with the emblem of the Phoenix Fire Department on it, a yellow slicker like we wear and rubber boots. They're all manufactured right here in Phoenix, so we can get them fast."

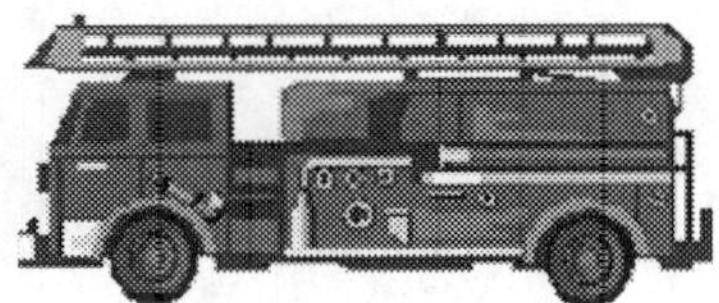

Three days later Fireman B picked up Billy, dressed him in his fire uniform and escorted him from his hospital bed to the waiting hook and ladder truck. Billy got to sit on the back of the truck and help steer it back to the fire station. He was in heaven. There were three fire calls in Phoenix that day and Billy got to go on all the calls. He rode in the different fire engines, the paramedics van and even the fire chief's car. He was also videotaped for the local news program. Having his dream come true with all the love and attention that was lavished upon him, so deeply touched Billy that he lived three months longer than any doctor thought possible.

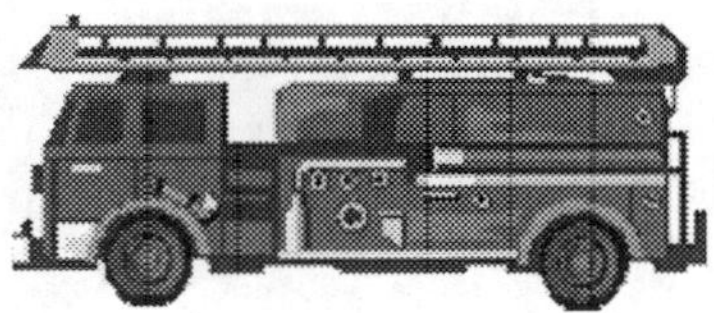

One night all of his vital signs began to drop dramatically and the head nurse, who believed in the hospice concept that no one should die alone, began to call family members to the hospital. Then she remembered the day Billy had spent as a fireman, so she called the fire chief and asked if it would be possible to send a fireman in uniform to the hospital to be with Billy as he made his transition. The chief replied, "We can do better than that. We'll be there in five minutes. Will you please do me a favor? When you hear the sirens screaming and see the lights flashing, will you announce over the PA system that there is not a fire. It's just the fire department coming to see one of its finest members one more time. And will you open the window to his room? Thanks."

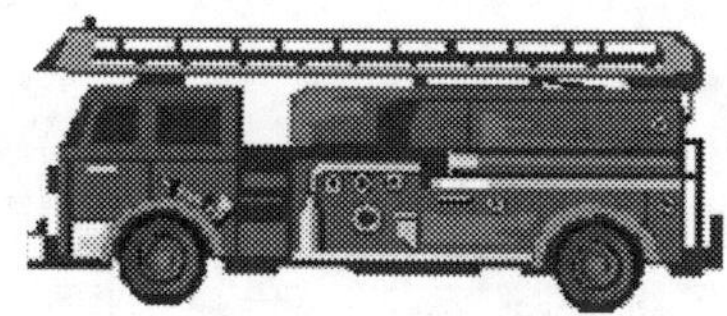

A bout five minutes later a hook and ladder truck arrived at the hospital, extended its ladder up to Billy's third floor open window and 16 firefighters climbed up the ladder into Billy's room. With his mother's permission, they hugged him and held him and told him how much they loved him. With his dying breath, Billy looked up at the fire chief and said, "Chief, am I really a fireman now?" "Billy you are." The chief said. With those words, Billy smiled and closed his eyes one last time.

Author Unknown

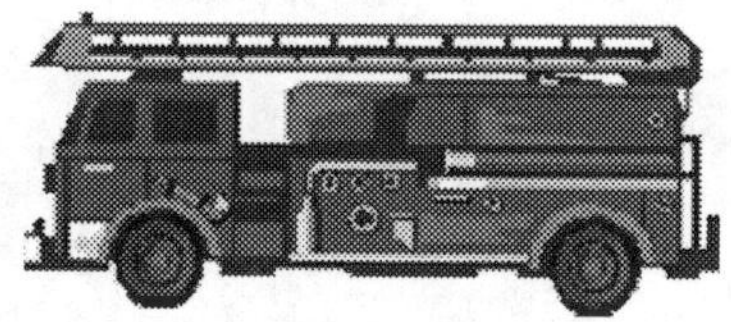

"This is why I tell you: do not be worried about the Food and drink you need in order to stay alive, or about the clothes for your body. After all, isn't life worth more than food? And isn't the body worth more than clothes? Look at the birds: they do not plant seeds, gather a harvest and put it in barns; yet your Father in heaven taken care of them! Aren't you worth more than birds? Can any of you live a bit longer by worrying about it?"

Matthew 6:25-27 (GNT)

Chapter 11: Another Answered Prayer

As I went into the New Year I prayed 2001 would be better than 2000. I wasn't getting depressed or complaining. I was just looking forward to a better year. It started off quiet, in a manner of speaking. I was not in the hospital however I did have to go back and forth to one of the clinics associated with the University of Chicago Hospitals, to have my memory evaluated by a neurologist who specialized in memory problems.

My first doctor's appointment, for the year, was scheduled on January 3, 2001. The place I was going to was called Windermere Memory Clinic. It was located in the same building that served the needs of the elderly. My primary care physician had aforementioned this information to me however, I refused to tell Momma. Momma and the family had already got to the point where the issues I was having with my memory had become the subject of many age jokes. If I had told Momma about the clinic, I would have never had any peace. When we arrived in the waiting area, I surveyed the waiting area and told my momma, "Don't say a word. Just go sit down while I get registered." She looked at me and smiled. Momma found seats while I registered,

The woman who registered me was quite surprised when she realized I was the individual seeing the doctor and not accompanying someone else. When I sat down, I felt quite awkward as Momma and I were the youngest people sitting in the waiting area. The room was filled with elderly people. Momma laughed. Here I was a 23 year old with short term memory issues. If I wanted to remember what I thought about, I had to make a note. I had to remain positive about the situation. If I didn't Momma would try to take over my life and really worry about me. She probably wouldn't never let me out of her sight. I smiled as I put it in God's hands.

The nurse responded with Momma's favorite joke, "you must be an 87 year old caught in the body of a 23 year old." I smiled. If he only knew. He took my vitals and place me in one of the exam rooms to wait for the doctor. This being a teaching hospital, I usually saw a medical student or resident, in addition to seeing my doctor, during clinic appointments. This was no exception. The medical student did an interview and full neurological exam. She then left to talk to the neurologist I was seeing. A few minutes later, she returned with the neurologist.

The neurologist was very understanding. He tried to assure me that the memory problems I endured were temporary and would resolve over time. As he said that I thought to myself, "Then why is it taking so long to come back?" after all it had been three years. He did a full neurological exam. The neurologist explained I would have some more tests that day to test my memory further. I would then return to see him when he had the results of those tests. Over an hour passed before the tests started. These tests were given by another individual. I was taken to another room for these tests. The tests took about three hours, if not more, to complete. There were no breaks given during the tests except when I had to stop because the alarm of my feeding tube was going off. I fixed the problem and the testing immediately resumed.

When I finally completed the testing, the doctor told me to wait and see if the neurologist wanted to see me again. When she returned, she informed me more testing need to be done, as well as, a blood test. I must say the front desk was very efficient as all of my appointments had been scheduled by the time I went to the waiting area.

When I got to the waiting area, Momma was no longer there. I was told she was in the office speaking to the doctors. Oh Lord! What was she telling them or vice versa? Momma came out and said, "I told you, you were a complicated case. The doctors want to do more tests." We then went to get something to eat.

The next day, January 4, 2001, was Sha's birthday. I received a surprise that I had been curious about for over a year, since after True Right went under new leadership. The new pastor actually came to visit me. It was an embarrassing visit that he could have kept to himself. I had called Momma beforehand to tell her, he was actually coming to visit me. She didn't believe me. HE CAME. HE SAW. HE STAYED FOR FIVE WHOLE MINUTES. HE STAYED IN THE HALLWAY BY THE FRONT DOOR WITH HIS COAT ON AND BUTTONED. HE KEPT HIS HANDS IN HIS POCKET, ALTHOUGH I WELCOMED HIM AND THE DEACON, THAT WAS WITH HIM, INTO MY PARENT'S HOUSE. HE SAID A SPEEDY PRAYER. HE LEFT. I called Momma again, who was at work. She thought I was joking. That evening, I told my daddy. He did not laugh it off like Momma and I did. He was not at all happy about what had occurred. The next day was even worse for me. I found out the true reason for his visit.

My parents celebrated their Silver/25th Wedding Anniversary the end of May 2001. During previous months, my parents and

I talked about what they wanted for their special anniversary. Shortly thereafter, my sisters started talking about planning an anniversary party for them. I told them, "I already asked Momma and Daddy about having an anniversary party. They made it plain and clear they don't want a party." During my conversation with them, my parents said they wanted a weekend away. So that's what I gave them: a weekend away. They wanted to go to the Sybaris for the weekend. When I called to make the reservations, because that was my gift to them, I was told the weekend packages was only Friday to Saturday or Saturday to Sunday. This was not long enough for my parents. I called back and made arrangements for them to stay the whole weekend. Now it was time to get even with them for what they did to me when I was in the hospital on my birthday. ☺ The customer representative was very helpful. In the end, Sybaris hung a banner in their room saying, "Congratulations Mom and Dad on your 25th Year Anniversary!" I also arranged for Momma to have roses in the room. They also had a bottle of wine and souvenir wine glasses, which they brought back home with them. To this day, NO ONE is allowed to touch their souvenir wine glasses. Everything was official.

When my parents got home, they were very happy. They enjoyed themselves tremendously. I thanked God for giving me parents that never stopped loving one another.

Lisette and I were almost inseparable during that time. She really encouraged me and we had a lot of fun when we hung out. During one of the Sundays she had off in July 2001, Lisette came to visit me. A few minutes after she got to my parents' house, we decided to go to the show. We looked at what was playing and decided on something to go see. Lisette was driving, of course. We were traveling northbound down Halsted. We had just stopped at the red light on 95th Halsted, right by Carter G. Woodson Library. We were talking and laughing. All of a sudden, Lisette said, "oh my God!" The next thing I knew, we were being thrown all around as the car was hit several times, until it finally hit the median strip and came back down. SHOCK was the WORD. Our instincts took over. "Are you ok?" "Yea, are you ok?" "Yea, your nose is bleeding."

"Yea I know. I hit it on the steering wheel." "Are you ok?" "My chest hurt." Lisette being the beautiful person she is was more worried about me than she was about herself. I still had the central line. She checked to make sure it was ok and didn't anything happen to it while we were being thrown around. This is where I must give rave reviews to the residents of the neighborhood. They came out of their houses and assisted people in the wreckage. It turned out to be an accident that lasted several blocks. The residents were the people directing paramedics to the injured. The police presence was scarce. In fact, I never saw an officer on the scene. I heard later on, police finally arrived on the scene. I called Momma. Momma and Sha came over immediately.

When the paramedics came, Momma went to the hospital with me. Sha stayed with Lissette. Momma called Daddy, who was doing prison ministry that day. He came right over. I was fine. I just wound up with a neck strain. Thank God, nothing happened to the feeding tube. I don't think I nor my parents wanted to have to deal with those repercussions. I stayed sore for several days but overall, I was fine. Thank you Jesus.

Thursday, August 9, 2001, I went for my follow-up appointment with Dr. Frim. For this appointment momma went with me because I was not feeling my best. During the last few days, prior to this appointment, I was also sleeping a lot more which was a cause for concern because I usually start sleeping a lot more (and a lot harder) when I am having issues with my shunts. My headaches were also worsening again. When we arrived, I checked in and we sat down. Momma's cell phone started ringing but she couldn't answer the phone in the area we were in (she kept losing her signal). She told me she would be right back so she could take the call.

While in the waiting area, people tend to talk to one another, while waiting to see the doctor. I was talking to another mother who was bringing her baby to see another neurosurgeon. I overheard another woman telling someone else about her son. I don't know why I heard what she was saying so clearly. I nearly jumped out of my skin as she said the words, "arachnoid cyst on the cerebellum with hydrocephalus." Could this really be happening? Had I finally found another survivor? She repeated what she said. Oh my God! I had to speak to her but I was so scared. How would she respond? Momma came back and I told her what I had just heard. "Did you speak to her?" Momma said.

I told her, "No, I was too nervous." We both smiled at the thought of finally finding another survivor. Momma went to the ladies room. I had to speak to the lady but I was so nervous.

I practiced in my mind, what I was going to say. Finally, I got up and somehow made my way over to the lady, who was in a conversation with another person.

I said, "Excuse me, miss. Did I just hear you say your son was born with an arachnoid cyst on the cerebellum with hydrocephalus for which he is shunt dependent?"

She looked at me and said, "Yes."

I then extended my hand to shake hers and said, "I would like to welcome you to the club of the elite few. My name is Shereice Garrett and I too was born with an arachnoid cyst on the cerebellum with hydrocephalus for which I am shunt dependent." She went speechless for a second as tears welled up in her eyes. She shook my hand and said, "Oh my God." Her name is Tammy and her son's name is James. We talked for a while about how James, who was 10 at the time, and I grew up. We also talked about how Tammy and I had searched for another survivor of the exact diagnosis. We talked about what I went through and what James went through growing up. By then, Momma made it back so I introduced Tammy and James to her. We continued talking. By the end of the conversation, we were all hugging and promising to keep in touch with one another. Thank you Lord for answering my prayer.

It was then I was called back to see Dr. Frim. When he came in, he asked how I was doing. I was going to stretch the truth just a little bit. However, my wonderful mother had a different agenda. She wasted no time telling Dr. Frim about the fevers, my increased headaches and, my sleeping patterns over the last few days. Dr. Frim gave me two choices: 1. Be admitted.—OR—2. Go home and come back tomorrow to be admitted through the emergency room. Either way, I was being admitted. Momma didn't give me a chance to respond as she told Dr. Frim to admit me that day.

Dr. Frim left out of the exam room so he could make the arrangements for me to be admitted to the hospital. I looked at Momma. She made a few comments about how I knew I needed to be admitted. I didn't say anything. A few moments later, Dr. Frim's nurse came in and sent us to the waiting area because they had not got me a room yet. While in the waiting area, Momma and I talked about the trip Kita and I had planned to go to Walt Disney World in a few days. Of course, now I wouldn't be able to go. I COULDN'T BELIEVE THIS! I had waited so many years to go to Walt Disney World! I couldn't believe the opportunity was being taken away from me. Ok Lord. I know you are in charge and you know the plan you have for my life but couldn't you have waited until after Walt Disney World for this chapter?

Shortly after we sat down in the waiting area, Tammy and James came out. Tammy turned to us, gave us the thumbs up sign. While Tammy was checking out at the desk, I saw James and waved at him. He must have asked Tammy if he could come by me because the next thing I knew he came over and gave me a big hug. Shortly thereafter, Tammy joined us. She told us James was doing fine. Momma told Tammy I was being admitted for a possible shunt revision. Tammy promised to keep me lifted up in her prayers. Thank you Lord. I always prayed that I would find another survivor of my condition. No. I never wanted any child to go through anything, or anything remotely close to what I went through during the last few years of my life. I just prayed that if I found another child who survived my condition that would mean doctors are closer to finding a cure and or preventive measures so that no other child will be born with this condition.

Sometime after they left, Dr. Frim's nurse came to talk to Momma and me. They were having trouble getting me a bed so Dr. Frim wanted me to go to the emergency room so an IV could be started. In the emergency room it took a little while for me to be called back. When I was finally called back, doctors wasted no time. They were very concerned about the shunts. They sent down neurosurgery, along with several other doctors. The supervising emergency room physician came to check on me. He assured me that I was going to be all right. He promised me the doctors would find out what was wrong with me.

Because it was so late, Momma got tired and went home. Momma said, "I hate to leave you by yourself but I am extremely tired. We have been gone all day. You will be all right. When they put you in a room, call me and let me know." Momma then gave me a kiss and left. I tried to rest but my head was hurting really bad and made it hard to rest. The emergency room doctor came in to check on me again. About an hour, or so later, I was moved out of the cubicle to the side to wait for a room. That's when it got very noisy and my head was pounding. About another hour or so later, the neurosurgery resident came to check on me. He had me placed in one of the private rooms because the emergency room had become extremely noisy by then. Sometime later, neurosurgery came back to tell me they were going to go ahead and perform the spinal tap in the emergency room, instead of waiting for me to get my room. They were again very nice and supportive as they tried to keep my mind off the spinal tap by asking me questions about myself. Finally, two hours later, I was admitted and put in a room. I talked to Momma to let her know I was in my room and they did the spinal tap. That was a very long day. My head was pounding. Lord, please give me the strength to endure and get through everything I have to do.

The following day was a little more complex than the first. I woke up with my left eye lid drooping badly. Initially, doctors had concluded it was because of my health, at the time, or I had slept on my eye the night before. As the days progressed however, doctors began questioning the possibility of me having another neurological condition called Myasthenia Gravis. Myasthenia Gravis is a neuromuscular disease. It occurs in stages, the first stage being ocular. At the time, doctors ran several tests, including the Tencilin test, which is used to diagnose Myasthenia Gravis.

Wednesday, August 22, 2001–University of Chicago Hospitals

My adventure at the University of Chicago hospitals continues. I am still no closer to finding out what happened to me than I was the day I was admitted. The doctors are still trying to use "depression' as a diagnosis. I have never been depressed a day in my life.

Anyway, Daddy called me this afternoon to see if I felt up to a visitor. I told him yes. Daddy went on to tell me he was bringing Dr. Burroughs with him. Dr. Burroughs was one of Momma's high school teachers. She is also a very dynamic writer and founder of the DuSable Museum. I felt very honored that she visited me.

When she arrived, I was taken back for a moment as I gazed upon one of the most beautiful African American women I have ever seen. She made me feel very special to have Joseph and Rosa Garrett as parents. Dr. Burroughs spoke highly of Momma. I had to call Momma and tell her Dr. Burroughs was visiting me. As usual, she told me to "be quiet" and we both burst into laughter. Dr. Burroughs and Momma talked for a little while. After we finished speaking to Momma, I received a surprise. Dr. Burroughs bought several pieces of her writings to share with me. She writes with such eloquence. In between pieces, she told me some more information about herself and her writings. She told me about her trip to Africa. We talked about my schooling. I told her I was a student at DePaul. She told me she received an honorary degree from DePaul. When I told her I write, she asked me to assemble some of my pieces so she could read them. It was then Dr. Burroughs asked me about letting others know about my life.

Dr. Burroughs and I discussed putting my life in a book. She even asked to publish it. Dr. Burroughs encouraged me to start thinking of a title for my book. It's funny. I had already though of a title, **"MY LIFE IS IN GOD'S HANDS."** *Dr. Burroughs spent a few more moments with me. She told me she wanted me to go to Africa to get the experience because I am a woman of color. She looked at my father and told him he would have to help me. he nodded in approval. I am planning to take this trip sometime in my life. I must remain in contact with Dr. Burroughs so I could get my book accomplished.*

Dr. Frim is back. Thank God! He is supposed to come see me this evening.

....

That following day, Thursday, August 23, 2001 was the day doctors gave up trying to find the answers to what happened to me. Neurology decided to transfer me to an in-patient rehabilitation hospital. This being my first experience in an in-patient hospital of this nature, I was very nervous. Once again, God sent people to stand in the gap. When I first became a patient of Dr. Frim, I met the social worker for his patients. For some reason, we immediately bonded. She always went above and beyond the call of duty to help me. As hectic as things were, she really helped to keep me calm. Issues arose that made my transfer almost impossible initially. The main problem being that my GI doctor had started me back on TPN (during this hospitalization) and no facility wanted to accept me while I was on TPN.

I think the best part of this scenario was meeting Cindy. For part of the time I was a patient, Cindy was my roommate. She remained my roommate until I was transferred to a private room. On the night she was brought in the room, after everyone left, she said, "I'm sorry for all the noise. My name is Cindy. I don't mean to be rude but I'm so tired. I will talk to you tomorrow." I then responded. "My name is Shereice. I look forward to talking to you tomorrow. Good night." We got along from the start. She was so sweet. I can remember one day Cindy pulled the divider curtain back so we could watch television together and not have to talk to one another through the curtain. When the nursing staff came in to take our vitals, the lady who took our vitals pulled the curtain across, separating us before she left out. Cindy said, "We did not ask her to pull that curtain back." Cindy got up and pulled it back like we had it so we wouldn't be separated. That's how it stayed unless the doctors were in the room. We became good friends very quickly. She introduced me to her family when they visited her.

Now the positive part of this health adventure. Dr. Frim and I had a long talk. All of the test results came back negative or within normal limits. This meant no stroke, no shunt malfunction, no hemorrhage, or no aneurism. So what happened to me? Still nobody knew. My family and friends continued to be very loving and supportive through all this craziness. Momma did what she did best. The nurses were wonderful, as always, with the exception of about 2 nurses, all of the nurses on the 4th floor remembered me from my back and shunt surgeries (1997-1998). They all noticed a difference, specifically with my balance and walking. It had worsened.

On Friday, August 24, 2001, a facility decided to accept me with the TPN (my GI doctor explained to the facility that I was independent with it and knew how to connect and disconnect myself). That afternoon I was transferred to an Inpatient therapy facility. Previously, I had heard only good things about this inpatient therapy facility. From when I got ready to be transferred from the University of Chicago Hospital, I knew that was going to be an adventure of its own. First, after the medics put me on the stretcher and wheeled me into the elevator, one medic made fun of one of the nurses, saying she was a man dressed up like a woman. On the ride over to the inpatient facility, the medics continued to play their radio loudly, ignoring the bad headache I had. The ride over was sickening as one of the medics admitted she spilled Chinese food in the ambulance earlier that day, so the ambulance smelled of old Chinese food. I felt very nauseated for the duration of the ride.

When I arrived at the Inpatient therapy facility, the woman at the security desk didn't have a clue. I was finally taken up to my room, given a white ID bracelet (your bracelet changes color as you get stronger and earn points, I was told), changed gowns, given a wheelchair, put in the bed and told not to get out of the bed without assistance. To enforce this, all of my railing was raised on my bed, making me feel like I was in a baby crib. My rehab doctor was not there, the day I was admitted, so I was examined by the doctor covering for her. Although they drove me crazy at times ☺ I couldn't wait to see my family that weekend.

That weekend, my family visited me. That was great but that wasn't the best part. My family bought my mail with them. It was then I found the greatest surprise. Tammy and James had sent me a Get Well card. It was hand-made and it was so cute. It had a hand sewn angel on the front. On the inside, James had written our favorite bible verse, Philippians 4:13. When my family left, I called Tammy and James. Tammy promised to say a prayer for me. I prayed I would not lose touch with them.

The positive part of this whole experience was my roommate. We got along very well from the start. She had been in the hospital for almost six months, after having half of her skull removed because of an aneurism. She took me to church with her that first Sunday morning I was a patient. I was very surprised to see the minister, who held the service I attended, stayed a while longer, following service and visited with the patients. He came to visit my roommate and myself. Before leaving, he prayed with us. My roommate was discharged from the facility the following week. She reminded me what I already knew. MY LIFE IS IN GOD'S HANDS ! ! ! Not man. That is why the neurologists couldn't tell me what happened to me before they gave up and transferred me to the inpatient therapy facility.

I continued working hard in all my therapy sessions. Unfortunately, progress was slow. Daddy visited me regularly, usually during his lunch break and or after he got off work.

I rarely saw Momma because of her work schedule. Momma called me regularly. Sha and Netta even called me regularly and relayed messages to me, through my parents.

My therapists worked me hard. They could also be a little harsh. For instance, my hair was not in the best shape due to all the tests that was performed while I was in the University of Chicago Hospitals. My headaches made it almost impossible to wash and/or comb my hair. One therapist had the audacity to ridicule me about my hair. Uh hello! I had been in the hospital for almost a month and on top of that I had an EEG. That therapist also forgot that when you point one finger at someone, there are three, sometimes four, fingers pointing back at you. Therapy was hard sometimes. Of course, I had to work hard if I wanted to go home. More importantly, I had to work hard so I could get out of that wheelchair. Thank you Lord for always being there. During my hospitalization, Mr. and Mrs. Trouble visited me. it was very good to see them. Mrs. Trouble did my hair during their visit.

As a result of this hospitalization, I learned a few important facts:

What occurred DID have something to do with the last shunt revision.

What occurred had a large part to do with everything that happened in 2000.

I have damage to my brain, bladder and stomach that was affecting my body as a whole.

As a result, I would not get 100% after everything that happened to me. My rehab doctor concluded that she would not keep me in the hospital trying to get me there, either. As a result, she monitored me and helped me regain as much as possible for a couple of weeks and then sent me home. Well what do you say after a conversation like that? Well I said, "Hallelujah anyhow!" because I was still going to praise God through the storm. God has been with me all these years so I was not giving up on God now. He never gave up on me.

Over time, my rehab doctor and I discussed what would happen after my discharge. The suggestion was made for safety rails, a wheelchair and a homemaker. When I spoke to Momma, she said if I needed a homemaker, she would stay at home with me. Oh my God! Here we go again. I know she is Momma and she gave birth to me. I was overjoyed that we became much closer however this was getting to be too much. I was getting sick and tired of all the sacrifices she made on my behalf, for my health. I was also tired of her watching me in pain and confronting doctors on my behalf.

It was determined that my target discharge date was September 7, 2001. As a result, every day until then, I got up, swallowed hard and threw myself into my physical, occupational and speech therapy sessions. I was not going to let the devil get the victory of this situation. I was victorious in Christ Jesus!

• •

Wednesday, September 5, 2001~In Patient Rehabilitation Hospital

Happy Birthday to me! Happy Birthday to me! Happy Birthday Shereice! Happy Birthday to me!

Today has been a fantastic day. It started with my nurse wishing me a "Happy Birthday." In therapy, everyone wished me a "Happy Birthday" as well. During my lunch break, two (2) bouquets of flowers and (2) bouquets of balloons were delivered to me. they came from Gerri (family friend) and my parents. Now I will just have to figure out another way to get them back. I guess their anniversary present wasn't enough. ☺

I was so excited about seeing everyone this evening, I couldn't wait for my afternoon schedule to end. When I got back to my room, I found a note on my bulletin board. It said, "Happy birthday Shereice from the 35W nursing staff." I went to the support group for people living with brain injuries. When I got back to my room, I practically stared at the clock until everyone started arriving. In the end, Momma, Daddy,

Nicole, Lavare, Sha (miracles do happen), Bri Bri, Nick, Lisette and John came. We then had to wait for Sara to bring the birthday cake. It was a wonderful evening of laughter and with my family. I must say there were some moments where they got me good. Now I will just have to think of a way to get even—ha, ha, ha. God has truly blessed me. Every present I received (almost) had a symbolic meaning behind it. My presents didn't end there.

I got back to my room in just enough time to receive my singing birthday wish from James. I then talked to Tammy for a little while. God has blessed me to see another glorious year. Tammy wants to get together with me when I get back on my feet (or stronger—whichever comes first). I told her most definitely. I them went to take my shower. I got out of the shower in just enough time to receive my last "Happy Birthday" for the night. It came from Kita. She sang to me. Today went very well. I didn't even let the headaches bother me. Thank you Lord for allowing me to see another birthday.

• •

September 7, 2001 was my last day at Inpatient therapy facility. Thank you Jesus! I completed my last therapy session. I also prepared for the road ahead of me. My occupational therapist ordered me safety rails, a shower chair and a temporary wheelchair (a rented wheelchair I would return when I no longer needed it). I was only supposed to be using the wheelchair until I got a little more stronger. My rehab doctor made me promise that when I came back for my return appointment in December, I would be out of the chair. That was something she did not have to worry about. I did not like the idea of using a wheelchair anyway. I said goodbye to the few friends I made while I was in the hospital and prepared for the road ahead.

When I was released to go home Friday, September 7, 2001 things were definitely different. When I got home, I was overjoyed to be home but unable to do anything because I was tired. It was evident that I would have a long and difficult (or so I thought) road to travel. Once again, Momma decided to stay home with me until I became stronger. The wheelchair and safety rails, which were ordered by my occupational therapist at the Inpatient therapy facility, never arrived. As time passed, no one from the Inpatient therapy facility answered the phone or returned any messages I left with regards to me resuming physical therapy and occupational therapy on an out-patient basis.

During my first days at home, Momma and I had some time to sit and talk about some things. One of the subjects that came up was the funeral of the former singer, Alliyah. Momma said her funeral was fit for a princess. She went on to say that's how she will have my funeral, complete with the release of one white dove for my age. I felt honored that she wanted to do something so special in honor of my memory. I don't want her to go overboard. My real reward will come when I get to heaven and see my Savior's face. Oh, how I love Jesus! Thank you Lord for giving me life, health and strength. Thank you Lord for giving me a spirit of peace during the storm. Thank you Lord for the positive interactions I did have at the inpatient therapy facility. Lord please help me to be stronger in you.

"Consider it all joy, my brethren, when you encounter various [a]trials, knowing that the testing of your faith produces [b] endurance."

James 1:2-3

Footnotes: a. James 1:2 Or *temptations, b.* James 1:3 Or *steadfastness*

One of the first things my mother and I did was go to Value City to look for my bedroom set. I couldn't bear sleeping on that chaise lounge chair any longer. Thank you Jesus for the money from the settlement. I had enough to get me a bedroom set, something I never owned, but badly needed. Unfortunately because of how my headboard was shaped, I had to switch bedrooms with Nicole. She was not happy about the change and made sure I knew how she felt. Nicole always had an attitude, even when she was younger.

The next day, September 9th, was even better for me. I relaxed in my room for the most part. However, during the day, I got to talk to Karen. She is such a great friend. We both have been through so much, with regards to our health, but never gave up. Meeting Karen is another positive result of my whole DePaul experience.

Tuesday, September 11, 2001

Today started out as a quiet day. Momma did my laundry for me; as she completed each load, I folded and put away my clothes. Just a little while longer, my bedroom set will be here.

What is this world coming to? It started early this morning and on throughout the day. Several federal buildings, in 3 states, were destroyed when aircraft crashed into them. One of these states was New York. I feel so sorry for all those people affected by this. I don't mean to sound selfish but I thank God my Daddy was here in Chicago and not in New York today. It looks like United States may be on the verge of another was as I heard a news report that the government plans to investigate and retaliate.

I rested today while I prepared to switch rooms. The truth of the matter is I was very tired and quite uncomfortable from pain. I won't tell Momma because she is already watching me like a hawk and worried about me.

Daddy turned 53 the following day. What a way to celebrate your birthday. I really prayed God's blessings over the people who lost love ones because of that tragedy. I thanked God Daddy was in Chicago and not in New York. He may drive me crazy at times but I thank God for his presence in my life. Daddy taught me a lot about the woman I wanted to be and the woman I didn't want to be. He also showed me what type of husband I wanted when God bless me with one.

"But the Lord says, "Do not cling to the events of the past or dwell on what happened long ago.
Watch for the new thing I am going to do. It is happening already you can see it now!
I will make a road through the wilderness
and give you streams of water there . . ."
Isaiah 43:18-19 (GNT)

Chapter 12: New Beginnings

Happy New Year ! ! ! Happy 2002. I brought in the New Year with friends. We went to Watch Service at one of their friend's church. It would have been fine except service didn't end until 3:00am. I also felt there were too much "man" and not enough God. I must say God had his angels encamped around me. There were two ministers who tried to approach me, while the prophetic word went forth. One of the ladies was stopped by my friend. The other woman started coming toward me and stopped dead in her tracks. Thank you Lord. After finally getting home, I went to bed. When I got up, I had a pretty laid back day with my family.

Sunday January 6, 2002

Can you say "new beginnings"? Well I can because that is exactly what occurred today. Daddy, Momma and I attended service at New Faith MB Church. This is the church my Aunt Dessa (Auntie) is a member. In the past, Momma and Daddy had visited this church several times, but this was my first time visiting. I knew there was something special about New Faith after coming through the front door. There was southern hospitality evident throughout the as members welcomed and embraced you as you came into the church. The choir sounded beautiful and spirit-filled. They sang "I Almost Let Go" and 2 other songs.

The pastor, Rev. Dr. Howard Randolph, is very friendly toward his members. He took time to fellowship with the members before service started. Service was spirit-filled even before Rev. Randolph delivered the word. He used one of my favorite scriptures.

Philippians 3:13-14 (KJV)

"Brethren, I count not myself to have apprehended: but this one thing I do, forgetting those things which are behind, and reaching forth unto those things which are before,

I press toward the mark for the prize of the high calling of God in Christ Jesus."

Basically, Rev. Randolph message was that we must leave our past behind and work toward the future. Yes, it hurts sometimes to let go of these things you have held on to for so long because you have become comfortable with it. However, God has a goal in mind and in order to reach it, you must let go of the past and move forward. While Rev. Randolph was preaching, Momma nudged me. We both knew God was speaking to us. Momma and I had begun having the almost identical conversation while at home. As he continued, we both kept nudging one another. It was almost like Rev. Randolph had been with us for the last few months and he used the scriptures to back up what he was saying. By the time Rev. Randolph extended the invitation, Momma and I both knew what we had to do.

We both nudged one another. We quietly discussed the decision. It was almost like God told him to wait for us because he extended the invitation a little longer. Finally, Momma got tired of fighting the Spirit, grabbed my hand, and we walked hand-in-hand to join our new family. Auntie Dessa was in tears. Daddy was happy with our decision and he nodded in agreement.

True Right was my elementary school and high school but, I have graduated and it was time to move to a higher education. New Faith is my higher education. Happiness is in my future.

New Faith brought about change for us. We were all going to Sunday service together, as a family again (because of changes it had been a long time since we all went to church together). We had also started going to Wednesday night bible class, sometimes together. We were happier. A weight seemed to have been lifted. The year 2002 was looking brighter to me.

On Sunday, February 17, 2002, we got up and went to early morning service. Netta even came to church that morning. Momma, Netta and I all sat together. Service was very spirit-filled. During service, a lady sitting directly behind me received an anointing of the Holy Spirit. I did not realize she was as close to my head as she was. She hit me in the back of the head. She did not hit my head hard. At the time, I thought nothing of it and just moved to the edge of the bench, in order to avoid being hit in the head again. Of course, Momma told Netta, who was sitting right next to me, to ask me what was wrong. I told her what happened. Momma, of course, asked if I was all right. When I said "yes," Momma asked me again to make sure I was all right. We stayed and enjoyed the rest of service. I completed my New Membership class that morning and then went back to my parent's house.

About an hour after we got home, I got a headache so Momma urged me to take my pain medicine and go take a nap. It was a long nap. When I woke up, my headache had worsened. Since I had slept almost six hours, I took some more pain medicine. I made it through the rest of the day, although it was very painful.

By February 18th, I could not bear the pain any longer and told Momma. After paging Dr. Frim, I went to the emergency room. As soon as I got to the emergency room, the triage nurse knew something was wrong. As soon as I told her I was having a possible shunt malfunction, I was immediately taken back. My vitals were taken. I had to endure the painful spinal tap. It revealed that my shunt level, on admission, was 26. This was dangerously high. Fluid was drained during the spinal tap and it brought the number down slightly. The usual shunt work-up was done.

Dr. Frim did not want to bother the VP shunts again because of the complications I had in 1997 and 1998. After discussing it with Me and Momma, of course, Dr. Frim placed an external lumbar peritoneal (LP) shunt on February 18, 2002. He placed it externally first, to make sure it would have a positive effect on my shunt pressure and headaches. By placing it externally, it would have been easier to remove if it didn't work. In the beginning, the LP shunt was not having a positive effect on my headaches or pressure. Normally, it is removed after day 3 but I was given 2 extra days. After 5 days, the LP shunt had a positive effect on my headache pressure. By this time the residents and Momma had decided the LP shunt was the right thing for me. Dr. Frim did not accept their opinion. He came to see me, without the residents. Dr. Frim was very serious. He said he knew how everyone else felt about the LP shunt. He wanted to know what I truly thought. I was silent, thinking carefully about my response. On the inside, I was very nervous. I did not want a repeat of 1997-1998. I told him since the external LP shunt had a positive effect on my headaches, I wanted it placed internally. This of course, meant surgery. After once again making sure it was truly my decision and not me speaking from pressure from my Momma, he decided to do the surgery. Dr. Frim and I decided to schedule the surgery for March 4, 2002. This would give the area on my back where the external shunt was placed, time to heal. Additionally, Dr. Frim went out of town for a few days and I didn't want anyone else to perform the surgery, except him. I was discharged on February 25, 2002.

....

Friday, March 1, 2002

1:11am – I am wide awake when I should be sleep. My back is killing me in the area where the external LP shunt was placed. Maybe if things were done a little bit differently in August, this would not have occurred like it did. Sunday wouldn't have occurred like it did, I wouldn't have been admitted to the University of Chicago Hospitals yet again. Maybe I wouldn't be having surgery. Maybe James wouldn't have had the dream he had. Lord please help me!

I am happy God allowed me to maintain my peace of mind. I am thankful God has blessed me with some wonderful people in my life. My Momma had been a major source of strength, education and acceptance. We may not always had the closeness I longed for, in the past, but when I needed her the most, Momma has always been there for me.

My Daddy love me very much and would do just about anything for me. he drives me crazy at times, with that attitude of his, but I don't know where I would be without him.

James is a little boy with a heart of gold. Tammy and Joseph raised him well.

Then there is Lisette. She is a mighty woman of God. She also has a heart of gold. God placed her in my life during a pivotal, yet stormy, part of my life. She has never wavered, sometimes going above and beyond what I could ever imagine. I can't wait to witness God use her even more than what he had already done.

There are numerous people at the University of Chicago Hospitals who have gone above and beyond the call of duty. I don't know where I would be without them. Thank you.

It is now 1:45am. I must really try to get some rest.

....

The following day, Saturday, March 2, 2002 was a very good day. That evening, I spoke to my good friend Karen. It was so good hearing from her. God really knew what he was doing (like always) when he put her in my life. When I first saw her prior to our first meeting, I never imagined a friendship such as ours. That day, we talked about some of everything for a little while. Of course, our main focus was about the upcoming week. I thought I had told her about James and Tammy but hadn't updated her on the bond that was established between us. She told me about her new job position. I was so happy she was doing well in her new job.

After talking to Karen, I received a message that Tammy had called. I called Tammy back. Before we could talk, I had to talk to James and his little brother. James said a prayer for me in school. I was touched. It still warmed my heart at the bond we shared in such a short amount of time. After receiving and giving "I love you" to the boys, Tammy and I got a chance to talk. I had to tell Tammy how she and James uplifted my heart when they visited me in the hospital. Tammy said the conversation I had with James about being honest about how he was feeling health wise) helped a lot. That conversation helped me too. I was so happy to have them in my life. When

I got off the phone, I went to talk to Momma. She said God blessed me with some wonderful people in my life.

Sunday, March 3, 2002

1:30pm – Well in approximately 17 hours, I will be having surgery for my new LP shunt, under the direction of Dr. Frim. I don't know what to say because so many things are running through my head.

Monday, March 4, 2002 my LP shunt surgery was performed. On the morning of the surgery, I was calm and at ease. I felt like I had made the right decision to have the surgery. After Momma, Daddy and I got to the hospital, we had a short time to wait. We passed time by bothering one another, in a good way, the make you laugh sort of way. When I was called back, Momma went with me. At this point, the weirdest thing to ever happen when someone is preparing for surgery occurred. It felt more like a family reunion as many doctors and nurses, who took care of me in the past and present was there, I even jokingly fussed at one of the residents because I had not seen him as much during that time. Momma just sat back, laughed, and shook her head. Later, when we were alone, Momma teased me about being able to go into a hospital for surgery and everyone know me by name. ☺

13. LP Shunt Placement – March 4, 2002

Initial response was very positive following surgery. After regaining consciousness from surgery, my headache pressure was very low, almost gone. I couldn't believe it! Dr. Frim came to check on me. "How did I do?" I smiled and gave him the thumbs up. He then said, "Did you see that? She smiled at me!" A couple of hours later, I went to join my wonderful nurses on the 4th floor. They were happy to see me looking better than before. The following day went just as well. My headache pressure went back up. I responded very well to the pain medicine. Momma and Dr. Frim was very pleased with the outcome of the surgery. Dr. Frim and I decided it was time to start working with physical therapy again.

Wednesday, March 6, 2002–University of Chicago Hospitals

Day 3 is going all right. Dr. Frim and his residents are doing a good job. Ayanna came to see me today. It was so good seeing her. She brought me a book of poetry by Maya Angelou, one of my favorite African American poets. As we were talking, Dr. Frim stopped by. He introduced himself. It was then trouble started jokingly. Ayanna told him I had told her some good things about him. Why did she do that?☺ Dr. Frim started smiling and told Ayanna she could stay as long as she wanted. He looked at me and I started laughing.

The following day I was evaluated by the rehab doctor. The conclusion was reached that I needed to do in-patient rehab. I needed to work on strengthening, balance and walking. I agreed as long as it wasn't the first rehab hospital I was a patient in. She suggested Weiss, which was also affiliated with the University of Chicago Hospitals, at the time. When I spoke to Momma, she agreed as long as it wasn't the first rehab hospital I was in. The remainder of my day was pretty quiet as I took it easy and rested.

Friday, May 8, 2002–Weiss Memorial hospital

This was my last morning at the University of Chicago Hospitals. The ride in the ambulance was smooth and quiet. I arrived at Weiss around 11:00am. My room and nurse was waiting when I arrived. A few minutes after I got settled, my physician, Dr. Linz, came in. She was very nice and attentive. Dr. Linz definitely seemed to be on top of things. After talking for a few minutes, she examined me and did her admission evaluation. She said that we would work together.

I will have physical, occupational and speech therapy. Because of the note written in my chart, the nurse will also teach me how to straight cath myself. I am receiving very good responses and I think this will be a far better experience than my first rehab experience. Thank you Lord!

....

The following day went just as well as the previous day. I continued following a therapy schedule that was printed out and given to me at the beginning of each day. Unfortunately, as Dr. Linz tried to find me another urologist, she could only find the one who performed the surgery. I just did not feel comfortable going back to see him. I never had a doctor so non-sealant as he turned out to be. In the beginning, he was very nice and forthcoming with information. He made it seem like he really wanted to help me alleviate the issues I was having with my bladder. Something about that surgery just wasn't right. I can remember he constantly ignored the residents and nurses in the hospital, when they kept urging him to check on me when I stopped being able to properly urinate. The day he finally saw me, which was also the last time he saw me, he was not happy to see me. He made it seem like everything was perfect and he sent me back to my hospital room (he saw me in his clinic). That was the last time I saw him.

....

Tuesday, March 12, 2002–Weiss Memorial Hospital

My roommate is Laine. She is an elderly Jewish woman. She is very sweet. The only thing is Laine sometimes walk around the room naked and don't care. Laine has a best friend name Norm. Laine says he is very nice except, when he's had something to drink.

9:55pm–The day went very well. When I finished my schedule, I came back to my room and took a nap. I have an appointment with another Urologist, here at Weiss, tomorrow.

Laine and I enjoyed the evening with Norm. he is very educated. Yesterday, I said I had a taste for some chocolate. Today he brought me some. Thanks Norm!☺

....

The next day I was able to see an Urologist at Weiss. When I got down to the Urology clinic, the nurse came out and prepped me for the tests HE was doing himself (instead of his nurse and resident). The tests were designed to test the size and strength of my bladder. The first test showed I held a large amount of fluid but didn't feel it. The Urologist and his nurses were surprised at the amount of fluid my bladder held, without me feeling it. He stopped the test and ordered my bladder drained. He then examined my bladder with a scope. The Urologist told me to continue learning how to catheterize myself. He said to stop trying to strain to use the washroom. He ended the conversation by saying he would take me on as a patient.

When I spoke to my Momma that evening, she was, of course not happy. That afternoon was very hard on me. I must say, by the time I ended my conversation with Momma, I was outraged with the Urologist who performed the surgery. I was mad at myself for trusting him. Well, what's done, is done. I couldn't lose sight of reality. I had to fight. I had to learn to straight cath myself and not rely on someone else to do it for me. I ended my day in prayer.

"Dear Lord, you have brought me through so many things already. Thank you for your love, grace and mercy. You are my life. You are my strength. Without you Lord, I am nothing. With you Lord, I am everything. Lord please give me the strength to move forward with my life. Thank you for the knowledge of my circumstances. Please help me Lord to use this knowledge to make the right decisions. Thank you Lord. In Jesus name I pray, Amen."

As my adventure continued, my roommate got some very bad news (in her opinion). Her daughter and her daughter's husband, who sat on the Board of Directors at Weiss at the time, decided to make Laine give up her place for an Assisted Living apartment. She was not happy at all. She was almost in tears as she told Norm (who was not allowed in the meeting) and me about the meeting. Sometimes family members think they are helping by trying to make decisions they think are right for their loved ones. Sometimes they are right in their decisions. Other times, family members need to take a step back and really listen to what the person in the situation is saying. Laine went from being high-spirited to being practically depressed within 24 hours time. She started talking in her sleep. She was miserable. I prayed her misery would cease and her happiness would return.

The following day, the Lord blessed me to have some type of positive impact on the people I met at Weiss. Everyone enjoyed working with me and I enjoyed working with them. The therapists enjoyed picking on me. ☺ That's ok. I enjoyed having nice people with good spirits around me, any day over people who were negative and mean-spirited.

By Day 12, I discovered the Rehab floor was a baby factory, literally. Everywhere I turned, there was a therapist, nurse and/ or doctor who either just had a baby or was pregnant. I would often joke, the stork must have a nest perched on the roof of the hospital. Vivian, my occupational therapist, was also pregnant. Day 12 was also my "AWOL" day. ☺ Dr. Linz took me off the floor for a little while. We went to the cafeteria and sat down and talked. She got to know me and I got to know her. I learned a lot about her. She loved her work, which was obvious from the first day I met her. She is the proud mother of six children. I remember thinking, when she first said she have six children, she don't even look like she had one. As we continued talking, I revealed to her, the in-patient facility I was a patient at during my not-so-great rehab experience. She apologized because she was one of the directors at the facility. We talked about the road ahead of me. I sat in amazement as I listened to this woman talk about me. Weiss really encouraged and assisted me. it was obvious, they cared about me and my well being. Later on that same day, I had my discharge meeting with my case worker. We had a long conversation about my discharge, which was taking place 2 days later.

Thursday, March 21, 2002~Weiss Memorial Hospital and Home Sweet Home!!!

Very Late Evening~Thank you Jesus! Thank you Lord! I am finally home. I got here late afternoon. Daddy came to get me while Momma stayed home and waited for my medical equipment~go figure. It felt strange, not in a bad way.

Yesterday, Laine went home. This morning, Laine and Norm surprised me and called me. it was good to hear their voices. Laine is a beautiful person. If I live to be 87 years old, or older, I pray I look as good as she does, or better. Today felt strange, I felt like I was leaving friends as I said good bye to all of the therapists, nurses and Dr. Linz. She sat with me for a little while before I left. Dr. Linz made me feel an even stronger sense of accomplishment as she talked about how I was when I was admitted and how I am now. In such a short time, we have bonded in a way that make me feel like she has been my doctor for a longer time than she has. Dr. Linz had a very busy schedule today but she made time for me. Thank you.

When Daddy came, I was still waiting on Dr. Linz. When she got to my room, she bought cookies with her so we could share one more time before I left. Daddy shook his head and smiled. Dr. Linz said many good things about me. He said "thank you" and did what he always do, started to change the subject and started talking about Lavare. Dr. Linz put the subject back on me as she said I had already told her about Lavare.

Anyway, I must remember to thank Momma for being honest with me about her feelings to the changes that occurred as I came home.

She sounded a little strange at one point while I waited for Daddy to pick me up. Momma admitted she would have to get used to the changes. I must admit, it felt strange to me, as well. God has not given me a spirit of fear, but a sound mind and a spirit of peace. Thank you Jesus!!

I waited for a few days, after I got home, to sit down and talk to Daddy about my latest adventure and the important information I learned during that last hospitalization, regarding my current bladder situation. I have learned through past experiences and observations, that Daddy has a hard time, sometimes, with my health issues. As a result he may not always respond in an expected manner or at all. So when I sat down to talk to him, one week later I tried to explain as best as I could, what was happening to me. Later that evening, my Momma and I discussed what happened earlier that evening. We both have a clear understanding of my Daddy and how he reacts to my health. It's funny. If you look at both of my parents, you would think their roles would be reversed. My momma is my weapon of mass destruction. She helps me question, understand and decide whenever I need her assistance with a medical decision.

In mid-April 2002, I returned for another follow-up appointment with Dr. Linz. When I arrived at Weiss, I went straight up to the rehab floor. When I got to the 4th floor, I felt like I was visiting friends, rather than going for a doctor's appointment. All of the nurses greeted me and complimented me on how well I looked. I then ran into Vivian, she walked with me over to Dr. Linz's office. On the way to her office, I finally noticed the stork had visited Vivian too. She was 4 months by then. While waiting to see Dr. Linz, I saw just about everyone, except Christy. When I did finally see Christy, she ran over and gave me a big hug. We talked for a few minutes.

Thank God, by the time I saw Dr. Linz, Daddy had went down to the cafeteria. By the end of that appointment, we had decided it would be better for me to continue using the walker for right now, instead of upgrading to the quad cane.

Her next goal was for me to get a motorized scooter, which I eventually received. She also reviewed my kidney ultrasound results. Unfortunately, it showed the right kidney to have the potential to be problematic. Dr. Linz decided she wanted me to have one more appointment with her, as well as, follow-up with the Urologist I saw at Weiss. We then said our goodbyes. I then said goodbye to the nurses and therapists.

The ride home was nice and quiet as Daddy never asked me about my doctor appointments. When Daddy and I got home, without giving any details, I called Momma and said, "we need to spend some quality time together this evening." She knew exactly what that meant. I needed to talk to her alone. I never saw Momma so quickly after she got home from work. We talked, behind closed doors, in my room. She laughed and counted backwards from 10. Momma was a little concerned. I couldn't wait to see what my other doctors had to say.

As I entered into May 2002, I began to think about change and how it affects us. I wondered what, if anything, would change about my bladder situation as a result of the kidney ultrasound. Lisette was graduating from medical school that June. How would things be after she graduated? We had become so close in such a short amount of time. Around this time, Lisette and I had lunch together. We talked about everything. We talked about the kidney ultrasound. As usual, she was very supportive as she promised to keep me lifted in her prayers. She also encouraged me as she told me I made the right decision by choosing another urologist. Lisette told me to always remember to do what's right for me, despite popular opinion. Thanks Lisette.

During that time, I endured problems with my shoulder, in spite of therapy and Motrin. It was initially believed to be related to how I held my walker when I walked. As a result I was referred to an Upper Extremity Orthopedic Surgeon for further evaluation and to see if I had somehow fractured it. It was later determined that I had developed a space in my shoulder that was most likely related to the Questionable Myasthenia Gravis.

Around this time, my parent's house became a little tight in space, as Netta and her children, moved back into my parents home temporarily. I really prayed that God blessed Netta. She had lost her job and her home. In the beginning, it was very peaceful.

By May 19th therapy continued to go well. It was going so well the therapists were preparing to release me 2 weeks later. I also had an appointment with my GI physician around this time. The appointment went fine except, she threatened to start me back on TPN if my eating habits didn't improve. I wasn't worried about that. It was still hard for me to eat because my appetite still hadn't returned. As a result, I often forced myself to eat, when I did eat.

Well my beautiful momma turned 52 that year, not that anyone could tell. She always looked young for her age. The evening of her birthday, my sisters and I bought her a birthday cake. Of course, everyone was at the house. As I went into June 2002, my spirits were uplifted. God was doing some wonderful things.

Friday, June 7, 2002 – Congratulations Lisette Lewis!!!

Today has been a busy, emotional day. Lisette became a pediatrician today.

I met her family early this morning at her apartment. It was on to the ceremony from there. Daddy surprised me and came to the graduation, during his lunch break. He stayed long enough to see her get her degree. He then had to go back to work. I didn't realize that so many people I knew was graduating.

University of Chicago Hospitals is going to feel a little strange without Lisette there. She looked great today. I sat with Collette, Lisette's best friend. It was great seeing her again. I met her mom today. I spent the day with Collette. After the ceremony, there was a luncheon. The second ceremony was long and boring. There was a break in-between the last ceremony and Lisette's dinner party. The dinner was beautiful! Congratulations Dr. Lisette Lewis (since I know this is the only time I can call you by your professional name. ☺)!!! I love you.

....

For the remainder of June 2002, I worked hard in therapy. Toward the middle of the month, I had my final appointment with my rehab doctor, Dr. Linz. As always, it was very good to see her again. We touched basis on how therapy was proceeding and how I had been feeling. Everyone at the hospital said I looked good. Thank you for the compliments. Dr. Linz and I talked about how things were going for me she watched me walk, of course. It was at that point I learned that Dr. Linz was leaving Weiss because she was about to head up a newly formed rehab center at another hospital. Everyone exchanged hugs before I left. Thank you Lord for allowing me to climb another mountain.

I continued physical therapy at Rehabilitation Achievement Center, RAC for short. There were some good days. There were also days that made you want to cry. Thank God these days were few. Thank you God for endurance to withstand the obstacles I endured. Without it, I wouldn't have made it through those tough days. During that time, my daddy and I went to Wednesday Night Bible Class. As usual, my spirit was fed and uplifted. On Wednesday, June 26, 2002, prior to class letting out, we were reminded that our pastor, Rev. Randolph, was speaking at a revival that evening. My daddy and I decided to go to the remainder of the service. I had a blessed time in the word of God. I was also reminded of the wonderful pastor I was blessed to have. Rev. and Sis. Randolph uplifted my heart each time I saw them by the words they said to me.

God has such a unique way of working things out. God gives us peace in the midst of the storm. Thank you Lord for continuing to give me peace in the midst of my storm called life.

Thursday, July 4, 2002 was our wonderful family dinner at my parent's house. I came out mid-afternoon (I was tired and slept late). Uncle Willie was looking for me. He was one in a million. He might not have always said it nice but he always told the truth. You will truly be missed Uncle Willie. I think I miss his family stories the most. We had a nice group that year. They tried to surprise me with Grannie (but I had accidentally overheard the conversation the previous night—nice try). Daddy barbecued. Momma fixed the side dishes. I really enjoyed myself.

I graduated from, or completed my last day of, therapy at RAC on Friday, July 12, 2002. I no longer used the wheelchair to get around. I was elevated to using my quad cane and walker, depending on how I felt that day. I was so happy. Thank you Jesus! For a moment, I actually missed that place but not enough to continue therapy. When I completed my therapy at RAC, I was given a binder with an exercise program for me to follow now that I had graduated. I thought to myself, I knew I wasn't going to keep up with the exercise regimen. I had tried in the past to keep up with the after therapy exercise program they send me home with on my last day. I always started slacking off after one month until I eventually stopped.

For the month of July I kept Tammy and James on my mind but didn't know why. I found out Tuesday, July 23, 2002. James had to have another shunt revision (surgery). His shunt malfunctioned again, causing him to sleep a lot and have increased headaches. Dr. Frim is great! I am so happy he stays on top of things. Tammy said James symptoms didn't get as bad as they usually do. I spoke to Tammy after James was put back in his hospital room, following surgery. In the beginning, Tammy said James couldn't stay awake. When he was awake, he vomited and went back to sleep. Otherwise, the surgery seemed to have gone well. The plan was for James to go home that Thursday, if not, Friday.

. . . .

Friday, July 26, 2002

Thank you Lord for a beautiful day. Thank you for your love. Thank you Lord for your healing power. Thank you for life, health and strength. Thank you Lord for the joy that the world didn't give me and the world can't take my joy away from me.

Today was a great day. Yesterday I was supposed to see Tammy and James however, James was tired so we switched to today. That's fine. After all, he is healing from surgery.

Tammy came to pick me up at 1:00. We went to a little restaurant that James and his little brother, Lucas like to go to for lunch. It really warmed my heart to see them again. James had a headache which is normal after shunt surgery. He looked wonderful. He gave me such a warm hug. Tammy hugged me. every time I see them, I feel like I have known them for a lifetime, instead of just a few months.

While we ate lunch, Tammy and I got a chance to get caught up on things. We talked about my appointment with my neurologist. We talked some more about James latest adventure. We talked some more about our experiences as we are still learning about one another. It didn't seem like we had been gone as long as we had. When they had dropped me off, four hours had passed.

• •

August started out very nice. My friend Vivian gave birth to a beautiful baby girl on August 2, 2002. She named her Jaime. Congratulations Vivian and Alvin. There wasn't too much happening around my parents house so I used the time to try and remain grounded in the word. I also looked forward to my birthday, which my friends had become quiet about again.

Toward the end of August, Tammy and I talked about her big surprise Christmas present she planned for James and his little brother, Lucas. She was planning to take them to Walt Disneyland in California. She was very excited as she told me about the details of the trip. She stopped abruptly. Then she did one of the most Christian deeds I have ever seen. She apologized for offending me (which she did not) by talking about the trip, knowing I missed my Walt Disney World trip I was planning to take when I was admitted to the hospital.

At that point, I thought that was one of the sweetest things anyone ever did. I was wrong. Moments later, she said, "if you can round up the money, you and Rosa (Momma) are welcome to come with us." It was her husband, Joseph's family trip. Tammy said she would have to double-check with Joseph and get back to me.

When Momma got home that evening, I told her about the trip. She said she wouldn't go because she would n't leave Nicole and Lavare. What about when she left me? Yes, I was in 8th grade but still. I didn't care. I was going to go on this trip and have a wonderful time. Now I had something to look forward to. Thank you Jesus!

September 4, 2002, I reached six months post-shunt surgery. I went six months with no complications, no hospitalizations, and NO MORE SURGERIES. THANK YOU JESUS ! ! ! You are a healer and a miracle worker.

• •

Thursday, September 5, 2002

Thank you Lord for allowing me to see another glorious year ! ! ! Thank you for allowing me to spend my birthday at home instead of the hospital like 2001, and under doctor's care, like 2000. For the most part, today was very boring. I only slept and watched television. My favorite conspirators are planning something for the weekend. I have no idea because they have been very quiet.

My Grannie called me two days ago to congratulate me. I hate that she go through so much emotional pain during this month. Uncle Mat died on my 13th birthday. I pray she will allow the peace of God to surround her very soon. Uncle Howard and Sara called to congratulate me. Nicholas and Momma congratulated me. I miss James. I look forward to the vacation.

• •

I was right. My favorite conspirators gave me a surprise birthday party at Gino's East, downtown Chicago. God blessed me with some wonderful people in my life. I got a chance to see many friends. I truly enjoyed myself. I was made "Queen for the day", complete with my crown. I just wish I had been able to put the planners in touch with Tammy and James. I received some nice gifts and heart touching cards. The part that really touched my heart was there were more people who RSVP'd but were unable to make it. Thank God, the rest of September 2002 was pretty calm.

Around the middle of October 2002, I spoke to Tammy. Her husband and his siblings didn't mind me going with them. Tammy put me in touch with her travel agent so I could get the same package they had. The trip was not cheap but, it was not as expensive as I thought. I paid for the trip using one of my credit cards. Thank God I still had a nice amount of available credit on the charge card I used. That evening I said a prayer for my finances, specifically a prayer that I would get my bills paid off in a reasonable amount of time.

Toward the later part of October 2002 I received a very special package in the mail from VIvivan. Conflicting schedules kept us from talking as much as I had hoped but when we do talk we have wonderful conversations. Her beautiful daughter was being Christened and she invited me to the service. Of course, I wanted to go but who could I ask to go with me and drive? When I spoke to Sara, she happily agreed. I called Vivian and RSVP'd for us.

On October 24, 2002, I had my return appointment with Dr. Frim. As usual, he was running behind schedule. To kill time, I ran some errands, I made some doctor appointments for Sha's children. I also ran up to the 6th floor where the GI clinic is located. Everyone was happy to see me doing better. They complimented me on how well I looked. I went back down to the neurosurgery clinic. I was relieved when I was finally seen by Dr. Frim. My appointment went very well. My headaches were controllable. My shunts were functioning well. He was satisfied that during my last neurology appointment, my neurologist started me on Mestinon, which is the medication used to treat Myasthenia Gravis. Momma dropped me off and Daddy picked me up, following my appointment. I had a long wait, following my appointment, so I sat in the lobby and waited.

The christening for Vivian's baby was Sunday, November 3, 2002. It was such a beautiful ceremony. Sara gave me a ride. Vivian greeted me like a friend she had known for a long time. She introduced me to her family. Sara and I found somewhere to sit and then got something to eat. The luncheon was held at Hong Kong Buffet. I surprised myself as I sampled several dishes (it was buffet style). We talked for a little while. After eating, everyone headed to the church for the christening.

The christening was held at Queen of All Saints Basillica. The church was beautiful. I really appreciated how the christening was carried out. The priest did not perform the christening. It was performed by the deacon. He explained everything (as the service commenced) out of respect for non-Catholics in attendance. I got a chance to see Christy. After the service Christy, Vivian and I talked for a few minutes. Thank you Sara for being patient. We took plenty of pictures before we said our goodbyes. Christy walked Sara and me out.

The rest of my day was pretty quiet. I talked to Tammy. I actually got a chance to talk to her. At that point, I didn't know who was more excited about the trip, Tammy or I. I couldn't wait to see the look on James and his little brother's face. Because I was at the christening, I missed the conference known as "Vision" that was also held that weekend. I learned a lot about it and began attending Vision when I became a member of the DePaul Gospel Choir.

* * *

Friday, November 15, 2002 – I Paid My Trip Off!!!

Netta has been going through changes all week because Momma said it is time for her to move out. Momma was nice. She gave her until January.

Anyway, I received a bill, or rather a confirmation in the mail. My trip is paid off. Thank you Lord!!! I wasn't sure at first but I ordered myself 3 outfits to take with me on the trip. I have been pretty good getting my bill paid. Theo only not so good thing is I now have 2 medical bills to pay. One from the accident. The other bill is from RAC. I found out RAC don't accept Medicare or Medicaid, only private insurance. I was angry because someone should have told me before I started therapy. I spoke to Pam, in the office, and worked out a payment plan.

This past Wednesday, Daddy and I went to bible class. I received a "thank you" note from Vivian. I didn't realize it meant that much to her as it did until I read her note.

• •

One week later, I had breakfast with Tammy and the boys. We decided to go to one of Momma and Daddy's favorite places to eat, Lumes. The food is always delicious. While eating, I slipped Tammy a note under the table about the trip (I couldn't tell her what I needed to say in front of the boys). Tammy and I laughed but the boys couldn't figure out what we were laughing about. We talked about many things. Tammy and I talked about many things. She asked me what I had decided to do about school, since I was so close to finishing when I got sick. At that time, I had just decided to just let it go.

Breakfast was nice. As we were preparing to leave, Tammy noticed that the end was missing off one of the legs of my quad cane. She took me to a medical supply store on West 95th Street to replace it. Thank you Tammy.

Thanksgiving 2002 was really nice. Momma cooked, of course. Once again, we had a housefull. It never mattered whether or not my parents invited people. On Thanksgiving, people always came out of the woodwork and ended up at my parents' house. That is mostly my Momma's fault. ☺ Sorry Momma, but it is. If you weren't such a wonderful cook people wouldn't always invite themselves over for the holiday.

For Thanksgiving 2002, the house was packed. Momma laid it out. My parents were all smiles. The food was plentiful: turkey, capon, dressing, gravy and all the other sides, too many to name. Of course, there was plenty of desserts too.

Everyone enjoyed themselves tremendously. My daddy did what he did best. He ate his food. He made himself full and fell asleep where he ate. That year, he fell asleep at the table and I have a picture to prove it. ☺ Thank you Lord, every day I wake up and see a beautiful day is a day to be thankful.

As I went into December, I thought the year went by fast. The other thing I thought about was I CANNOT WAIT TO GET TO WALT DISNEYLAND ! ! ! I admit, I was, and partially still am, a big kid at heart when it comes to Disney. I looked forward to having so much fun on my vacation.

On December 6, 2002, my energy level was low so I felt fatigued all day. I woke up that evening, after my 2nd nap, to my cell phone ringing. I looked at my caller ID but did not recognize the number. Something said pick up the phone. I am happy and sad that I did. I couldn't believe who was on the other end of the phone. It was a family member of my dear friend Cyndy, calling to tell me that she had died that morning. I couldn't believe it. She had been in my thoughts frequently then but between sleep and memory, I didn't get a chance to talk to her. It had actually been several months since I had talked to Cyndy. When I got off the phone with her family member, I cried. Sha and her daughter Bri Bri came and asked me, "What's wrong?" I told them. Daddy surprised me as he volunteered to take me to the funeral without me asking. Her brother gave me the funeral information.

Her funeral was Saturday, December 14, 2002. Daddy gave me a ride, as promised. He stayed in the lobby until the funeral service started and then he came in and sat next to me. Cyndy has such a beautiful family. The first people I noticed was her three nieces. I don't think they remembered me. I had actually met them when her brother visited her in the hospital, while we were roommates. To give you an example of how Cyndy was, I never had the opportunity to meet her family except, her brother and three nieces when they visited her in the hospital. However, several of her family members embraced me like I had known Cyndy for a lot longer than I did. I had just met them at the memorial service but because Cyndy loved her family so much, I felt like I had known her family for a lot longer. Many of them remembered me either from the stories

Cyndy told them about me or the Christmas card I had sent Cyndy the year before. During the memorial service, because it was not a funeral, there was singing. People told stories of their memories of Cyndy. People were there celebrating Cyndy's life. She was loved by all who knew her.

In my opinion, the best part of the service came when Cyndy's mother told how she died. The evening before she died, Cyndy fell out of the bed. When her family found her, Cyndy's hands were extended toward heaven and she said, "I'm ready." She had accepted Christ into her life a few months before she died. Thank you Jesus! Cyndy was cremated. She wanted people to remember her like she looked in her early days, before the cancer ravaged her body. I will always remember that red hair of hers. The service was beautiful. It was very deserving of Cyndy. God bless you Cyndy. Until we meet again, your partner in crime. ☺

December 21, 2002 was my friend John's birthday party. During the party, I got a chance to see Lisette because she came in town to surprise John for his birthday. The party was nice. He loved it. i also got a chance to see my friend Stephanie, who I met through John.

Happy Birthday King Jesus! Christmas 2002 was a beautiful day. By the time I got dressed, the hurricane had already swept through the Garrett house and the kids were playing with their presents. I received a purse to take with me on my trip. Momma cooked. Uncle Howard and his future wife came over. They looked so nice together. Kita was in town visiting the rest of her family and she also came over. She looked very well. Kita had me worried for a little while when she got sick. I know God is a healer so that was short lived. It was also good seeing my cousins Gerri, Deidre and Derrick. Everyone laughed and talked the evening away.

I was so excited by the time my vacation came up, I hardly slept the night before I left. I had an early flight so on Sunday, December 29, 2002, I got up early so I wouldn't miss my limo ride. I put the rest of my luggage in the living room and that's when Daddy came upstairs to wait with me until the limo came. Just before my limo driver rung the bell, Momma came upstairs too. Then the bell rung and I met Mike for the first time. At that point, I didn't realize how many trips I would take with his company providing the transportation to/from the airport. He gave my parents his business card and started putting my luggage in the limo. Momma and Daddy told me to have fun on my trips. Hugs and kisses. Of course I had to say, "See you next year ! ! !" They laughed. WALT DISNEYLAND, HERE I COME ! ! ! Mike was so nice and talkative (Daddy said most limo driver are like that, very friendly) on the ride to the airport. Mike was very friendly. When we got to Midway Airport, Mike got me curbside check-in so I wouldn't have to do all that lugging with my scooter. They promised to take good care of my luggage and scooter. The flight was very smooth. I slept most of the way like I usually do.

When I got to Los Angeles, I was the last person to get off the airplane as it took airport personnel forever to come with my scooter. The pilot, who waited with me, joked he could have got me to baggage claim much quicker than waiting on airport personnel. When I got to baggage claim, I began looking for my bag and Tammy because baggage claim was our meeting spot. I eventually found my bag but enlisted the help of airport personnel to help lift it off the conveyor belt. Thank you.

Tammy got turned around in the airport so it took us a few extra minutes to find one another. The boys were happy to see me as I was to see them. I finally met Joseph, Tammy's husband and the boys daddy. I also met one of Joseph's sisters. We spent the rest of the afternoon and evening in Disneyland and neighboring parks. It was during that time, I met Joseph's other sister and brother-in-law. I rode my scooter. Some people were considerate whereas, others were very rude. Tammy decided that because of the amount of people in the park, it would be easier for her to wheel me around the parks instead of using my scooter for the remainder of the trip. I rented a wheelchair and Tammy and her brother-in-law took turns pushing me around. Thank you. During this time, a character assistant sent us to Guest Services to get a Special Assistance Pass so we wouldn't have to wait in line as long. I had to get two passes because only six people are allowed on a pass. We had eight in our group. For the most part, these passes proved to me very helpful.

I overslept the next morning but thankfully I woke up in enough time to have the character breakfast. We had breakfast with Minnie Mouse, Mickey Mouse, Pluto and Max. That was very fun. Pluto was biting everyone's head. Lol. ☺ I took pictures with the characters. As our trip progressed, I also took pictures with Geppetto, Winnie the Pooh, Tigger and Eeyore, just to name a few. Due to a play on words, on the part of Tammy. I also got a chance to take pictures with Minnie Mouse and Mickey Mouse in their houses, without having to wait as long (the average wait time was 2 hours for Mickey Mouse and 1 hour for Minnie Mouse in their houses). We took pictures with our cameras, as well as, professional ones. Unfortunately, we were having so much fun we forgot to pick up our professional pictures. We had so much fun. I hated to see my vacation end. Thank you so much, Tammy and James.

"You see that a man is justified by words and not by faith alone. In the same way, was not Rahab the harlot also justified by words when she received the messengers and sent them out by another way? For just as the body without the spirit is dead, so also faith without works is dead."

James 2:24-26 (NASB)

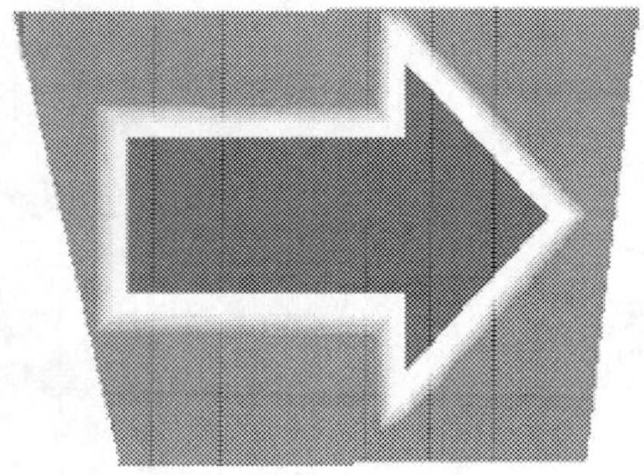

Chapter 13: A Step In The Right Direction

Happy 2003 ! ! !!

The parade down Main Street was beautiful. The only problem I endured was a woman who allowed her daughter to come in the section specifically sanctioned for people sitting in wheelchairs. The little girl stood directly in from of me, hindering my view of most of the parade. She ignored me each time I said, "Excuse me," The New Years' fireworks were beautiful. The sky was so colorful. It was spectacular! It was like a scene out of a Disney movie. At the stroke of '12' everyone started blowing party favors (that was provided by the park), kissing their loved ones and, singing the usual song. Thank you Lord! I called my parents and wished them "Happy New Year!" The new year indicated that I had less that 12 hours before my vacation officially ended. I hated to end my vacation. As that old saying goes, "all good things must come to an end."

Well January 1, 2003, I overslept. I woke up literally running. Tammy came to walk out with me. Because I overslept, I missed my ride to the airport. Tammy was able to get me a ride on another van going to the airport. Tammy and her family was going somewhere else before heading back to Chicago.

My family was excited to see how I enjoyed my vacation. They loved the fact I got caught on the ride, "It's A Small World." I had the added bonus of listening to the song in 8 different languages. The positive part was the decorations inside the ride were beautiful!! I had so much fun in Walt Disneyland! Now my next goal is to take my trip to Walt Disney World.

On Saturday, January 4, 2003, which is also Sha's birthday, I went to the Winter Retreat sponsored by Sankofa Ministries. One of the scriptures used was one that I consider to be the theme of my life, **Jeremiah 29: 11.**

"For I know the plans I have for you," declares the LORD, 'plans to prosper you and not to harm you, plans to give you hope and a future."

The theme was "People of Purpose, Men of Mission, Daughters of Destiny." The main text was taken from the book of Daniel chapter 1. We spent the day talking about our roles as men and women in the body of Christ. We placed emphasis knowing and acting upon that which the Lord has given us to do in life.

January 4, 2003 was especially nice because I got a chance to see Mack. His hectic schedule had made it very hard for me to talk to him in the month, or two, before the retreat. I really thanked God for allowing Mack to stand in the gap those past few years whien I needed encouragement and prayer.

One of my dear friends, who is called by God to the ministry is Rev. Ayanna. We had a problem with playing phone tag. Trying to catch up with her was like getting my wisdom tooth pulled (and that was hard to do). When I did catch up with her, it was always a blessed experience. Toward the middle of January, January 12th to be exact, she invited me to go to church with her. We went to the church of one of her friends in the ministry. Service was very nice. Following service, we got to socialize with the other members and her friend because there were refreshments for everyone after service.

Toward the end of January 2003, I became ill again and developed a sore throat. On January 23, 2003 I went to Urgent Care. The doctors were a little worried because my tonsils appeared swollen. The right tonsil, which is the same side my VP shunt is located, was larger than the left. Thank God the x-rays came back clear for pneumonia. I also tested negative for strep throat. I was given anitibiotics to take twice a day for ten days. At my new follow-up appointment I met my new primary care physician. She suggested I see a doctor in the Ear, Nose and Throat Clinic (ENT) so I could be evaluated to have my tonsils removed. On a brighter note, I was able to see my dear friend Lisette. She visited Chicago in February and came to visit me February 12, 2003. She was doing her residency in another state so I didn't see her as much.

February 24, 2003, was my appointment for the ENT doctor. I almost wound up spending seven hours down at the University of Chicago but due to a compromise with Momma dropping me off and my dear sister picking me up, I only stayed down there for four hours. Thank you momma and my dear sister. The doctor initially said I did not need to have my tonsils removed but after reevaluating my medical history and symptoms, I had been exhibiting for the last few months leading up to the appointment—hoarseness, sore throat, infection—he decided to do the surgery. During the surgery, both tonsils would be removed. Since the right tonsil was larger than the left, the doctor also ordered a pathology report to make sure nothing else was wrong.

I spoke to Michelle B during that time. She had endured some complications with the health of her oldest son that had him in the hospital after he was born. Thankfully he had improved. We had breakfast to talk and give me a chance to see her son, William, on Thursday, February 27, 2003 at one of my favorite restaurants back then, Bob Evans. Michelle B and William looked great. William reminded me of Lavare. Both boys had dealt with some health issues but one look at their smiles, you couldn't tell they had endured anything. We had so much fun that day.

March 8, 2003 was the anticipated DePaul Gospel Choir Winter Dinner Musical. I was amazed at how the campus had changed. This was my first time on campus in over three years. I saw many new faces and some old faces. I sat with Mack and his wife. That gave us a chance to talk. Mack had been so busy, we hadn't been able to talk much during that time.

One of my favorite moments came when I saw a security guard name Karen. Karen was a very kind-hearted woman. When I was a student at DePaul, she always looked out for me. As the choir sung their first song, I was reminded of my days as a member of the choir. I enjoyed myself tremendously. Keep up the good work DePaul Gospel Choir!

On the day prior to the scheduled surgery, Sunday, March 23, 2003, I went to church with Daddy. We went to early morning service. Service encouraged me and uplifted my spirit. I spoke to my pastor and left with my daddy when service ended. Later that evening, I spoke to Michelle B as we still had details to fill in for William's christening reception. I was happy everything was falling into place. I knew it was God who allowed things to work out as they should have.

Monday, March 24, 2003 was the day of my tonsil surgery. The day of the surgery was somewhat challenging. My tonsils were found to be asymmetric. Momma and Mack stayed with me at the hospital. The doctors watched me for several hours before they decided to admit me for one-day observation. Mack left after the decision was made to admit me. He had spent the whole day with Momma and me. Daddy got over to the hospital just after Mack left.

14. Tonsillectomy – March 24, 2003

I got through the month of April. It had its share of ups and downs. Thank God for the strength he gives us. Toward the end of April, Sara and I decided to go to Chicago Ridge mall. This day was hilarious but nice. First, we went to the show and saw "Bringing Down the House." That movie was hilarious. A good laugh was just what I needed. After we left the show, we had lunch. During lunch, Sara developed a plan while we walked around the mall. I did not think she was going to really do it but she did. We finished lunch and stopped at the first jewelry store we saw. We walked around the store looking at the ring cases. Finally a sales associate said, "Can I help you?" Sara's response was, "This is my friend (pointing at me). I was not suppose to tell her but I had to tell her or what I'm about to do would not have worked. Her boyfriend wanted me to find an engagement ring that she looks good in and like. When I find it, I have to let him know." Oh my God! It was so funny. I felt like such a princess for the day. The sales associates were so nice to me as they gave me their best service and helped me find the perfect engagement ring so Sara could tell my "Boyfriend" what to buy. I was so sorry to every jeweler we did that to but by the end of the day, I was very happy. More importantly, I found out that Rogers and Holland have the best customer service. I also found out I look good in diamonds and the best style/cut for me is diamond cut. ☺

....

Thursday, May 1, 2003

Today was a wonderful day. The only thing I could think about was this evening. This evening I got a chance to see my buddy, Ed K. Ed and I had therapy at Rehabilitation Achievement Center (RAC). This evening I met his wife as she joined us for dinner. We had a great time. On the way to the restaurant, we talked a lot. Ed's wife is just as sweet and friendly as he is. We got along right from the start. I learned a lot about Ed. I didn't realize how much I missed him until this evening. Ed is doing pretty well. His right side is somewhat permanently affected by the stroke (which is how he ended up at RAC where we met). Otherwise, he is going through the same thing I went through with Social Security. I told him if the lawyer he was planning to speak to didn't work out, call me and I would give him my lawyer's telephone number. The food this evening was delicious but the people I had dinner with was even better. I hated to see the evening come to an end. Ed and Dorian want to get together in the future. I will definitely look forward to that. I spent the rest of the evening helping Nicole study.

Thank you Lord for your continued blessings thank you Lord for blessing me with wonderful people you have allowed to embrace my life at one time or another. Thank you for allowing me to be a friend and encourage so many people.

• •

Mother's Day 2003 was beautiful, as always. In my eyes, Mother's Day is everyday because a mother stays up late, wipes noses, blows noses, takes temperatures, gives baths, cooks food, helps with homework, listens to stories, reads stories, stays up late when needed, mends cuts, bruises and scratches every day, not just one day out of the year, which is supposedly meant to honor Momma. I love you Momma. Thank you for all our ups and downs. Thank you for teaching me how to be a woman and mother. I love you.

I tried to take it easy for the first half of May as we prepared for William's christening which was Sunday, May 18, 2003. I must thank his beautiful parents for allowing me to assist in the preparation process because it blessed me in ways I cannot put into words. Suday, May 18, 2003 started out very busy. I went to church with Michelle B and her husband that day. Service let out a little later that usual. As a result, we had to literally run to the banquet facility where the christening was being held. We changed clothes. I then had to step out and handle a slight guest problem. As I did, I ran into one of Michelle B's good friends. She helped me by going to calm Michelle's nervousness while I handled some behind the scene work. The evening turned out very nice. Wonderful, in fact.

I thanked God every year, every month, every week, every day, every hour, every minute, every second my parents are happily married. We may not always agree but they created me and gave birth to me. They did not give up on me when the world did. I thanked God because at the end of May, Momma celebrated another birthday and my parents celebrated another year of marriage. Thank you Lord.

Sunday, May 24, 2003 was DePaul University Gospel Choir Spring concert. Michelle B and I had already discussed riding together for the concert and staying for the choir reunion. Can you say, "Healing?" that is exactly what took place but I am getting ahead of myself. The choir reunion began with some ice breakers that allowed us to get caught up with one another's lives. Afterwards, we had some powerful praise and worship. Something started happening in that room. Now this is where I must stop because before this portion began, a rule was put in place, "what is said in this room, stay in this room." Thank you Lord because something great happened that night.

Memorial Day 2003 was very nice. I went to the show to see "Daddy Day Care." That movie was cute and family friendly. I really enjoyed hanging out with my little sister. By the time we got back to my parent's house, it was getting full. Among the people I saw, Uncle Howard came over with his girlfriend. Netta also came over with my cousin Neicy and the kids. We had a nice time.

During the later part of June 2003, Lisette came to Chicago to visit. This gave me a chance to see her little sisters and Collette, all of whom I hadn't seen in a while. As we hung out, we saw more of Lisette's friends. The following day, I got together with friends and went to Chicago Ridge Mall. We had fun as we went to the mall and the movies. Afterwards, we went back to my parent's house. Around this time, Kita, who I jokingly said was becoming an international traveler, left on another trip. She got back in just enough time for my vacation I took during the beginning of July.

Thursday, July 3rd - Sunday, July 6, 2003 ~ Atlanta, Georgia

Today I woke up to see the sun shining brightly. I got up as soon as my alarm clock went off and got ready. I think I finished getting ready quicker than usual. I listened to the radio while I sat on the end of the bed waiting. Daddy came up to wish me a good trip before he went to physical therapy. I took my things into the living room as it came close to time for us to leave. I went to see Momma before the limo got the house but she was getting ready for work. The limo came. Mike was usually my driver but not this time. I had another driver. He deemed to be in a hurry. I tried Momma one more time but she didn't answer her cell phone. The driver loaded my stuff. Just as I was getting into the limo, Momma called me from the front door. We hugged. I got into the limo and we were off to the airport.

I did curb-side check-in. An airport employee helped me get to the Delta gate. The Delta employees were very courteous. They tagged my scooter, without me having to ask. For my return flight, they switched my seat so I could be closer to the door. When I got to Atlanta, the stewardess helped me off the plane and found an airport employee to take me to the luggage area where Kita was waiting. Bwefore we went to her house, Kita and I visited 2 of her friends. Afterwards, Kita went to the store, as she had to keep up the tradition and give me one home cooked meal. ☺

Kita's house is immaculate. She designed it herself and had it built from the ground up. She gave me the grand tour as this was my first time in the house. We got settled and while she cooked, we got caught up on one another's lives.

The 4th of July was a lazy day for us. Kita cooked breakfast. We went to the show to see "Charlie's Angels 2." It was not as good as the first movie. Later that evening, we went to see the fireworks. It was not as big as the show you see in Chicago. Kita cooked another delicious dinner.

Saturday, we ate breakfast. We then spent the day with one of Kita's friends and her roommate.

My trip came to an end quickly. Sunday was my last day with my sister. We went to church. Service was nice. I med the Praise and Worship Team which Kita sings with. I also met one of the Associate Pastors of the church. After service, we had just enough time to run through McDonald's drive-thru before heading to the airport.

At the airport, Kita was given a special pass so she could wait at the gate with me until my flight boarded the plane. I slept most of the flight. When we landed, I got my luggage and an airport employee helped me to the platform where limos pick-up passengers. Mike, my limo driver was not there. I had to call and page him 3 or 4 times before he called me back. This was the first time that ever happened. He said they were having phone problems that day.

When I got home, I called Kita to let her know I made it home. Thank you Lord for allowing me to have such a wonderful vacation. The only bad part is I didn't get to see Lisette. She sent me a message *saying she wouldn't be able to see me because she was going home, due to death in her family.*

• •

July 2003 ended on a low note. DHS came over to evaluate me for a ramp because my scooter was too heavy to keep trying to lift. Unfortunately, I failed the interview (I didn't score enough). Towards the end of the month, my family experienced the loss of a loved one. My great-aunt Willie Mae, Grannie's sister, died. Everyone in the house went to funeral, except me. Momma felt that because of my health, at the time, I couldn't handle it. The funeral was held in Alabama.

Initially, Momma didn't want to leave me alone. I told her I was going to be all right. Momma asked Uncle Howard to look in on me. in addition, Daddy asked his friend, Lou, who lived up the street from their house, to watch out for me. My Uncle Howard called me every day while they were gone. He even picked up my medicine for me. Thanks Uncle Howard.

At New Faith, God allowed some very special people to become a part of my life. Among them was a family that always looked out for me (I won't say their name but you know who you are. ☺). As was the case when my parents were in town and couldn't bring me to church because of work and prison ministry, this family picked me up for Sunday service while my parents were out of town.

Around August, my friends Sara and Michelle B. started talking about my birthday. I was very happy to see Sara doing something else because that meant she was healing from the loss that she had recently experienced. Sara and I went to Chicago Ridge Mall to have lunch and just walk around. At lunch, she asked permission to do the wedding ring joke one more time. Initially, I was going to say, "no" but then I thought she needed a good laugh so I let her do it. it was just as hilarious as the first time.

During the later part of the summer, I went to Chicago Ridge Mall again because two of my friends were getting married and I was going to the wedding. Thank God I found the presents. The rest of the week, leading up to the wedding was nice and quiet. On Friday, August 22, 2003, Daddy and

I had dinner with Christine, Uncle Willie's granddaughter. We had a nice time. I'm not sure who talked more, Daddy or Christine, because they both talked a lot. At one point, I just sat back and listened. Christine and I got together before she left the following week.

Sunday, August 30, 2003

Thank God for allowing me to get through another glorious week. Thank you Lord for showing me the meaning of true friendship through the people you have placed in my life.

This evening was very nice as I had my birthday dinner with Ed and his wife, Dorian. Ed and I spoke about one week ago. During this time we talked about getting together again. When I told Ed about my birthday being on the 5th, he asked to take me out to dinner. They took me to a restaurant called The Paragon. I got another surprise as Ed's younger brother joined us. He looked like a younger version of Ed. He is just as nice as Ed. I always have fun when we get together. Every time we get together we plan to get together again. The meal I chose was inspired by the suggestions Ed and his brother gave me, since this was my first time in the restaurant. I had orange ruffie for dinner. It was delicious. I don't understand why God allow some of the people he allows to come into my life but I thank you for people like Ed and Dorian. I met him at RAC and he has always been wonderful to me. I also met another wonderful friend, Kylie, who brightens up my day each time we talk.

September 5, 2003 was finally here. I thanked God for allowing me to see another year. I was officially 26 years old. It amazed me how many people didn't know that. Many people called to say "Happy Birthday" throughout the day. Momma bought me flowers. Sha bought me a birthday cake. Mmmm good! Thanks Momma and Sha.

My conspirators, also known as my very good friends, decided to have my birthday party at Gino's East. I was running late because I took a nap earlier that afternoon and overslept. I got ready as quickly as possible so I wouldn't be too late for my party. When we got there, Vivian and Alvin, Christy and Ben, and Michelle and Terrell were already there. We were then joined by several other friends. I had so much fun. That year people really had a hard time remembering my age. It was so funny. As long as I have known some of the people there, it was funny how many people got my age wrong. I didn't make it any better because I never told I made 26 years old that year.

In November 2003, I began getting sick again. The question of whether or not I had Myasthenia Gravis was never answered. I had been taking medication for it, for several months because my eyes seemed to respond to the medication. The only problem (or should I say blessing) was doctors never got positive test results when they did the Tencilin test, which is one of the ways Myasthenia Gravis is diagnosed. I wasn't complaining by no means. I just wanted to know what happened to me.

On the morning I was admitted to the hospital in November 2003, I woke up with a very bad headache. My pain level was 13 on a scale of 1 to 10. When I went to the washroom to prepare for my day, I couldn't brush my teeth because I couldn't hold the toothbrush in my mouth. The toothbrush fell out each time I tried to put it in my mouth. I tried to spit but I couldn't spit. Oh my God! What's wrong with me? After several failed attempts I realized I had no feeling on the left side of my face. Although very weak, I went and found Momma to tell her. It was then I realized I could barely talk.

Momma said, "Why are you talking like that? What's wrong with your face?"

It was at this point I realized that the left side of my face had tightened up. When Momma realized I couldn't move the left side of my face, she paged Dr. Frim.

I had a scheduled appointment with Dr. Linz that day. Although the appointment was just so she could give me a new catheter prescription, when she saw me, she immediately knew something was wrong. She examined me as she noticed I had virtually no movement on my left side. She immediately paged Dr. Frim. When he called back, Dr. Frim told her to send me to the emergency room at the University of Chicago Hospitals immediately.

To say the least, I was admitted when I got over to the University of Chicago Hospitals. Doctors placed a NG tube for feeding because I had swallowing difficulties. They ordered a MRI non-infused scan of my brain on November 26th. They did the shunt series, which came back negative for a shunt malfunction. After waking up with problems breathing, doctors began IVIG treatments Thursday, November 27th-December 2nd. Momma spent the night with me because she wanted to make sure I had no problems with the IVIG treatments. For several days, I also had to wear a C-Cap to bed at night. Not comfortable. By Wednesday, December 3rd, I tolerated a clear liquid diet and the NG tube was removed. One of my last days there, a neurologist, who I had seen in the past for the same test, did the test again. She was also able to see a difference. Physical therapy was called to evaluate me and treat me while I was in the hospital. After several days of treatment, the physical therapist called the rehab doctor so I could be evaluated in order to see if I needed in-patient therapy again. By the end of the evaluation, the rehab doctor decided I needed in-patient therapy to work on walking, balance and strengthening. I decided to return to Weiss again. Neurology tried to do a spinal tap but was unable to do it because they could not place the needle correctly (because of the LP shunt, doctors have to be careful not to hit it). They did succeed in putting me through a lot of pain and making my back sore. Radiology did the spinal tap on Thursday, December 11th. That same afternoon I was transferred to Weiss for rehab.

Since Dr. Linz was no longer at Weiss, I had a different physician once I was transferred there. I had physical, occupational and speech therapy. Although my doctors would never tell me while I was in the hospital, all my records sent over to Weiss indicated I had a myasthenia gravis crisis. I was given a wheelchair and used it for the duration of my hospitalization. I had all new therapists as Christy and Vivian was now on the out-patient floor. When I had some free time, my nurse and therapists let me go down to the out-patient therapy department to see them. Of course, it was wonderful to see them again, I just wished it wasn't in the hospital that I saw them. Vivian and Christy had become so close to me, I prayed that out friendship would remain intact.

Because Christmas 2003 occurred while I was in the hospital, my doctor gave me a one day pass to go home and spend the day with my family. My cousin, Vernetta, and her son, came over and spent most of the day with me. Of course, it was great seeing my family. The kids were so happy to see me, as I was to see them. The little boy I sat with and tutored until his mother got off work, came over to see me. He was so happy to see me. I must admit, I felt funny being in a wheelchair in the house. It was hard getting through the hallway to the washroom. When I was carried in the house, it felt very scary because as I was being laid back and carried up the stairs, I kept feeling like I was falling (it would take a few years for me to find out what I was feeling was actually vertigo). Overall, it was a very nice Christmas, despite the fact I had to look forward to going back to the hospital. I thanked God I was able to come home, for even that short amount of time, and spend Christmas with my family. Momma cooked a great dinner, as always. Sha braided my hair. Thank you. After dinner was the hardest time. I told Daddy, "it's probably time for me to start heading back to the hospital, because it's getting late." Daddy said, "you have plenty of time." He then disappeared downstairs.

Momma and I didn't say anything. I stayed for a couple more hours until the hospital called the house looking for me. I had to tell him again. Once again, my daddy dragged his feet. It eventually took Momma getting him out of the house to take me back to the hospital. I love you Daddy! When I got back to the hospital, I was one of the last people to check back in. ☺ I had two weeks left. I continued working hard in all my therapies. I saw Christy and Vivian whenever possible. By the day of discharge, I was elevated to using the wheelchair only when I wasn't being supervised. When I was being supervised and my energy level was acceptable, I could use my quad cane. I was discharged on January 10, 2004. Upon discharge, I resumed therapy on an out-patient basis at CRS in Munster, Indiana, everyday, Monday thru Friday. As I improved, it was changed to three times a week.

"Just as Moses lifted up the snake in the desert,
so the Son of Man must be lifted up, that everyone
who believes in him may have eternal life.
For God so loved the world that he gave his one
and only Son, that whoever believes in him shall
not perish but have eternal life.
For God did not send his Son into the world to
condemn the world, but to save the world through him."
John 3:14-17 (NIV)

Chapter 14: My Life Is In God's Hands

I resumed going to therapy at CRS after my discharge. On January 24th, my nephew, Nick, had his birthday party. I was so happy to be home to enjoy celebrating his birthday with him. Things looked like they were moving in the right direction. I thanked God for being a healer. I thanked God each day I woke up for life, health and strength. Therapy was hard, some days harder than others, in the beginning. I continued taking the Mestinon. It seemed like it was helping, or maybe I was just praying that it helped. By the end of February, I started getting sick again. It was almost like the previous hospitalization. My biggest problem was now I was not just having problem with my left jaw but, I was having problems with my right jaw, as well. I was admitted on February 22, 2004. By then Momma wanted answers immediately. I had jaw weakness in my left and right jaws. Facial x-rays were done to compare the previous x-rays. I was re-evaluated by speech therapy. Thicken was added to my diet to make swallowing easier. I was released from the hospital February 25, 2004. Of course, just like the previous hospitalization, I resumed therapy at CRS.

Therapy went well. As I worked hard, I made some friends. Among them was a beautiful lady name, Kylie. I think we kept one another on our toes. In the beginning of March 2004, Michelle B., my dear friend from Maranatha and DePaul, came to visit. I hadn't seen them in a while. By that time, William was such a big boy. We enjoyed our day together.

My health looked like it was trying to improve as I went into March. Thank God. By the end of the month, however, I started coughing again like I did when I had throat infections. How could that be when my tonsils were removed? My breathing was clear so I knew my asthma wasn't flaring up. To make sure everything was fine, I made an appointment for Urgent Care on March 24, 2004. As it turned out, it was just a virus.

June 2004 was a time of celebration. My baby sister, Nikki, as well as my oldest nephew, Lavare, graduated from eighth grade. My babies were growing up. I was so proud of them. Nikki graduated from Kipling Elementary. Lavare graduated from Neil Elementary school. I was able to attend Nikki's graduation but, due to ticket limitation, I was not able to go to Lavare's graduation. I was very proud of him. He overcame so much. Thank you Lord for being a miracle worker and working miracles in my nephew's life

During 2004 my play brother Fred, who serves actively in the military, came home to visit. It was so nice seeing him. I spent the rest of my summer

As I came into November 2004, things started out very hectic. I had a doctor's appointment to further follow-up October's visit to the emergency room (woman's issue). Momma was unable to take me back and forth to my doctor's appointments. I went in search of a ride and found three.

Unfortunately, by the morning of November 1st, the day of my appointment, I was without a ride again. Thank God for reconciliation. I was able to call Netta and get a ride to the hospital. I got a ride back home from another friend who just happened to have an appointment the same day.

During this appointment, I also had my annual exam. Because of what occurred in October, my gynecologist decided to order an ultrasound. She also decided to have me try hormones at a low dose to try to regulate my cycles. I just wanted some answers. I was 27 years old. I should not have been going through the changes I went through.

The ultrasound of my uterus came back normal. I had to wait until my follow-up appointment to find out the full results and details. I took the hormones my gynecologist prescribed but felt no side effects except, the mood swings. Some of my friends tried to be very helpful and understanding.

My prayer was that the Lord would help me make the right decisions in my life. Please Lord help me to get my financial situation straightened out so I won't live from one check to the next. Please Lord direct me as I complete this book. Guide me Lord so that every word I write will be ordained by you. Guide me so that when others read my book, they will be encouraged and want to serve you more. If they don't know you, my prayer is they will come to know you for themselves. Thank you Lord for my family and true friends. Help me to determine who I should help and who I should allow to put the pieces of their puzzle together by themselves, regardless of whether or not they are family. Help me get out of my financial dilemma. Thank you, Lord, for all you are in my life. In Jesus name I pray, Amen.

....

Sunday, November 14, 2004

Thank you Lord for a wonderful day. Mom nor Daddy got up and went to early morning service. I had to miss out. That's alright because I needed the extra rest anyway for Mack's Retirement Celebration. This evening Mack's Retirement Appreciation was held at Western Springs, the church Karlos and Michelle Dodson was married at. The program was beautiful. At one point, there was probably not a dry eye in the building as different people got up and spoke about how Mack had a major impact on their life and blessed them greatly. Thank you Lord for people like Mack who you use to stand in the gap.

Now I just need to get out of this financial dilemma I am in presently. At which point, I will say "no" to anyone who approach me, unless they are someone I know I can trust. This includes family and supposed-to-be-friends (you know who you are). I place everything in God's hands—my bills, my finances, my health and my relationship or lack thereof. I just realized I lost my medicine.

....

The next morning I got up and made calling the church my first priority. Thank you Lord! The lady answering the phone said she had just called my parents house and left a message on the voicemail regarding finding my medicine. The next issue was finding someone to go get it for me. I didn't want to because I knew he probably was still tired and/or still had company but, I called Mack to ask if he could get it for me. He graciously agreed.

When Mack got to my house, one of his guests was with him. Mack decided he wanted something to eat and so we all went to McDonald's. Once there, his guest volunteered to pay for our meals. Thank you, Lord. We talked about many things. Mack got a chance to read his book of appreciation letters that was presented to him during the service. He said he had forgotten about the day I made reference to in my letter. I could never forget that day. Mack said I touched his heart by what I said in the letter. There are hardly any words to express my gratitude for all he did for me. Thank you, Lord for placing Mack in my life.

Once I got back home, I spoke to another person who has been a huge blessing in my life since I first met him, Rev. Randolph. I thanked God for having him in my life. He had been such a huge blessing in my life in such a short time. Thank you, Lord, for everyone you place in my life to bless me.

I went into December 2004 on a positive note. My friend Christy was preparing to enjoy motherhood for the first time. I was so excited for her. If her character was any indication of what type of mother she was going to be, I knew she would make a beautiful mother. She had been so wonderful to me since we first met at Weiss. I am happy to say on December 6, 2004 Christy, and her husband Ben, welcomed the newest member of their family into the world. They named her Anja Elizabeth. Congratulations, Christy!

December 22, 2004 was the date my gynecologist scheduled the D&C. My mother went to the hospital with me and stayed with me. My gynecologist came out to speak to my mother and I before the procedure. She told us it would be a minor procedure. After the surgery, my gynecologist spoke to my momma and myself in recovery. The surgery was successful. She did not see anything that would require any further attention. Hopefully, this would manage the woman's issues I was having so I would be comfortable again.

15. D & C with Hepetroscopy–December 22, 2004

"I may be able to speak the languages of human beings and even of angels, but if I have no love, my speech is no more than a noisy gong or a clanging bell.
I may have the gift of inspired preaching; I may have all knowledge and understand all secrets; I may have all the faith needed to move mountainsâ but if I have no love, I am nothing.
I may give away everything I have, and even give up my body to be burned â but if I have no love, this does me no good.
Love is patient and kind; it is not jealous or conceited or proud; love is not ill-mannered or selfish or irritable; love does not keep a record of wrongs;
Love is not happy with evil, but is happy with the truth.
Love never gives up; and its faith, hope, and patience never fail.
Love is eternal. There are inspired messages, but they are temporary; there are gifts of speaking in strange tongues, but they will cease; there is knowledge, but it will pass.
For our gifts of knowledge and of inspired messages are only partial; but when what is perfect comes, then what is partial will disappear.
When I was a child, my speech, feelings, and thinking were all those of a child; now that I am an adult, I have no more use for childish ways.
What we see now is like a dim image in a mirror; then we shall see face-to-face. What I know now is only partial; then it will be completeâ as complete as God's knowledge of me.

Meanwhile these three remain: faith, hope, and love; and the greatest of these is love."
I Corinthians Chapter 13 (GNT)

Chapter 15: A Year to Love

January 1, 2005

Happy New Year ! ! ! Service was beautiful. My favorite part of service was when I saw my Uncle Tony walk in the church. I was surprised and happy to see him. I was the first person who noticed him sitting in the last row. I told Momma and Sharonette. I then went and got him so Uncle Tony could sit with us. Service was nice. As it progressed, Uncle Tony became emotional and got up and left. We motioned to Daddy, who was in the pulpit, so he could go get him. Daddy was able to get him to come back in and stay for the remainder of the service. Daddy and Uncle Tony stood at the back of the church. He left just before service ended.

My favorite part of service was watching a couple renew their wedding vows. They really loved one another and it was evident as they spoke their vows to one another. My pastor then went a step further and offered to renew the vows of any married couple in the church at that very moment. Several couples went forward, including Momma and Daddy. Of course, Sha and I had to convince Momma (she is still so shy after all these years) to go when Daddy came to get her. Following service, we came home, ate and, went to sleep. This afternoon I called several friends to wish them a happy new year.

• •

Saturday, January 8, 2005

Blessed be the name of the Lord! He is the source of my strength and strength of my life. It is from God, all my blessings flow! Thank you Jesus!

Today was an awesome day. Sankofa had its Annual Winter Retreat at Grace Baptist Church. Thank you Lord for the word that went forth. The day began with breakfast and a getting to know you fellowship. We then went to Praise and Worship led by several DePaul Gospel Choir Alumni. We then received a word from Curtis. The theme this year was, "Can You Be Loved?" Curtis message came from II Corinthians Chapter 5 as he spoke about reconciliation. Curtis said for true love to be achieved, reconciliation must first take place. The Praise and Worship Team came back once more to prepare us for the keynote speaker. This time I helped Zaneta lead Praise and Worship. The keynote speaker was an awesome woman of God name Janice Tuck Lively. She was wonderful as she relayed her own personal experiences to emphasize the joy of the Lord is our strength. After giving her word from the Lord, she ended with a question and answer session.

We then had a break. During this time God revealed himself again as Mack embraced me and took me to meet Janice. It was during this time Janice said Mack told her about me (and my ministry). She said my life was a testimony and I had blessed her by what I said. She said my smile through my storm is a blessing to others. It even blessed her. I told her, "the joy of the Lord is my strength."

The afternoon session was awesome, as well. We had more Praise and Worship. We then broke into small groups for bible study which was great. Afterwards, we came together for one last time to reflect on the day. Curtis ended with Popcorn Intercessory Prayer. Powerful!! God is so wonderful. God gave me confirmation regarding some things in my life i.e. my health, my ministry and, my finances. Thank you Jesus!! We ended the day with Poetry to Praise.

....

The year was 2005. It was turning out to be a year to love. The month of January was laid back for the most part. I worked out when I was able to. My health was stable, for the most part. I dealt with the usual medical issues but nothing major. Thank you Lord. I was supposed to do some billing for a medical transportation company so I could earn a few extra dollars but, that didn't work out. That left me more time to work on my book. As I did, I prayed the book would bless and encourage those who read it. I also prayed the negative aspects of the book would not offend anyone because I did not mention them to offend anyone but to show how the Lord brought me through the different aspects of my life.

While walking to the store one day, I met a guy, unofficially. At the time I thought he worked on the property he was standing in front of. We spoke to one another and I kept going about my business. A few days later, I ran into the same guy again. This time, I learned he lived on the block. He lived in the house of a long time resident on the block. His family lived in the house next door to that house, which belonged to another long time resident on the block, before she passed away. He decided to give me his telephone number and asked me to call him.

Collette was the first person to call me and tell me she was getting married in 2005. She was so excited! I was happy for her. I told her to make sure she sent my invitation in enough time so I could find a reasonable airplane ticket. Collette gave me her information over the phone so I could work on my airplane tickets. Collette and her mother let me stay with them so that helped me out financially. She wanted me to wear the same color as the bridal party. Thank God it was purple. I had the perfect dress that I had only worn once before the wedding.

Approximately one week before I left, on March 2, 2005, Whitney came to Chicago to visit. It was good to see her again. It had been almost 8 years, if not more, since I had saw her. Whitney's baby was beautiful. Of course, she was still crazy as ever. I don't think that will ever change. God bless my crazy God-sister.

When I spoke to Collette, regarding the wedding, we had decided that I would come down a week before the wedding so we could have a few days before the wedding to hang out. When I arrived, we did just as planned. We went to Sea World. This was my first visit and I had so much fun. Of course, we took plenty of pictures. She looked so happy. I only prayed for the best for her. When Lisette and Shaunda arrived, her bridal party (in addition to her sister), it seemed like time flew by. Her wedding was March 12, 2005. Collette was a beautiful blushing bride. In the end, the ceremony was beautiful. As always, it was nice seeing Lisette and spending time with her. I didn't see her as much anymore, since she no longer lived in Chicago. Therefore every chance I got to see my sister was special to me.

When I got back to Chicago I had a little over two weeks until the next special wedding in my life. My Uncle Howard decided to marry his sweetheart, Valerie. Their wedding was April 2, 2005. His wedding festivities were somewhat smaller, as he got married at City Hall. My Daddy was his best man. Uncle Howard and Valerie had a wedding reception at their house, later that evening. My Daddy and I went to the reception together. I got to meet Uncle Howard and Valerie's family members, for the first time. It was a very festive event. Congratulations Uncle Howard and Aunt Valerie!

By July 2005, I had begun worrying about my relationship with my boyfriend. Something didn't seem right. He wasn't opening and closing doors for me like he did when we first started dating. He wasn't as attentive as he was in the beginning. My boyfriend, if that's what I could call him, stopped calling when he was running late or needed to cancel a date. He didn't leave messages on my voicemail as frequently as he did when we first started dating. Something didn't seem right. My mom, as well as, all the important women figures in my life, always taught me to listen to that inner voice, that instinct that tells you something is wrong. I wish I had. That inner voice kept telling me something wasn't right. Even when My boyfriend was with me. I started having funny feelings, like something wasn't right. I decided to ignore this feeling, after all, we had been together for a little over 6 months.

On Wednesday, July 27, 2005, the Lord blessed me to wake up and see another glorious day he created. I had planned to watch Trell and then go over to Family of Hope that evening.

After Elaine, Trell's mom, came to pick him up, my boyfriend and I were supposed to have dinner together. It was nice. My mother and I were in the kitchen cooking dinner for our men; Momma was cooking for Daddy and I was cooking for My boyfriend. I called him three times about dinner but he still did not show up. I went over to his house. Nephew one said he was in the back yard. I walked into the back yard and found my boyfriend talking to a lady, who was sitting in her car. I know he saw me but he didn't say anything so I called his name. He half-heartedly said "One moment." The woman in the car asked if he was going to introduce us to one another. Once again, he half-heartedly did that. This disturbed me and showed on my face. My boyfriend finished his conversation with her. He then promised to meet me on his front porch, after he put his truck in the backyard.

Instead, after I went to sit down on the front porch, he hopped in his little black truck and went to the gas station—so he said. The same woman he was talking to, when I walked into the backyard drove back around looking for him. I told her he was gone and she left, but she came back around again, a few moments later. Thank God she did. She finally introduced herself to me. "My name is—. I am his' girlfriend. We've been together for 1 ½ years." I was a little stunned as I replied, "Nice to meet you. My name is Shereice and I'm his girlfriend. We have been together a little over 6 months." The lady continued. "I mean no harm. I am a grown woman and don't have time for the foolishness. May I speak to you please?" I replied, "I am a grown woman too so I do not have time for any foolishness." At this point, I got up from where I was sitting on the porch to stand near the curb, where her car was. Lord Jesus. He had been lying and cheating on both of us with each other. We figured out his phone scheme. We even figured out he divided his time between us.

We then decided to catch him in the act. She had told him she was going to the club with her girlfriends so she turned her car radio up loud so it could sound like she was in the club with her friends. I listened to the conversation. "Hey baby." "Hey baby." "Me and my girls are having so much fun at the club so I know I won't see you tonight." "Ok baby, just call me when you get in."

Now it was my turn. I called him sounding a little upset. "Hey baby." "Hey baby." "Where are you? You had me cook dinner, my Momma even gave me some of her vegetables to make sure I had enough, and you are not even here to eat it!" "I'm sorry baby. I'm at the gas station. I'll be home in a minute." "You better. Your food is already starting to get cold." "Just warm it back up for me baby." He promised to be home in 10 minutes. We then got in her car and drove to the end of the block so he wouldn't spot us and run.

We saw him drive up and park his truck, in front of the house. We jumped out of the car, I walking in the street, the other woman walking on the sidewalk. He was speechless. He tried hard to lie his way out of it but it didn't work. We had already put two and two together and figured everything out. He then tried to lie and say he and I were never dating. At that point, I almost slapped him with my keys in my hand. Thank you, God, for restraint. I then stated some facts that proved we were dating. I went a step further and went into my cell phone voicemail and played some of his messages where he called and said, "I just called to say I was thinking about you. I love you." "I just called to say I am running late baby. I will be there in a few minutes." The other lady snapped on him. I snapped on him. I had to later pray for forgiveness because I got so angry I said some things I pray will never come out of my mouth again. After everything was said and done, the other lady and I told him, "Bye." I went home. The other lady got in her car and left. I knew he was embarrassed because his family as well as, several people who lived on the block were standing outside watching everything.

I was furious. When I went in the house, I went straight to my room and closed the door. I tried so hard to sit down but I had become so furious, I couldn't sit down so I paced my floor, back and forth. I was clinching my teeth. I needed air. Who could I call this late at night? I called Ayanna. She said she was on her way. I then called Elaine. She told me to come over. As I was leaving to go over to Elaine's, my sister Sha walked up. She said, "What's wrong with you?" I told her what happened. My sister being crazy as she is ☺ said, "Man! Why couldn't I have drove up sooner? I would've loved to have seen that." There was a reason why God didn't allow my sister to drive up any sooner. Her name is Sha. We may not always get along but when it come to having her sister's back, for the most part, Sha is there. I then went to Elaine's house so I could talk to her while I waited on Ayanna.

Elaine got me calmed down a little. Ayanna was wonderful as always. We drove around, talking about what happened. We then went by the church to relax and talk some more. Thank God for Ayanna. She is a great listener. She had a feeling something like this was going to happen. We ate ice cream, talked, laughed and prayed. This was a surprisingly long day. I prayed the days to follow would be better.

The following day, Thursday, July 28, 2005, I woke up saying, "The joy of the Lord is my strength." I began to have a little peace about the previous night. Sha and I talked, in more detail about what happened. She was not surprised by what happened but felt bad that it happened to me. She still said she wished she could have got home sooner so she could have seen it for herself.

As usual, I babysat Trell, while Elaine was at work. He was no problem. When she picked him up that evening, we talked some more about what happened. It was at that point I realized he still had my parking PLACARD. Elaine made me promise to get it from him and immediately leave. I promised. When I got to the door, his niece answered the door. He was not home but she promised to get the placard from him and give it to me.

At 11:00 that night my doorbell rang once like My ex-boyfriend used to do, when we were dating and he wanted me to come outside with him at night. I went to the door and My ex-boyfriend was standing there with my CD's and placard. I took them from him. My ex-boyfriend tried to apologize for what happened the previous night. Before he left, he tried to soften me up by saying, "Call me if you need anything." WHATEVER. My God shall supply all my needs according to his riches in glory. Thank you, Jesus!

Despite the break-up, he remained on my mind. I had taken the lock and chain off my heart in this relationship because I thought I was dealing with a real man. I had to continually pray to my heavenly Father for comfort and direction. I also learned a very valuable lesson: you cannot tell all of your friends your business.

About a week, or so, after hand I broke up I learned another valuable lesson. Immediately after we broke up, I went on a hiatus from his family. This was partly due to the other woman saying his family knew about her all along. The family said the night of the confrontation with him was the first time they saw her. I didn't know who to believe. I went to finally visit his family like I did when he and I dated. His mother thought I was upset with her, as well. Oh my God! I felt so bad. I had to explain to her that I needed some time to be alone and get things in order for myself. I knew she had nothing to do with him cheating on me. I wasn't blaming anything on her. The relationship I had with her was separate from my relationship with Him.

I began to throw myself into the work I did at the church Ayanna was pastor at, Family of Hope Christian Church. That way I did not have to think about him as much. I prayed God would get me through this chapter in my life. Watching Trell also provided me with ways to occupy my time and mind.

• •

Sunday, August 21, 2005

Praise the LORD.
Praise God in his sanctuary; praise him in his mighty heavens.
Praise him for his acts of power;
praise him for his surpassing greatness.
Praise him with the sounding of the trumpet,
praise him with the harp and lyre,
Praise him with timbrel and dancing,
praise him with the strings and pipe,
Praise him with the clash of cymbals,
praise him with resounding cymbals.
Let everything that has breath praise the LORD.
Praise the LORD. Psalm 150 (NIV)

Today was so wonderful!! Thank you Jesus! There is not enough words in the English language to express my joy. Service was beautiful. Today was the reunion service for the former members of Orchard Street Christian Church. Ayanna, or should I say, Pastor Ayanna, envisioned a special service so they could know that although Family of

Hope Christian Church now occupies the building. Orchard Street Christian Church members are always welcomed. Tears of joy rang through the building and throughout the service. I learned some important history regarding Blue Island, the church building and its members.

Ayanna got a nice surprise today. Armon, who was on vacation, showed up in town to give her a surprise visit. Everyone knew, except Ayanna of course, so it was especially great watching the surprise and joy in Ayanna's face. ☺

• •

As I came to the end of August 2005, I began thinking about my birthday. Earlier on, Ayanna and I discovered that our birthdays is 2 days apart. I also learned that Ayanna hardly celebrated her birthday. I convinced Ayanna to celebrate our birthdays together. We decided to go to the Grand Luxe Café. Unfortunately, none of the people I invited showed up. The evening was nice and fun except the heel of my shoe got stuck in a man hole and broke.

The following week, My ex-boyfriend dropped by my house. He wanted to talk. Lord please give me the strength. Since there was no place to talk in private, he asked me to go to the store with him. We didn't make it to the store. Instead, he drove several blocks over and parked. He gave me the option of starting the conversation. I began by stating the obvious: what he did when he cheated on me was wrong and I wasn't going to put up with it. He agreed and apologized. I still had some feelings for him but I was not going to be treated without respect. A relationship is based on love and trust. If we didn't have these, then what kind of relationship did we have? I then went back to when we first started dating. We promised to always be honest with one another. This included if the feelings we had for one another changed, we would let the other know. He said he never meant to hurt me. He still loved me and wanted to work things out. I told him certain things had to change IF we got back together:

1. Communication must increase.
2. He must never cheat on me again.
3. He must be honest about his feelings about me.
4. If he's running late, he better call.
5. If he want to break up, he better tell me.
6. The other woman better not call me again and give any indication he was cheating again.

By October, things looked like they were improving between my boyfriend and me. We were spending more time together. He was still bad at calling to let me know when he would be late. I got two calls from the other lady saying He was with her again, but she did not behave like she did previously (let me hear him talking to her in the background). I stopped accepting her calls and started trusting my own instincts again. I just thanked God because I knew in my heart that if He messed up again, that would be the end, FOR GOOD.

Therefore, as God's chosen people, holy and dearly loved, clothe yourselves with compassion, kindness, humility, gentleness and patience. Bear with each other and forgive one another if any of you has a grievance against someone. Forgive as the Lord forgave you. And over all these virtues put on love, which binds them all together in perfect unity.

Let the peace of Christ rule in your hearts, since as members of one body you were called to peace. And be thankful. Let the message of Christ dwell among you richly as you teach and admonish one another with all wisdom through psalms, hymns, and songs from the Spirit, singing to God with gratitude in your hearts. And whatever you do, whether in word or deed, do it all in the name of the Lord Jesus, giving thanks to God the Father through him.

Colossians 3:12-17(NIV)

Chapter 16: "Say What?"

Thursday, October 6, 2005, I woke up with a very bad headache. My pain level was 8.5 on a scale of 1 to 10. My head was really hurting badly. I took two Fioricet tablets (the pain medicine I took for my headaches) and went back to bed. At 9:00am, I got up. Because the pain continued, I took two additional Fioricet tablets and rested. For the remainder of the day, I took two Fioricet tablets every 4-6 hours for headache pain (when I was awake).

Monday, October 10, 2005, I woke up at 4:00am with headache pain so severe my head was pounding, my ears were ringing and I had become severely sensitive to light and sound. I took two Fioricet tablets. At 8:00am, feeling no change, I took two additional Fioricet tablets. At 9:00am, I got up to do my morning catherization but was unable to stand because in addition to the pain, I was lightheaded and dizzy. I tried to walk, using my quad cane for assistance but fell, breaking my quad cane in the process. Something was not right. Having trouble with transportation, I did not find a ride to the hospital until noon. In times like these, I wish I had a video camera so I could tape and show the world how my family is truly. NO I wouldn't because that is not my style but it did hurt that my family didn't take me a little more serious about how bad I felt. Sha, Momma and Daddy refused to take me to the hospital because they refused to take any time off work. My boyfriend got on my last nerve, as well, as he claimed he was too busy to take me to the hospital. When I finally got to the emergency room, I was immediately taken back as doctors and nurses suspected I was having possible trouble with my shunt. My stats were taken. The usual shunt work-up (x-rays, CT scan) was ordered, blood was drawn, and a urine sample was obtained.

Moments later, the nurse attending to my care returned with one of the emergency room doctors to tell me my urine culture resulted in a positive pregnancy test. I explained how I was on birth control pills (for my irregular menstrual cycles) as well as used a condom the few times I engaged in sexual intercourse. They told me the test was repeated for accuracy and came back positive each time. At this point, I was asked if I planned to keep the baby. I explained that I did not believe in abortion but I was not sure what I was going to do. I then enacted my rights under HIPAA and told everyone not to reveal the details of my pregnancy to my family. It was noted in my chart. The doctors gave me some time alone while I waited to be taken to radiology.

As I lay there waiting, many thoughts flooded my mind. Maybe that was why my patience was very thin lately. Maybe that's why I exploded like I did when I discovered He cheated on me because by my calculations, which the doctors would later confirm, I got pregnant on a very special night, prior to the night he was caught cheating. What would my family say (here I go again worrying about my family instead of myself)? Is my baby going to be healthy, given the medication I was taking, prior to discovering I was pregnant? How would he respond? Is my baby going to be alright? Where would we live? I did not want to raise my child under my parent's roof. I wanted a place of my own to raise my baby. What would my friends say? Is my baby going to be alright? Oh my God ! ! ! I'm going to be a mother. Years ago, doctors said that children would not be in my future. Thank you Jesus! Once again you have allowed your miracle working power to overpower me and this time, instill a beautiful new life in me.

My thoughts were interrupted by the arrival of transportation to take me to radiology. The radiology techs refused to do the CT scan because of my pregnancy and sent me back to the emergency room. Back in the emergency room, a Heplock was placed and I was given medications, for pain, through it. During this time, my sister Netta arrived. My mom had sent her to check on me because my Momma was still at work. Of all the people she could have sent, why did she send Netta, knowing that we didn't always get along very well? Unfortunately, she arrived while a doctor was in the room checking on me. We were talking. His back was to the entrance, although I was facing it. I put my finger to my lips, indicating not to say anything else about my pregnancy. Unfortunately, he continued to talk and Netta concluded what we were talking about.

When the doctor left, Netta wasted no time putting her nose where it didn't belong. She said negative things about him, as if the men she dated in the past were so wonderful. She continued talking. I think what irritated me the most was when she told me to get an abortion because I was not ready to be a mother. Excuse me, who did she think she was trying to offer someone advise as if the decisions she's made in her life were so smart. At that point, I tried to be as nice as I could, given the circumstances, and told Netta to go home. Who did she think she was? I was in pain and I had enough thoughts running through my mind, without having to deal with her. Thanks Momma.

Due to crowding, I was not taken up to the floor until two days later, October 12, 2005. That evening, the always painful spinal tap was done by one of the neurosurgery residents. Knowing my preferences, the neurosurgery resident made sure I knew Dr. Frim was consulted by phone because he was out of town. The spinal tap showed my shunt pressure to be 12, which was good and at its original settings. Neurology was consulted regarding options for getting rid of, or dealing with, my headaches. OB/GYN was also consulted with regard to my pregnancy and the medication I was taking. An ultrasound was done which revealed I was nearing the end of my first trimester. It also revealed that I was having a girl. My due date given was April 15, 2006.

I didn't know how or what I was going to tell anyone about my pregnancy. After all, I had some wonderful people in my life but some of them were very judgmental. Ayanna came to visit me first that evening. I decided to use the element of surprise to tell her. She was getting ready to leave. She was just about to open my room door when I said, "Oh Ayanna, by the way, I'm pregnant." She was hilarious! Ayanna turned around, came back to the chair she was sitting in and sat back down. She then looked at me. She repeated this three times. I was cracking up. Ayanna ended up staying an additional hour. Ayanna was very supportive about my feelings and concerns. We also concluded by saying, I would tell people when I was ready.

Sha surprised me. I told her about my pregnancy when she called to check on me, later that day. I was surprised at her response. She was very supportive. Sha even agreed to keep it to herself and support my decision to wait to tell our parents. I only needed one headache at a time.

My boyfriend came to see me the following day. I told him about my pregnancy. I could tell by his facial expressions that he had a lot of things on his mind. He became very nervous. He knew my baby was his. He was concerned about our financial situations. We both had been struggling with our finances. I told him, with us taking all the necessary precautions, except abstinence, God was watching over us. God had watched over me all my life. Look at all the miracles God performed. He asked me if I planned to keep the baby. I must say, adoption did cross my mind, in the beginning because I was concerned about financially caring for her. I then reminded myself about the miracle of the situation. I was pregnant, for three months at the time I found out I was pregnant. Preliminary tests revealed my baby was healthy in spite of the medication I had been taking. She showed no signs of any of the health conditions I had experienced, past or present. This was a definite miracle from God.

Just about all of the doctors whom I saw regularly came to see me. They all congratulated me about my pregnancy. Above all, my doctors promised to respect my privacy and decision to wait to tell my parents about my pregnancy. They agreed not to say anything to my parents about it. Some of my nurses, who cared for me during the past hospitalizations, congratulated me as well. I was surrounded by positive people and this helped me so much. By the time I was discharged from the hospital, I had decided to keep my baby and not give her up for adoption.

At that point, the doctors I saw regularly, Ayanna and Sha all promised to respect my privacy and not reveal my pregnancy to anyone, without my permission. Thank you for honoring your word and respecting my privacy.

After several days of pain management and observation, I was discharged home on October 17, 2005. Due to balance problems (that I was told would worsen as I got further along in my pregnancy), I was given a walker, to be delivered to my home later that afternoon. Some of the medication I was taking had to be altered or discontinued due to my pregnancy. I was referred to a high risk obstetrician that I was scheduled to see two days later, October 19, 2005.

At home, I spoke to my friend Deirdre. (I had told her, as well, about my pregnancy while I was in the hospital) She had a son who was only a few months old, at the time. We laughed as our thoughts took us back to the first Sunday of October 2005. We had concluded church service and were sitting in the office talking. I was holding Deirdre's son, which I did a lot. Out of the blue, he went to my breasts like I was breastfeeding him (at the time, Deirdre was still breastfeeding). At the time it happened, we thought nothing of it. Deirdre and I laughed as we reminisced about that afternoon. Maybe that was God's way of telling me I was pregnant. We also discovered the high risk obstetrician I was referred to, was the same doctor who delivered Deirdre's son.

At home, it was very hard keeping my pregnancy from my parents, especially Momma. She always had questions. Why did my headaches increase? Did I need a shunt revision? When was it being scheduled? Why was so many of my medicines being changed? . . . Just to name a few.

My first prenatal appointment was scheduled for Wednesday, October 19, 2005. Because I still had not told my parents about the pregnancy, I got him to take me to the appointment. In spite of me not being aware of my pregnancy, my weight and vitals were good. My baby's heartbeat also sounded good. The doctor moved my due date up to April 10, 2006. The doctor told me what to expect. I had to look forward to OB appointments every month (here we go again), sometimes more frequently as needed. Due to my need to self-catheter for my bladder situation, the OB would not be able to check my urine for Urinary Tract Infections because they would render false/positive results every time. Therefore, I had to tell her if I suspected a UTI. I had to move my appointment with my neurologist closer to make sure my anti-seizure medication didn't need to be altered. She also needed a straight answer to the dilemma of the previous three years, did I have Myasthenia Gravis?

The other issue my OB raised was my balance and walking. During that last hospitalization, physical therapy worked with me on a regular basis. We did some strengthening exercises, practiced walking and keeping my balance. We also reviewed safe ways for falling so I wouldn't hurt myself or my baby. I was given a prescription so I could continue physical therapy on an out-patient basis. I was warned because of my diagnosis at birth, my pregnancy would have an impact on my balance. My balance (and walking) would worsen as I got further along in my pregnancy and got bigger.

Following my neurology appointment on October 23rd, Sha and I talked again. She felt it was time for me to tell my parents about my pregnancy. She told me to go ahead and tell them. Approximately two days later, I got the opportunity to tell Momma. She did not fly off the handle like I thought she would. I still had to tell her husband, my father. I took a different approach with him. Later on that same day, my father was standing in the kitchen fixing himself something to eat. My parent's kitchen has two doorways. I made up my mind I would walk in one entrance, tell him while I was walking through the kitchen, and walk out the other door. I had my chance. In one breath I told him I was pregnant and walked out of the kitchen, just like I planned. He didn't blow up at me. All he said was, "Thanks for being honest with me."

Sha was in her room. She was surprised my parents didn't fly off the handle like they did with her. I later learned, my parents responded the same way with Netta. So why did they respond to me like they did. Maybe they just wanted to be more understanding. Maybe they realized the responses they gave Netta and Sha didn't improve their relationships. Maybe unlike Sha and Netta, they realized I would respond to them. Maybe they really just didn't care. Oh well . . .

My Precious Gift
(An original poem by Shereice Garrett)
November 19, 2005

I often dreamed of motherhood
I often dreamed of the love I would share.
I would wash and keep you clean.
I dreamed of the joy you would bring.

But why dream of something I know is not true?
Man came and took that away in just one swoop.
"Your health is bad.
Because of this, a child you cannot have."
A story I began to hold true.

I gave up on the dream.
I forgot about my heavenly Father.
Who holds the world in the palm of His hand.
If he did it for Rachel, why can't he do the same for me?

So one month ago,
You showed me again,
You hold the world in the palm of your hand.
As I thought I was going for one thing,
But out of this a precious gift you would bring.

A little girl you gave me.
Ten fingers, ten toes,
You cannot tell me God do not know.

Now I say, "thank you."
For the joy she brings.
Each time she moves,
I know whose word is true.

So I know when she is born,
Joy to THIS WORLD she will bring.
For she has already brought joy to me,
THE PROUD MOTHER TO BE.

My pregnancy was hard. Some of the reactions I was getting from some family members and friends made me want to throw my hands up and scream to the top of my lungs. I did not do that. Don't get me wrong. There were some very good, positive reactions. But those that weren't made me want to throw my hands up and scream. I had to remember that I was carrying my precious gift from God and I needed to protect her at all costs. I cried. I prayed. I cried some more. I continued reading God's Word for direction. Thank you, Lord.

I did have some very encouraging reactions. Lisette was very excited and happy for me. As usual, she always had a word of encouragement. Kita was wonderful and supportive. Ayanna kept me grounded spiritually. She was a wonderful friend who helped me concentrate on the joy of the situation rather than the responses the world was giving me. Deirdre remained crazy as always. My favorite comment that she would always give me was, "why are you worried about what people are saying? Their words are not going to change anything are they? [of course not] So why are you worrying?" Candyce loves babies so she was excited too. She always questioned me to make sure I was taking care of myself. Thanks, Candyce. Armon and Lewis, thank you for being real men of God. Thank you, my extended family at Family of Hope. I couldn't have done it without you.

And to my family . . . Thank you, Sha. You are a beautiful person when you allow people to see your true heart. Lisette . . . . What can I say without crying because you are a God-send. Kita, God knows the plan HE has for our lives. Man cannot stop what God said will be. You are one in a million. Thank you for all of your support. Daddy thank you for all of the bake potatoes and chicken nuggets from Wendy's. Thank you for the tuna subs from Subway. Thank you, Daddy, for fulfilling my cravings. Netta thank you for driving me crazy. I love you. Momma, thank you for doing what you do best, getting mad and worrying. I love you. Thank you Grannie. Thank you Uncle Willie. You are in a class by yourself. You will truly be missed. To everyone who was not individually named, thank you from the bottom of my heart. To my DePaul family, what can I say, I love you.

I cannot forget those of you who tried to test my faith and patience. Thank you for calling me a sinner. Thank you for telling me I was no longer a child of God because I was pregnant. By doing this, you helped me gain more strength to endure. Thank you because I am better person as I learned to turn the other cheek even more. I truly pray a special blessing on your lives.

• •

Sunday, December 18, 2005

Only 13 days left in this year. Thank you Lord for allowing me to make it this far. Thank you for life, health and strength. Thank you Lord for blessing me with food and shelter. Thank you Lord for blessing me with my beautiful daughter that has brought so much joy, on the inside and she hasn't even made her appearance on this earth yet. Thank you Lord for those people you have placed in my life to be a blessing to me.

Thank you Lord for clarity. Thank you Lord for wisdom and guidance. I believe it take all those things, and of course having the Lord on your side, when you are making life affirming decisions. Today was a good day. Just by speaking my mind I was better able to see things for what they really are/were. In doing so, I came to the decision I believe will be healthier for me in the long run. I decided that I need to leave some "things" behind when move to start my new life with my child. Among these things, I will be leaving some people behind. There is a time and a season for everything. When that season ends, one usually put, or throw away, things that are no longer usefull to them. The same can be said for people. Through observations, talking over with my dear friend Ayanna and of course, praying, I have began to see who some of these people are. I just pray that God will continue to give me wisdom and revelation if there is anyone else I need to leave behind.

• •

Happy Birthday King Jesus ! ! ! Christmas 2005 was fun. I was five months pregnant by then. I began my day at home, with my parents. I then went to Deirdre and Lewis house for their Christmas party. I really enjoyed myself that evening.

Unfortunately, December 26th, which is also Lavare's birthday, I began feeling sick. I spent 3 days on complete bed rest due to increased headaches and stomach pain. On December 28th, I woke up with increased shunt pressure and stomach pain. I called my OB's nurse and she switched me to her resident. The resident conferred with my OB who immediately sent me to L&D (Labor and Delivery) so I could be checked out.

My vitals were taken and I was checked to make sure I wasn't in early labor. Labs were also taken. I wasn't in labor however; my labs showed I had a very bad kidney infection. Doctors went back and forth regarding whether I should be admitted or sent home on antibiotics. At 1:30am on December 29th, I began to feel worse. I became extremely cold and shivered. My nurse wrapped me in two heated blankets but I still shivered. My nurse spoke once more to the doctors about admitting me.

When I was finally admitted and taken up to my room, my temperature was rising higher. An IV was started and antibiotics were given. The next day, I was transferred to the Perionatal Unit so I could be monitored more closely. During this time, my baby's heart rate increased and I could tell the difference. Ultrasounds were done at regular intervals to watch my baby.

On January 1, 2006, I was transferred back to the Prenatal Unit after my fever broke. Antibiotics were continued intravenously. On January 2, 2006, doctors were satisfied that my fever had broken and my temperature stayed down. Blood work showed my white blood count had come down. Satisfied that my temperature stayed down and my lab work improved, doctors released me from the hospital on January 2, 2006.

Toward the end of the month, January 24th, I saw my OB. All went well except my blood pressure was higher than usual. I wondered if it had something to do with the antibiotic I was taking. She had me come back to have my blood pressure checked the following week.

Bible class that week blessed my spirit. When I got home, I started thinking about Tammy and James quite a bit but I couldn't figure out why. Maybe it was because I hadn't talked to or seen them in a while. The weirdest thing happened when I went to sleep that night. I dreamed I saw them at my upcoming appointment with Dr. Frim. I put my thoughts aside thinking it was just because I met them during one of my appointments to see him.

The day of my appointment with my neurosurgeon, January 26, 2006 I got up and got ready. When I got to the clinic, I registered and sat down in the waiting area. As usual, Dr. Frim, my wonderful neurosurgeon was running behind schedule. Surprise. Surprise. As I looked up, I saw a boy and a lady that looked just like Tammy and James, except the boy was much taller. That had to be James. I then saw Tammy and knew that was him. When I called them the first time, neither of them heard me. James heard me the second time and got Tammy's attention. Tammy was just as excited as she was the day we met. James gave me a big hug and so did Tammy. They sat down and we started talking. Tammy kept asking about Momma so I called her. It was at that point I was a little embarrassed because although I mentioned my appointment to Momma, more than once, she still forgot and couldn't figure out how I ran into them. Tammy and Momma talked for a few minutes.

When she got off the phone, Tammy and I talked some more. James talked in-between his studying. Since Dr. Frim was still behind schedule, we had lunch in the cafeteria. When we got back, Dr. Frim saw James first. Before they left, they came to see me. Tammy said she would try and make my baby shower. I prayed she made it.

My appointment went very well. All my shunts seems to be functioning properly. He agreed with my refusal to have an epidural (an epidural is inserted in your back and my LP shunt is in my spine. I refused to risk it being poked). Unfortunately, at that point, he said he wouldn't be in town on my anticipated due date (Passover started that Thursday before). If I had any problems after he got back, he would have me come in for a spinal tap or something. All I have to say is I do not want to have to be away from my baby any longer than necessary.

Friday, February 3, 2006

Thank you Lord! You always amaze me. My baby is getting so big. She is growing and is healthy. I never thought I could experience this much happiness in my life. I am having a baby! I'm going to be a mother. What a miracle! Time is flying by. April will be here before you know it.

This week I thought about Godparents for Christina—yes I have been calling her by her name. I made sure no one knew what I was doing because I really didn't want to hear what anyone had to say about it. This is my decision. I took out a piece of paper. On one side of the paper, I wrote down characteristics I was looking for in Godparents. On the other side, I wrote down potential Godparents. I then prayed to God for direction. I began eliminating people from the list, according to characteristics the person or couple lacked. By the end only two names remained, Kita and Lise. I then thought about how tradition molded Godparents to be a married couple. However, all of my dreams had me seated at a table with Christina, Lisette and Kita. In the dreams, Christina always said she have 3 mommies. So I prayed and asked God for confirmation. I called Lisette and Kita. Neither one of them answered their phone. I left them both the same message: "I have something important to talk to you about. It is nothing bad, I assure you. I cannot tell you what it is in this message. Please call me back as soon as you can so we can talk. Love you."

I must have done something right. Lisette called me back first. I told her what I was calling about. All I can say, is I made the right choice. When Kita called me, I did the same thing. It's funny; they both gave almost identical reactions to my request. They both cried and they both were extremely honored. By the time I finished talking to Kita, I knew I had made the right choice.

February 11, 2006 turned out to be a very good day. Sara knew she wasn't going to make it to my baby shower that was planned for the following Saturday so she asked to take me out on February 11th. Sara started running behind schedule. That turned out to be a blessing in disguise. My doorbell rang about 30 minutes later and I thought it was Sara. Lavare answered the door and called me. I came into the dining room, then the front door to find Lisette and Felicia standing there hollering "Surprise!" I couldn't believe it. They came up to surprise me because they wouldn't be able to make it the following weekend for my baby shower. I was just so happy to see them. We talked and laughed until Sara got here. Sara invited them with us, which is what I wanted, of course.

We went to Bennigan's. I had so much fun. I felt like I was having my baby shower that day, instead of the following week. Sara, Lisette and Felicia all gave me their gifts before we left. Lisette and Felicia bought me the stroller and car seat combo I wanted. Sara bought me the Winnie the Pooh bedding set and night light. All my presents were so cute. We took plenty of pictures. I only wish Lisette and Felicia could have stayed longer but both of them had to work Monday morning. Initially, Lisette got to see everyone except Momma because she was at work. I called her at work but she didn't answer her cell phone so I left her a message telling her Lisette was at the house and wanted to see her (since they missed one another the last time Lisette visited). Just as the bill for the food was being paid (I was being treated, thank you), Momma called me back and said she would be home in fifteen minutes. That was perfect because Lisette was using Cory's car and he had made plans that evening. He was very understanding and let Lisette have the extra time to see Momma. We took plenty of pictures. We took pictures at home and at Bennigan's. I prayed they all came out, which all of the pictures did. ☺ Thank you Lord for such a special day. Kita also called to tell me she wouldn't be able to make it to my shower. I was a little sad she wouldn't make it but I understood.

Saturday, February 18, 2006—MY BABY SHOWER ! ! !

Still feeling wonderful about spending the evening with Sara, Lisette and Felicia, the previous week, I was actually nervous about my actual baby shower. So much unnecessary drama arose prior to my baby shower. If it had not been for Ayanna and Deirdre, I would have found a closet to hide in and cancelled my baby shower. As the week progressed, numerous people, some people who were and were not aware of my pregnancy and baby shower let me know how they felt. What happened to that old saying, "don't stress the mom to be." By the time the day of the shower got here, I had to first confer with my beautiful friends throwing the shower, and then have a long talk with God because I almost just said "forget it" and went to bed for the rest of the evening.

I woke up early that Saturday morning so I could go get my hair done. Thank God, Sara gave me the money so I could get my hair done because a certain male species was full of cow manure that day. I asked him for some money to get my hair done weeks prior to the shower, but he claimed he didn't get paid until the following week. I was *so* sick of him.

Sha took me to get my hair done at a beauty shop chain that was becoming more and more famous around that time. The wait time wasn't too bad. My hair was done by a man. He did a good job. Unfortunately, it took so long to get my hair done, I was running late for my own baby shower. I had to hurry up and get dressed so I could get to the church before all my guests arrived.

When I first got to Family of Hope Christian Church, I got really excited. The first thing I saw when I walked inside was the picture they hung on the wall. They really got creative as they took lavender, blue, green and yellow streamers and hung them from the ceiling so they hung over the staircase. People had to walk through the streamers and down the stairs into the dining room where the shower was. When I got to the dining room, I was so happy. I spoke to Kita. It took me about 5 to 10 minutes, after I sat down, to realize Kita was at my shower. "Wait a minute! What are you doing here?" I asked. Then Deirdre said, "I thought you said she called and said she wouldn't be able to make it. When I saw her, I thought I was wrong." Kita was all smiles. She had got me good.

The baby shower was nice, especially when my friends and I hung out later that evening. Overall, I had so much fun at my baby shower. Deirdre and Ayanna were fantastic. They were the ones who gave me the baby shower. They decorated the place so nicely and purposely left out pink because they knew how much I disliked pink. The colors were baby blue, baby green, yellow, orange, and lavender because everyone who knows me well know I love purple. Thank You. Deie cooked one of my favorite dishes. Thanks Deie. In fact, Deie prepared all the food. It was so delicious. Everyone loved the food.

That poor gift table looked like it had been hosed down with Pepto-Bismol. My family went pink crazy. I don't know if they did it on purpose or accident but by the end of the shower, I wanted to scream. I cannot stand pink. That's why Deirdre and Ayanna decorated like they did. I received some of everything. Diapers, clothes, t-shirts, blankets, bottles, just to name a few. Of course, Lisette and Felicia gave me the stroller and carrier combo the week they came to visit. Sara gave me the Winnie the Pooh bedding. Thank you everyone for all the beautiful gifts.

Among the people who attended the baby shower was Christina's dad oldest brother, Butch, and his youngest sister, Pam. They have always been nice to me, regardless of how he acted. They were so excited when I first told them I was pregnant. Dorothy was also very excited. My true school friends were great. After my family left, we sat around and reminisced about all the miracles God has performed in my life. God is such a healer. God is so merciful. God is so kind. God is better to us than we have been to ourselves. Thank you Jesus!

After everyone left, Ayanna, Deirdre, Lewis and I hung around the church. I had to thank Lewis again. Back then, he worked nights. He got, literally, no sleep so he could be at the church for my shower (except for that precious moment when he couldn't hang anymore and he found a corner to take a nap in). I thanked Deirdre and Ayanna for doing a wonderful job. By the time I got home that night, all my energy was gone. I was so tired. My bed felt so good. Sweet dreams.

On February 21st, I prepared for the two doctor's appointments scheduled for that morning. My first appointment was in the Neurology clinic. The second appointment was in the OB clinic. Transportation picked me up at 7:30am with no problems. However, after about 7-10 minutes riding in the vehicle, I was overcome with extreme dizziness and lightheadedness. Because of the lightheadedness and dizziness I began to pass out so the driver kept me conscious by talking to me and rubbing my hands with ice.

Upon arrival at the University of Chicago Hospitals Emergency Room, they took me to L&D because of my pregnancy. In L&D, my vitals were taken and I was examined to make sure I wasn't in labor. Blood and urine cultures were also taken. I wasn't in labor but the fetal monitor showed I had a few contractions. I was admitted under OB. Neurosurgery was called to confirm I wasn't having a shunt malfunction (I didn't feel the symptoms I usually felt when I was having a shunt malfunction). Test results and examination confirmed I wasn't. Thank you God. Neurology was called to consult and could give no answers to the lightheadedness and dizziness.

Doctors suspected preeclampsia and test results came back negative. Thank you, Lord. The OB did regular daily ultrasounds of my baby to check my baby's breathing and heart rate. I had that mother's instinct to start talking to her and call her by her name, "Christina." I felt miserable. I noticed, however, that when I talked to Christina, she calmed down. So I did that regularly when she was awake.

The attending physician began discussing labor and delivery options. My neurosurgeon and my OB discussed what would be safe. During this time, I spoke personally to my neurosurgeon and my high-risk OB associates but never to my OB directly. This irritated me somewhat. Anesthesia also came in to confer what medicine could and should not be used for delivery. I told him, I definitely did not want an epidural because of the LP shunt. He explained other medication could be used but may not be as effective as an epidural. However, given the location of the LP shunt, I still did not feel comfortable with having an epidural. I was transferred to neurology Friday, February 24, 2006. After finding no answers in OB, I was finally discharged home February 25, 2006.

"For the gifts and calling of God are without repentance."
Romans 11:29(KJV)

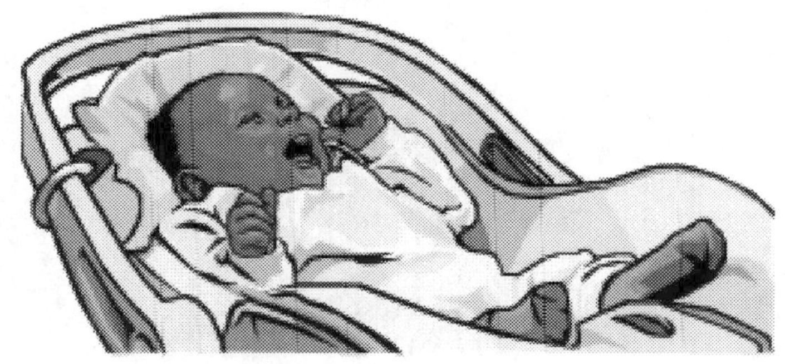

Chapter 17: Precious Gifts

My due date given was April 10, 2006. On April 9, 2006, as I sat and lay around the house, I had a feeling that Christina was not coming out on April 10, 2006. I was right. ☺

April 10, 2006

I don't believe this! I'm due today and I am not even feeling any labor pains. I pray my baby comes out soon.

After 10:00 am—My legs are cramping and I don't know why. I went to the washroom and I was spotting a little bit. I think I'll call Momma, since nobody's home and see what she says.

Moments Later—Momma said page my doctor because I'm high risk so she doesn't know what to say. When the doctor on call returned my page, she said the same thing: because of my medical history, she doesn't know what to tell me so use my best judgment.

My day continued like this, all the while my leg cramps increased. By 6:00pm, my leg cramps became unbearable. I paged the doctor one more time, the doctor on call repeated the same thing she said the first time I paged her. I tried to lie down but couldn't. I went to talk to my family. They told me to call my baby's father. I called him. He said he couldn't take me to the hospital because he was going to see his older brother.

I was in my bedroom when I decided to go talk to my family. I went to talk to my parents and Sha. This is when I got extremely mad. I begged them to give me a ride to the hospital, while everyone sat in the dining room talking.

Someone said, "I'm tired. I just got off work gas costs money."

Someone else said, "I'm tired too. I just got off work." She waited a few moments and then said, "Where's he at?" I replied, "He just told me he couldn't give me a ride because he is going to his brother's house.'

Still someone else said, "Gas costs money. I just got off work. I'm tired."

I went back into my bedroom. A few minutes the doorbell rang. It was my boyfriend. Surprised, I made my way to the front door. He was bringing me a minute cup of strawberry ice cream that he promised to bring me almost two weeks prior to that day. "Are you kidding me? I asked you for this ice cream over one week ago . . ." I then asked, "You changed your mind?" Without hesitation, he said, "No, I'm about to go see my brother now. I just thought I would bring this before I go." He walked away. *Are you kidding me? Does someone have a hidden video camera on me so they could record my reaction to this bad joke?*

I went back into the dining room to ask my parents and Sha again. "Will someone please give me a ride?" They gave me the same responses as before.

"I just got off work. I'm tired. 'I'm not wasting gas."

"Gas costs money. I just got off work. I'm tired."

My leg was still cramping quite a bit. I stood in the dining room waiting to get a "yes" from someone. They got very quiet. They continued resting their head on their hands with their elbows on the table. Finally, after several minutes, my Daddy grudgingly gave me a ride.

When I got to Labor and Delivery, the registrar asked me my due date. When I said, "today," they took me straight back.

My vitals were taken. The OB on call checked me. He said, "Ma'am, you are dilated 6 centimeters."

I said, "Are you trying to say I'm in labor?"

The OB responded, "Yes." Everyone laughed. One of the nurses said, "if everyone came in acting like you, our jobs would be much easier."

I continued "Will you please do me a favor? There is a man sitting in the waiting area who is probably driving everyone crazy with his snoring . . ."

The nurse said, "I'll get him for you."

When my daddy came back, I said, "I'm dilated 6 centimeters." Daddy said, "Are they keeping you?" I said, "Yes."

I continued, "I know you still have to finish packing and are tired so you can go back home."

Daddy said, "I'll call you later." He kissed my forehead and left.

After being admitted, the fetal monitor was placed on my stomach so they could watch Christina. An IV was started. They noted that I refused an epidural. The doctor said I had other options for pain management. Later that night, I tried to sleep but couldn't. Those leg cramps, or should I say contractions, made it hard to sleep. Sometime that night, the OB on call came to check on me. He decided to give me some medicine to slow down my contractions and to decrease my pain. This was because I was told I needed to be well rested to safely deliver my baby so he wanted me to get some sleep.

On April 11, 2006, the nurse came in early to take my vitals. I was given more medicine to increase my contractions and decrease my pain. The doctor was paged. Moments later, a very familiar voice came into the room. It was the OB/GYN I had before I got pregnant. I was so happy. She was very happy. This was when she said for the first time, "Make sure my name is listed as the doctor who delivered this baby." Thank you. I was so happy she was there too. She continued. I would deliver my baby in three pushes. I said ok.

Everyone was wonderful. My nurse from the previous night wanted to see the birth of my baby so she stayed later. My nurse on duty was also in the room. There was also a pediatrics team off to the side ready to get Christina when she was born. There were also some residents in the room. I began pushing. ONE. Push. TWO. Push. THREE. Push. BREATHE. FOUR. Push.

On April 11, 2006 at 12:11pm, I, Shereice Garrett, gave birth to a beautiful baby girl. At birth she weighed 6 pounds, 9 ounces. She was 20 inches long. Because of my health status, they would not let me hold her. I had to literally beg to see her before she was whisked away. Thank you Lord for blessing me with a beautiful daughter. I decided to name her Christina Sherrie. About five minutes after I had Christina, my high risk OB came in ready to deliver my beautiful baby, who was already in this world. After she realized Christina was delivered, she told me I had to stay in the hospital three (3) days.

I was told I would have to wait one hour to see my daughter. It was suggested I try to take a nap. That was impossible. I was high on adrenaline. All I could think about was seeing my daughter. One hour later, I put on my call light and asked for my baby because they had not brought her to me. About 5 minutes later, my Daddy walked in. He said, "Did you have your baby yet?" I responded, "I had her an hour ago." Daddy asked where Christina was. I told him she was in the nursery. He tried to see her in the nursery but hospital nursery rules state, no one is allowed to see the baby in the nursery unless they are wearing the same arm band that the baby and mother is wearing. I called my nurse again. She apologized. This time she promised to go get my baby and ring her to me, personally. Moments later, she brought Christina to me. That was the last time we were apart from one another, except when they had to take her to the nursery to do her vitals.

Christina was a beautiful baby. Daddy couldn't wait to see her. Netta came to see her. Momma came to see Christina. Since momma and Daddy would be gone out of town when I was released from the hospital, Sha brought us home. By the time I was released from the hospital, Christina's father still had not come to the hospital to see her.

After Sha brought us home from the hospital, Christina and I shared some quality time together. She was a very peaceful baby. If Christina cried, I knew she was crying for a reason. It was usually because she was hungry and/or needed her pamper changed. The first few days after I came home from the hospital, I still did not see him. His family made it their priority to come see Christina. Christina's father's family was among the first people to visit Christina. It took him well over a week to come see Christina. I believe it was one week after I came home from the hospital, Lisette and Felicia came up to see me. Well, let's be honest, they did not come to see me, they came to see Christina. ☺ Just kidding. They were so happy for me. While they were visiting us, another friend of Lisette called and came over to visit.

It seemed like attitudes simmered down in my parent's home, after Christina's birth. Thank God.

The only issue I dealt with was the position Christina slept. Christina did not like sleeping on her back so she was never peaceful unless I put her on her side. I know experts say that is not a safe for a baby to be on their side at that early age but someone should have told Christina that. I felt comfortable with her on her side because she was always within my reach so I watched her closely.

I knew Christina was blessed by God because I was in the dining room one evening watching television while I put her to sleep. Actually I was listening to the Gospel Music Channel. All of a sudden "The Battle Is the Lord's" by Yolanda Adams began to play and I kid you not, it sounded like my daughter was humming the song as she went to sleep. The other song she had to listen to at night was "Imagine Me" by Kirk Franklin. She would be irritable and fight sleep until she heard those two songs. When she heard that song she would sip her milk until she spit her bottle out and went to sleep. When my parents changed cable companies and the music was not offered, Christina fought sleep that first night until I found the CD's for her to listen to with the songs on them. As she grew a little older, "Never Would Have Made It" and "The Best In Me", by Marvin Sapp became songs she enjoyed and uplifted her spirit.

May 4 2006 – Heavenly Father,

Thank you for your grace and your mercy that sustains me. Thank you for keeping me. Thank you for my beautiful daughter, Christina. Thank you for keeping her safe and healthy. Thank you Lord for allowing my bank account to go back on the positive side so I can be able to take care of myself and Christina. Thank you Lord for always making a way when I don't see a way. I love you Lord. I give everything – my life, my health, my strength, my finances, my baby's health – I give it all to you Lord. In Jesus name, Amen

The same people, within my household, seemed to have started softening up as they bonded with Christina. However, he was not changing, for the better. By May 19th, Christina was continuing to develop into a beautiful little girl. Motherhood was challenging times, but it was also the most beautiful experience a woman can experience in her life.

That following day, May 20th, started off nicely. That evening, momma surprised me. I wasn't really surprised because I knew it was going to happen eventually. I didn't expect it to happen so soon. She asked to give Christina her bath that night. Of course. She smiled as she bathed her grandbaby for the first time. Momma's birthday was the following weekend. She told me don't buy her anything. Since she didn't have any plans, I asked her if we could be excused that evening to go to Lawrence's birthday party. Momma said yes.

However a party was being planned for momma I knew nothing about. I had told Deie we would be at Lawrence's party after I spoke to momma. For the most part, momma didn't mind but she wanted to show Christina off. I told her I would come back in enough time for everyone to see Christina.

Lawrence's party was nice. Everyone was excited because Lawrence turned one year old. They were also excited to see Christina. Everyone complimented me on how beautiful Christina was. When we got back to my parent's house, momma's birthday party was winding down. People had started leaving. Those that were still at the house were happy to see Christina.

The following day, Sunday, May 28, 2006 Deirdre and Lewis families were special guests for Lawrence's Dedication. It was so beautiful. After service, everyone met up at Deie and Lewis house. We then went to dinner at Leona's. I was a little nervous as money was tight for me. I decided to take a little money from my account and eat light that night. Good thing my appetite was still not that great. Ayanna and I sat next to one another so we could share desserts. Christina was a good baby as always. Everyone always said I had a sweet baby that hardly cried. I thanked God because I knew if she was crying it was for a reason. At the end of the meal, we all got a big surprise when Lewis' brother and sister-in-law paid for everyone's meals. Thank you Jesus! Thank you Mr. and Mrs. Jones.

Still that following Wednesday was very unusual. He came over and volunteered to look after Christina while I rested and did whatever I needed to do. "Shock" was the word for the day. At this point, Christina was asleep in my bed. He watched television while she slept. I was in the dining room when she woke up and started crying. Usually he didn't touch her, let alone pick her up and hold her. Today he picked her up and consoled her. He went a step further. He got her bottle. He fed Christina and burped her when he got finished feeding her. I couldn't believe it. Had he finally come to his senses? I had to take a picture of this.

That evening, bible class was nice as always. Ayanna and Deie didn't believe me until I showed them the picture.

Well June 8, 2006 turned out to be better than I thought it would be. I had to take my baby for her first set of immunizations. Yuck! I did not want to see my baby get stuck. Her pediatrician teased me but I survived it. Following her appointment, I had to run by the neurosurgery clinic so I could pick up a new prescription for the pain medicine I was taking for my headaches. Initially, I was supposed to see his nurse because he was supposed to be out of the office that day. When I got to the clinic, I received a surprise; Dr. Frim was in the clinic. When I got back to the conference room where he was, he said one of momma's favorite comments, "Don't nobody want to see you, let me see the baby." ☺ Lord, thank you for blessing me with a caring doctor who know how to treat people. He then did his other favorite thing and joked about momma. He asked me if she acted the same way as a grandmother as she does as a mother. I looked at him and said, "now you already know the answer to that question she also had plenty of practice. My baby makes grandchild number seven." After we got home, we ate and took a nap. Later that evening, Christina woke up running a fever so I gave her Infant Fever Reducer and she went back to sleep.

In the beginning, Christina started out being a Pa Pa's baby. I guess that's because my father drove me absolutely crazy during my pregnancy, except when he was bringing me the food I craved. ☺ Christina did not like my momma in the beginning. She cried every time momma came near her. The other person she love (and still drive me crazy about) is my baby sister Nicole, her "Auntie Nikki." Nicole would come in the house looking for Christina. They would sometimes play until Christina fell asleep. Sometime, Nicole volunteered to put Christina to sleep.

By June 2006, when Christina was two months old, she was very observant and made good eye contact, in response to sound. She also enjoyed lying down and kicking her feet up in the air. Christina was generally a happy baby. If she cried, you knew it was for a reason. She loved taking baths. I loved when she took a bath too because she would be so relaxed and fall right to sleep. I miss those days. ☺

During my six-week appointment, I told my high-risk OB, who I saw for prenatal care, that I was initially scheduled to have a tubal ligation after Christina was born. At the last minute, they cancelled it because the doctor said I risked infection to the shunt. My high risk OB stepped out of the exam room for a few minutes. When she came back in, she referred me to another OB, who she said would give me another option.

During my appointment to see this OB/GYN I was referred to, he reviewed my medical history and medication I was taking at the time. He asked me if I wanted the procedure or was someone forcing me to have it. I lied. I told him it was all my decision. The truth was my mother was bugging me to have it done. I didn't want to risk having any more children however I was not in a rush to have my tubes tied. He told me it was usually not done in women as young as I was. Due to my medical history, however he would do it if I was sure I wanted it. I reassured the doctor I wanted the procedure. He then explained a new procedure called ESSURE. It is an alternative to the traditional tubal ligation. It is especially beneficial to women who because of their medical history, was unable to undergo the traditional tubal ligation. I decided to have the procedure.

By August 2006 Christina continued to fill my life with joy. We went to church Sundays at Family of Hope Christian Church, as I still helped out with Sunday service. On Wednesday evening, if Christina and I weren't too tired, we also went to bible class at family of Hope. I was so proud of my dear sister. She was working hard to maintain her ministry.

Of course, September is always the best month of the year. I guess as Christina matures and grows older, April will become the best month of the year. That year, 2006, my wonderful friends and I decided to celebrate and have my birthday party at Friday's. This year was especially nice as my play brother was in town. He, along with many of my closest friends, came out to help me celebrate. Of course, Christina helped me celebrate. That following week, Christina made 5 months old. She got a clean bill of health each time she went to the doctor. The only time I hated was when she had to get her immunizations. She looked so pitiful afterwards. However, my baby's health is very important to me. I will do all I need to do to ensure Christina's well-being.

Nikki loved my baby. She loved playing with her. One of Nikki's favorite things to do was "cook" my baby. She loved taking momma's big roaster out and sitting Christina in it. Christina would be cracking up. My daddy spoiled my baby like he did my niece Brianna. In the past, Brianna could never do anything wrong. He was starting to do Christina the same way.

October 17, 1006 turned out to be a very good day. I went to the University of Chicago Hospitals for the HSG. This is the test done to make sure the ESSURE procedure was successful. The staff was still at lunch when I arrived in Radiology so I had a nice wait. While waiting for the staff to return from lunch, I spoke to June. She helped me replace my baby's birth certificate that Social Security lost when I sent it in.

After I was called back and changed for the test, I still had to sit outside the exam room and wait. I then sat in the exam room and waited. This is when I got a big surprise. A lady, who looked very familiar to me came in the room and spoke. Where did I know her from? Who was she? After waiting for me to try and figure out who she was, the lady said, "It's Me Sharice." Oh my God! I couldn't believe it. It had been twenty years since the last time I saw her. We were in the 5th grade at Henton. Time sure does fly. She looks the same. She has two sons now. We talked for a quick minute then she had to go tend to her patients. She wanted to come speak to me because she noticed my name on the schedule. I am so happy she did. I had thought about her over the years, after we lost touch with one another. She was one of the few friends I made while at Henton. The HSG was a breeze. It confirmed the ESSURE was a success. That was one less headache.

By November everyone was looking forward to Thanksgiving. My first Thanksgiving with my baby or so I thought. I developed a woman's issue that was becoming more of a nuisance and making it close to impossible for it to be ignored. As a result, I was recommended to surgery to correct the problem. The surgery was scheduled for November 20, 2006. This was one day before my family was scheduled to leave. Of course, I would not be able to go. Momma and daddy, or should I say Christina's Nana and Papa, decided to take her with them so I could rest. She enjoyed herself tremendously. My family couldn't wait to come back home so they could tell me about it. Christina spent her days hanging out on the golf course with my Uncle Mike (Aunt Odessa's husband).

Christmas Eve 2006 was the Garrett Family Dinner. Initially I was not involved with the planning process. That was done by my parents, Sha and Nicole. Everyone started arriving around the same time, 5:00pm. I was still in my room getting Christina, as well as, myself ready for the evening. It was during this time, someone temporarily tested me by banging on my door and walking away. This was repeated two additional times. I remained under control and continued getting ready. I came out and everyone complimented me on how beautiful Christina looked. Overall, that evening went well. The food was prepared by one of the world's greatest cooks, my momma. It was so good; in fact, people took plates home, leaving no food to be put away at the end of the evening. Attendance was beyond expectation, once more, for a Garrett Family Dinner.

• •

Monday, December 25, 2006 – Merry Christmas ! ! ! Happy Birthday King Jesus ! ! !

Thank you for coming down to earth just to save a sinner like me. Thank you for giving me the right to eternal life.

I really enjoyed today. Christina kept me up All Night. She did not go to sleep until 4:30 this morning. Thank God I made it extremely clear that NOBODY was to come wake neither Christina nor myself up. We got up around noon. I had three text messages wishing me "Merry Christmas ! ! !" Everyone i.e. momma, Nicole, and Lavare wanted to take Christina to open up her presents. How could they deprive me of that FIRST with my daughter? NO way ! ! ! I spoke up for myself as I told them that

Christina was my daughter and I would open up presents with my daughter after I got dressed. Where would I be without this house of BIG kids?☺

Christina received some great presents. Momma and daddy bought her a playpen. They also bought her the same toy I was getting my baby (if I hadn't run out of money while shopping), some pajamas and bibs. Nicole Bought her another pair of gym shoes. Sha bought her a learning toy, as well as, another toy. Netta bought her a play set for the bath tub. Chris actually bought her some clothes that actually fit.

This evening, I took Christina to Dorothy's house for their Christmas dinner. The house was packed with Chris family, some of whom I met today for the first time. Overall, the dinner was nice. Dorothy looked so pretty. Chris had his video camera out taping. He pretended to be a good father as he got excited and taped Christina opening up her presents from him. Is Chris actually trying to improve? I will reserve my judgment until later. Well Christina has fallen asleep so I am going to try and get some sleep.

•••

As I approached New Year's Eve, I thanked God for bringing me another year. I thanked God for this wonderful gift of life he gave me through Christina. I thank God she was healthy and happy. Oh my God, I am a mom! I am still amazed by this miracle. That evening, Christina's paternal grandmother invited Christina and me to bring in the new year with her. Since my parents were planning something private, Christina and I went to bring the New Year in with Dorothy and her family.

10... 9... 8... 7... 6... 5... 4... 3... 2... 1...

HAPPY NEW YEAR ! ! ! HAPPY 2007 ! ! !

Thank you Jesus ! ! ! We made it.

"Children, obey your parents in the Lord:
for this is right.
Honour thy father and mother;
which is the first commandment with promise;
That it may be well with thee,
and thou mayest live long on the earth."
Ephesians 6:1-3 (KJV)

King James Version Public Domain
www.biblegateway.com/passage

Chapter 18: One Year Old

The months leading up to Christina's first birthday were wonderful. I enjoyed watching my baby smile, play, sing and try to walk. This showed me she was all right. Because of her spirit of happiness that seemed to surround her, I was able to tell those rare moments when something was wrong with my baby. For instance, Christina was a hard crawler. When she crawled through the house she could be heard very clearly. One day she crawled so hard that she banged her foot on my momma's coffee table. That same evening she developed a small bruise on her foot. I showed her Nana. Momma said it would be all right. Unfortunately it was not. 24 hours later I was in her pediatrician's clinic with her because her foot started to blister. This began several trips back and forth to the doctor until her foot healed.

The biggest issue I had was my family. Everyone knew everything and I knew nothing. I know they were only trying to help, sometimes, but their comments were making me upset, at times. With my daddy, I could not do anything right when it came to taking care of Christina. As a result, he always interfered. He sometimes made me feel like a little girl again. The other thing is Christina could do no wrong. He always protected Christina when I was teaching her right from wrong and he was around. This continues to be an issue. Momma was not as bad as daddy but she also interfered. Momma, Daddy, Sha and Nicole surprised me. They help out quite a bit with Christina.

Around the end of February 2007, my sisters and momma asked, "What are you planning for Christina's party?" I started planning for Christina's first birthday party. It would be in my parent's house because we did not want to chance the weather. I had so much fun shopping for Christina's party. Since she fallen in love with Nicole's Winnie the Pooh, I made Winnie the Pooh the theme for her party. Party City . . . Wal-Mart . . . Toys R Us. They all broke me but it was alright because I wanted her party to be nice.

Lisette and Felicia came up to Chicago for Christina's party. Timothy and his wife were also there. Michelle B brought the kids. Her kids had gotten so big and beautiful. Christina's father, and as always I use that term loosely, did not attend Christina's birthday party but, his family did attend. He had taken me to the store earlier that afternoon to get the food I ordered, prepared, from Jewel's Chef's Kitchen. When we got back to my parent's house, I called my nephew Lavare, to help take the food in the house. Christina's father was in such a rush he was about to put the food on the ground for Lavare to come and get so he could leave. I stopped him. He got mad. After everything was removed from the car, He left and did not return for his daughter's first birthday party. People asked me where he was but at that point I did not know where he went because he would not answer my phone calls either.

Anyway, we had so much fun that afternoon. One of my spiritual mothers, Momma Tucker, came over. I was so happy to see her because it had been a while since I saw her. Food was plentiful and guests were abundant. At one point, we had so many people in the house, that Christina got shy and started crying. She did not want to be around anyone. As the party winded down, Christina became happy again. I guess she did not like the crowd that year. It was just too many people for her. Well we will see how next year is. My crazy sisters are already talking about next year and we had just finished that year. That's my family. I don't know what to say about them. I do know they do know how to love even when they pretend they don't.

"Brothers, I do not consider that I have made it my own. But one thing I do: forgetting what lies behind and straining forward to what lies ahead, I press on toward the goal for the prize of the upward call of God in Christ Jesus."

Philippians 3:13-14 (ESV)

Conclusion

Today is June 3, 2011. I am holding back tears of joy as my daughter receives her final diploma from Orchard Street Christian Church Child Daycare Center. Oh my God! My baby is getting to be such a big girl ! ! ! I can remember her first day at Orchard Street. She cried because she did not want me to leave her. One of the teachers would coax her away from me as I eased out of the door. She did not realize I watched her for a few seconds before I actually left out of the right. She was only two then.

The last three months have been a challenge for me, health wise. In March 2011, I woke up with a very bad headache and I felt funny. I took Christina to school and immediately came home. Thank God my friend was with me. He watched television while I took a nap on my couch. The last thing I remember is lying down on my couch. I woke up in the emergency room of the neighborhood hospital. I was told I had a seizure in my apartment. I remembered my friend was in my apartment and they told me he was in the waiting area. Of course, I called Momma and she came right over. After all, this was the first seizure that I had experienced in almost ten years! Since then, I have had two more seizures and my anti-seizure medication had to be increased. "Thank you Lord for always watching over me!" A few weeks later, I had to send my baby to stay with her Nana and Papa because I also went through a battle with my headaches where I couldn't get any control of them. Thank God my shunts continued to function properly during this time. My pain medicine had to be altered to alleviate the problem.

Now my big girl is five years old and graduating from pre-K. Oh how I love her. She looks so beautiful today. She is still upset with her Nana and Papa but she got over it as soon as she put on her new graduation dress and shoes they bought her, before they went on their anniversary vacation. Good going momma and daddy. ☺ Only 24 days until the next chapter of her, or should I say, our life begins. She was accepted to Morgan Park Academy for the 2011-2012 Kindergarten class. She is on the waiting list until a spot opens up. When we took our first tour of the school a few months ago, she said, "Momma I want this to be my new school. I like it here." Days later, she started saying, "Morgan Park IS my new school. I want to go to summer camp at my new school." She continued proclaiming Morgan Park as her new school before she was even accepted.

Thank God she was accepted because I don't know what I would have done. Now my prayer is that she gets off the Wait List and gets an actual spot before the regular school year began. That is one storm I do not want to battle because Christina will be very upset if I have to tell her they do not have a spot in the kindergarten class for her yet. Being the big girl that she is, my daughter reiterated, "Momma I want to go to summer camp at my new school." Summer camp starts June 27th. I don't know who is more excited, Christina or me. as her mother, I only want and pray for the best for my beautiful gift from God. I can see already that she will be very strong-minded and smart. Her strong-mindedness already gets her in trouble because when she makes up her mind to do or not do something, she responds accordingly, regardless of the consequences. I only pray that she will use these gifts to be everything she can be and not be deterred by the negatives of this world. I only pray she will work hard in school and excel. Of course, I pray for her happiness because ". . . the joy of the Lord is your strength." Well, I have 21 days to sleep late. Yeah right. My daughter never sleeps late on the mornings she should. I won't complain. I will be overjoyed at being awakened each morning by my baby.

Thank you Lord for allowing Christina to enjoy five healthy and happy years with her momma. Thank you Lord for allowing my daughter to remain healthy. I know the road may get rough sometimes. I know there will be hills to climb. I also know that everything will be all right.

Marvin Sapp has song entitled, "Here I Am," which is the title track on this awesome, anointed by God, CD. It came out in 2010.

"Here I am. I'm still standing.
Here I am. After all I've been through.
I've survived. Every toil. Every snare.
I'm alive. I'm alive.
Here I am."

I love that song. The words say it all. I'm Shereice Garrett. I'm still standing. I'm alive! I'm alive! Even through all the diagnoses, pain, hospitalizations, surgeries and, heart breaks. I'm still standing. Why? Because MY LIFE IS IN GOD'S HANDS.

"Blessed is the man that endureth temptation: for when he is tried, he shall receive the crown of life, which the Lord hath promised to them that love him."

James 1:12

King James Version (**KJV**) Public Domain
www.biblegateway.com/passages

Epilogue

There is an old saying, "home is where the heart is." I know that is certainly true in my life. When my time at Family of Hope ended, or should I say, I had been away from home long enough, I went back home to my New Faith family. Of course, I saw many old faces. I also saw many new faces. Going home has allowed me to reconnect with Momma Merrill. Nothing bad ever happened between us. I just somehow lost touch with her when I got really sick, prior to me finding out I was pregnant with Christina. It has been such a blessing to her back in my life. We talk like we used to at True Right. We probably talk a little bit more. I have my other spiritual mom back. However now I have gained more than a spiritual mom. I have gained a friend. Momma Tucker will always be my other spiritual mother, as well. Our schedules clash and we may go a few weeks without talking to one another. When we do, my heart is overjoyed and my spirit is fed each time.

I love Ayanna and will forever thank God for her friendship. We have gone back to what we do best: playing phone tag. ☺ I am so thankful to her because during the time I worked with her ministry, she encouraged me to speak the word God had given me. Under her leadership, I preached my first sermon. That was definitely ordained by God. I worked with the Children's ministry and had an awesome time doing it. I also did a little office work. Thank you Ayanna for seeing something in me I probably would never have seen for myself. Above all, thank you for your friendship and your sisterhood. It is priceless.

Deirdre and I are soul sisters. I thank God for allowing our paths to cross. She sees in me everything I see, plus more. She is an awesome woman of God. I cannot wait to see her ministry in full force. Look out Chicago ! ! ! Look out world ! ! !

Momma is wonderful. We play phone tag a lot. We have our best conversations through text messages, sometimes. However, I know when I truly need her, she is there. She helps me so much with Christina. Daddy will never change. He can be a big teddy bear at times with a big heart and a wonderful sense of humor. He can also be a thunderstorm you pray would quickly pass over so you can see the sun again. I can talk to him when I need to. He continues to drive me crazy when it comes to Christina. ☺ In his eyes, Christina can practically do no wrong.

Grannie is my heart. She means the world to me. Unfortunately, the last few months have been hard. She suffered a heart attack, while alone in her apartment, so no one knew what happened. My Aunt Kat called me and asked if I had heard from her. I told her, "no." Concerned because no one heard from her for several days, my Aunt Kat and Uncle Leon went to check on her in her apartment. They found her passed out. After that, she seemed to start having issues with her health. She had to be placed in a rehab facility so I don't get to talk to her as much anymore. The facility is on the north side of Chicago so I have only seen her once, since she moved there.

I could get upset. However, I really don't have a reason to be upset. Grannie is almost 100 years old. She has lived through a lot, from the cotton fields of Alabama to the city of Chicago. She raised seven children on her own, after my granddaddy was killed. She has seen and done it all. You could never tell Grannie what she could or could not do. I am honored to have had her as a permanent fixture and source of strength in my life for so long. I love you so much Grannie.

Lisette and Kita are wonderful sisters to have in my life. Christina loves her God-parents very much. When Lisette got married, Christina welcomed her God-father with open arms. When Lisette gave birth to her first child, Christina was very excited and welcomed her God-sister with open arms. As Christina gets older, she amazes me with her love for her Godparents. I guess the dream I had, prior to me choosing Christina's Godparents, will come to pass. I am so blessed to have Kita and Lisette in my life. I used to wonder why it took so long for these two ladies to become a part of my life. I am then reminded of that old saying, "there is a time and pace for everything."

Nicole is crazy. She shows the world a hard, mean exterior. When you get to see her heart, you see a maturing woman who has a loving heart. She cares so much for Christina. The family joke is I had Christina for Nicole.

Sha and Nicole should have been twins. They sound alike, at times. They act just alike a lot of times. Sha has a big heart but I think she is just afraid sometimes to allow it out in the open. She has been a great mother to my niece and nephew. She has been a great aunt and she has become a great sister.

Netta has blossomed into a beautiful flower. She has grown up. Nobody's perfect. She has allowed the mistakes of her past to pave the road to her future. She has found love and I am so happy for her. I wish my sister greatness.

Everyday is a new adventure with Christina. I just enrolled her in a Chicago Public School because my financial situation didn't allow me to keep her enrolled in Morgan Park Academy. The transition has been a lot smoother than what I anticipated. Her teacher seems nice thus far. It has not been a month yet so I will see how things look by Thanksgiving. I am working on her behavior. As I have heard so many times from parents,

Christina tries new things all the time. Her new thing is temper tantrums. When they are minute, I ignore her. When they are loud, I intervene.

Only God knows what tomorrow, or the next day, will hold. I pray for strength to be the best mother I can be. I pray for my health. I also pray Christina will always do her best. I pray for Christina's safety. I pray she will remain healthy. I know everything will work out fine as long as MY LIFE IS IN GOD'S HANDS.

“For I know the plans I have for you, declares the Lord, ‘plans to prosper you and not harm you, plans to give you hope and a future.”

Jeremiah 29:11 (NIV)

Medicare Basics Today

Your One-Stop Source

FLORENCE M. GOGEL

Archway Publishing books may be ordered through booksellers or by contacting:

Archway Publishing
1663 Liberty Drive
Bloomington, IN 47403
www.archwaypublishing.com
1 (888) 242-5904

ISBN: 978-1-4808-6355-2 (sc)
ISBN: 978-1-4808-6354-5 (e)

Library of Congress Control Number: 2018946806

Print information available on the last page.

Archway Publishing rev. date: 7/18/2018

CONTENTS

Introduction ix

Chapter 1 What Is Medicare? 1

Chapter 2 What's New in 2018? 9

Chapter 3 Eligibility and Enrollments 14

The Initial Enrollment Period 16
Lack of Employment Quarters 20
General Enrollment Period 21
Special Enrollment Period (SEP) 22
Delaying Enrollment in Medicare, if There Are Special Circumstances 23
Retiree Plan 29
Disability 35

Chapter 4 Medicare Premiums and Cost 42

Chapter 5 Medicare Savings Programs/State Assistance Programs 53

Chapter 6 Medicare Part A and Coverage................61

Mental Health 64
Skilled Nursing...66
Home Health Services 70
Hospice Care 72

Chapter 7 Medicare Part B and Coverage............... 78

Clinical Research Studies 80
Ambulance Services..................................81
Durable Medical Equipment (DME)........83
Mental Health Services.............................85
Medicare Part B may help cover the
following outpatient medications..............89

Chapter 8 Preventive Services/Laboratory Testing Coverage.................................... 97

Medicare Screenings Offered.................. 102
Laboratory Criteria and Restrictions....... 124

Chapter 9 Medicare Part C (Medicare Advantage Plan) and Coverage 128

Medicare Advantage Plan
Enrollment Period 129
Medicare Advantage Disenrollment
Period 130
There Are Different Types of
Medicare Advantage Plans Available....... 133

Chapter 10 Medicare Part D and Coverage 143

Medicare Part D Plan Enrollment Period 144
Medicare Advantage Disenrollment Period 146
The 2018 Medicare Part D plan's coverage is as follows 146

Chapter 11 Medigap Plans and Insurance Supplements 151

Medigap Plans 154
Medigap Coverage outside the United States 156
Medigap Enrollment Period 157
Medicare Supplements/Secondary Retiree Plans 169

Chapter 12 Medicare and Travel Coverage 178

INTRODUCTION

Medicare can be a nerve-wracking experience when trying to determine the best process and coverage. I understand how frustrating this can be. I have over thirty years' experience working in the medical profession and specializing in insurance benefits. I have assisted and currently assist my patients with the selection process of interpreting and understanding this complex medical benefit. I hope this book will make it easier for you to navigate through and understand this complex process. This book breaks down the Medicare system into a simpler format, to assist you in making the correct decisions, whether or not you are just about to become Medicare eligible or currently have Medicare. This book will provide you with the tools you need to understand your Medicare benefits. Knowledge is power, and having power over your decisions and choices can eliminate costly errors.

Common Errors

The following are the most common errors I see when working with my patients.

Believing more insurance is better than less

Example: A common misconception among patients is that having more insurance will cover everything and eliminate all out-of-pocket costs. Unfortunately, it's not that simple.

- Too much insurance can hinder your treatment and does not necessarily eliminate all out-of-pocket costs for some or all of your medical services.
- Here is an example of the number-one common mistake I encounter on a regular basis, involving patients who have the Original Medicare with a retiree plan. The patient changes his or her Original Medicare to a Medicare Advantage Plan and retains the retiree plan as secondary insurance.
    - A patient has Original Medicare and Tricare for Life. Both plans do not require a prior authorization. Tricare for Life covers both Medicare's deductible and coinsurance on covered services. There is no cost to you, as long as the services are covered by Medicare. Tricare for Life offers prescription plans.
    - The patient switches Original Medicare to a Medicare Advantage plan. As a result, some tests, expensive injections, and infusions may require a prior authorization through the Medicare Advantage Plan. This causes a delay in treatment while waiting for the decision of the Medicare Advantage plan to approve the request.
    - The Medicare Advantage plan may deny the request, resulting in denial of treatment or test.

- *If the patient had stayed with Original Medicare and Tricare for Life, the covered service by Medicare and Tricare For Life would have been performed, and the patient would not have a delay.*

Conclusion: Signing up with too many plans can hinder your treatment. Always make sure the insurance plan you select provides you with sufficient coverage for both your medical and prescription health-care needs. If your existing insurance covers what you need, you *do not* need to add additional insurance.

Bundling symptoms with your yearly Medicare wellness appointment

Example: A common mistake made by Medicare patients is that during their yearly Medicare wellness exam, they also have their doctor treat them for symptoms of a current illness or chronic condition.

- **Be Advised!** The yearly Medicare Wellness exam can only be 100 percent covered by Medicare Part B if the wellness visit is for prevention and screening exams for disease, **Not for any treatment of an illness!** During the Medicare Wellness exam, you *cannot* be symptomatic, i.e. (experiencing any signs or symptoms of an illness) and request treatment for an unstable chronic condition during the Medicare Wellness exam. Your doctor may need to charge an additional code in addition to your Medicare wellness visit. ***To be clear, you may be charged for any medical service or treatment that is not part of the Medicare Wellness exam!***

- The Wellness Exam will be 100 percent covered, but the physician can charge an additional code for the evaluation and management of the illness or the chronic condition if it requires testing, evaluation and medication management. Your doctor will code this charge with a modifier advising the insurance company that you were treated for something in addition to your wellness visit. The diagnosis code associated with this additional code will define which condition was treated. The second charge will go towards your Medicare Part B deductible of $183 and/or your 20 percent coinsurance. You may see two charges on your explanation of benefits (EOB) that you receive from Medicare after they process the claim.
- **To recap:** The very act of the patient requesting an examination and treatment for any illness or an unstable chronic condition during a wellness visit, can add an additional charge which will result in a balance to be paid by the patient if he or she does not have a secondary insurance to cover that balance.

Conclusion: The medical providers are in the business of treating your health and not to serve as your insurance benefits advisor! You need to know for yourself and understand how your insurance benefits works. Knowing in advance what is covered and what is not will help you avoid unnecessary charges. *Please refer to Chapter 8 for more information and specific details.*

Enrolling in a Medicare Advantage Plan (Part C) when your particular health care situation requires high-end treatment for your medical conditions

Example: Some of my patients have switched from original Medicare to a Medicare Advantage plan without researching how their high-end treatments are covered. A common example I encountered while working in the rheumatology clinic in Killeen was the following scenario.

- **A patient was diagnosed with osteoarthritis of the knee. The patient was given Visco supplementation knee injections. Visco supplementation injections is a procedure whereby a lubricating fluid is injected into the joint in the knee.**
- **Medicare Part B covers this Visco supplementation injection without a prior authorization under the current benefits of a deductible and coinsurance. There is, however, a frequency restriction that requires this injection to be done every six months. If you have a secondary insurance, then depending on the benefits provided by the secondary insurance, it would probably cover a portion of the cost or the balance secondary to Medicare.**
- **Medicare Advantage's plan most likely will require a prior authorization for this type of injection and medication. This plan may have a preferred method for the treatment of the diagnosis of osteoarthritis of the knee.**

- The plan may have a preferred medication that they require the patient to use, and that might not be the same one you have been receiving.
- The plan may have a different coverage and cost for the medication, as well as the administrative procedure. The procedure, however, may not be covered under the office-visit benefit. Sometimes an office visit has a copayment, but this procedure may fall under a deductible and/or a coinsurance.
- The plan may not cover the medication under the Part B benefit on this plan but instead on the Part D prescription services. If so, you need to find out if you have to purchase the medication through the pharmacy and pay upfront and have it mailed to your medical provider to administer to you.
- The plan may deny the prior authorization and the treatment and **require** you to **try** other treatment options first.

Conclusion: Remember—before enrolling in any plans, find out what your coverage is for expensive treatments and how it will affect your treatment plan. If your plan requires a different option for your treatment than what you were receiving, check first with your medical provider to see if that option is sufficient for your medical treatment.

Common Medical Terminology You Need to Know:

Original Medicare—The traditional Medicare insurance offered by the government. It pays for services directly to your medical providers, facilities, or suppliers.

Deductible—The amount of money your insurance requires you to pay up front for your medical services, prescriptions, and/or supplies before your insurance plan starts paying on your behalf.

Coinsurance—A percentage of the cost that your insurance requires you to pay for your medical services, prescriptions, and/or supplies.

Copay—A fixed amount that your insurance plan assigns to specific covered services that you are required to pay for those specific medical services, prescriptions, and/or supplies.

Out of Pocket—The amount you will have to pay for covered medical services performed in a plan year. After you paid the amount assigned as your out-of-pocket limit by your health plan, the health plan may cover 100 percent of your covered medical benefits. Your copays, deductible, and coinsurance **may or may not** apply to your out-of-pocket charges. You will have to check with your health plan to find out how much applies toward the out-of-pocket maximum.

Accept Assignment—A contractual agreement between Medicare and your doctors, providers, facilities, and/or suppliers to forward the bill directly to Medicare. They will accept the contracted "agreed-upon" amount for your services paid by Medicare and will not bill you for the cost difference. They agree to only collect or to bill you for the Medicare deductible and your 20 percent coinsurance (cost share) that is applicable after the deductible is paid. You are also notified if a benefit is not covered by Medicare and given the option to accept or decline the service by providing you an advance beneficiary notice (ABN).

Advance Beneficiary Notice (ABN)—This notice is required to be given to the patient who has original Medicare by your medical providers, medical facilities, and/or suppliers to inform the patient in advance that a service may not be covered by Medicare. This notice gives the patient several options regarding services and includes the reason for a possible denial of services. Please refer to **chapter 1** for a detailed explanation of the ABN.

CHAPTER 1

What Is Medicare?

Medicare is a single-payor, federal health insurance program for people who are sixty-five or older, certain younger people with disabilities, and people with end-stage renal disease. Medicare was created in 1966 and is administered by the federal government. For the past five decades, this insurance program has been funded by you, the American taxpayer.

- The government uses the payroll tax (FICA) to fund Medicare, which is based on a percentage calculation of your salary. This percentage is deducted from your wages, and your employer matches the contributions and sends this tax to the Internal Revenue Service (IRS). Your employer forwards and reports your wages to the Social Security Administration.
- If you are self-employed, you pay the IRS the employer *and* employee portion of the Medicare estimated tax on a quarterly basis, along with social security and income tax.
- Once you are eligible for Medicare, the federal government will pay for 100 percent of your Medicare Part A premiums and 75 percent of the cost of your Medicare Part B premium if you meet the following criteria:
    - You have worked forty quarters (ten years).
    - You must see only Medicare-approved doctors and medical practitioners or use a facility that is approved and contracts with Medicare. This is called "accept assignment."

- Medicare coverage is based on federal and state laws. Medicare decisions (as to whether or not something is covered) are determined by each state's insurance companies that process Medicare claims. They will decide if something is medically necessary and should be covered by their state.[1]

Medicare Consists of Different Parts

The different parts are Medicare Part A, Medicare Part B, Medicare Part C (Medicare Advantage), and Medicare Part D (prescription plan), Medigap, and Medigap Select (Medicare Select). Both individual state assistance plans and retiree plans combine to complete the Medicare coverage.[2] Each part of Medicare is discussed in detail in specific chapters.

Advance Beneficiary Notice of Noncoverage (ABN)

Not all services are covered by Medicare. If something is not covered, you will be asked to sign an advance beneficiary notice (ABN) that will explain which tests or services are not covered by Medicare, the specific reasons why the tests or services are not covered, and the associated costs of those services. Those services may include certain laboratory tests, outpatient services, skilled nursing facility (SNFABN), hospital-issued notice of noncoverage (HINN), and durable

[1] See the official Wikipedia site for Medicare, https://en.wikipedia.org/wiki/Medicare_(United_States).

[2] See the official US government site for Medicare, https://www.medicare.gov/, for the different parts.

medical equipment. The ABN will give you the following three options:[3]

- **Option 1:** If you still need and choose tests or services that are not covered or paid by Medicare, your provider or facility may ask you to pay for the test or service in advance or out of pocket while the claim is submitted to Medicare for consideration of payment. If Medicare denies the payment, then you are responsible for the cost, and you can expect no refund of what you have already paid. Submitting a claim automatically entitles you to appeal Medicare's decision.
- **Option 2:** You still need and choose the tests or services that are not covered or paid by Medicare. Your provider or facility may ask you to pay for the test or service now, but you do not want them to file a claim to Medicare. In this case, since a claim is not submitted to Medicare for denial, you cannot appeal Medicare's decision.
- **Option 3:** You do not want the tests or services that are not covered by Medicare. You are not responsible for payment, nor will a claim be submitted to Medicare for consideration. It is in your best interest to inform your doctor that you have decided not to do the requested test or service because your Medicare plan does not cover that specific test or service.

---

3 . "Your Medicare Rights," https://www.medicare.gov/claims-and-appeals/medicare-rights/abn/advance-notice-of-noncoverage.html.

It is very important to know that the ABN gives you information to make an informed choice and help you determine whether or not to receive the test or service. An ABN is not an official denial of the claim. Please remember that some of your secondary plans follow Medicare guidelines. A rule of thumb on secondary plans' coverage: if Medicare denies coverage, then more than likely, the secondary insurance will too. Always double-check your secondary coverage to see if there is an option that the plan will cover or consider payment, even if Medicare denies the service. If you choose not to have the test or service performed, please advise your medical provider. It may be something you need for your health, and the medical provider may need to change the diagnosis code or add additional codes to have the test or service covered.

Appeal Process

You can participate in the appeal process only if you elected to select option 1 on the ABN. You will need to collect from your doctor, health care provider, or supplier all the information and documentation that may help your case in appealing Medicare's denial of payment. There are five levels of the appeal process. If you disagree with a denial decision during any of these levels, you will receive a decision letter explaining how to proceed to the next level of appeal.[4]

[4] "File an Appeal," https://www.medicare.gov/claims-and-appeals/file-an-appeal/appeals.html.

Who do I contact for help or questions?

Medicare—for questions regarding:

- Benefits and claims
- A replacement card
- Authorization setup for anyone other than yourself or to call on your behalf

Contact Medicare at 1-800-633-4227 or TTY: 1-877-486-2048 or visit Medicare.gov

Social Security—for questions regarding:

- Eligibility for Medicare Part A and Part B and enrollment
- Changes to Medicare Part A and Part B benefits
- Replacement of a Social Security card
- Questions regarding your premiums for Medicare Part A, Part B, and/or Part D
- Changes or updates to your name or address
- Applying for the Extra Help Assistance Program with Medicare prescription drugs
- Reporting a death

Contact Social Security at 1-800-772-1213 or TTY: 1-800-325-0778 or visit socialsecurity.gov

(BCRC) Benefits Coordination and Recovery Center— to notify Medicare that you have other health insurance or to report changes in your insurance information.

Contact BCRC at 1-855-798-2627 or TTY: 1-855-797-2627

(BFCC-QIO) Beneficiary and Family Centered Care-Quality Improvement Organization—to report or file a complaint about quality of care received by a Medicare-approved doctor, facility, or hospital.
Contact Medicare at 1-800-633-4227 to have them give you your BFCC-QIO number or visit Medicare.gov/contacts

Department of Defense Questions on Tricare for Life benefits or Tricare Pharmacy Program
Please call TFL (Tricare for Life) at 1-866-773-0404 or TTY: 1-866-773-0405 or visit tricare.mil/tfl or tricare4u.com; Tricare Pharmacy Program at 1-877-363-1303 or TTY: 1-877-540-6261; or visit Tricare.mil/pharmacy or express-scripts.com/Tricare.

Department of Veterans Affairs—If you are a veteran and have questions regarding your VA benefits and/or Champva. Please call: Veterans Affairs at 1-800-827-1000 or TTY: 1-800-829-4833 or visit va.gov[5]

(OPM) Office of Personnel Management—for current or retired federal employees who have questions or need information about the Federal Employee Health Benefits (FEHB) program. Please call OPM Retirees at 1-888-767-6738 or TTY: 1-800-878-5707 or visit opm.

---

5 · See US Department of Veterans Affairs, https://www.va.gov/landing2_contact.htm.

gov/healthcare-insurance. Active federal employees can call their benefits officer or obtain a list from the website apps.opm.gov/abo.[6]

(RRB) Railroad Retirement Board—if you receive benefits from RRB and have questions on:

- Eligibility and/or enrollment in the Railroad Medicare
- Making changes to your name and address
- Requesting a replacement Medicare card
- Reporting a death

Please call: RRB at 1-877-772-5772 or TTY: 1-312-751-4701 or visit rrb.gov.[7]

---

6 · See OPM.gov, https://www.opm.gov/healthcare-insurance/contact-healthcare-insurance/.

7 · See Medicare & You 2018, https://www.medicare.gov/pubs/pdf/10050-Medicare-and-You.pdf, 17–18.

CHAPTER 2

What's New in 2018?

Cost-of-Living Raise: There will be a 2.0 percent cost-of-living adjustment (COLA) in 2018.[8]

New Medicare Cards: A new Medicare card will be sent to you in the mail between April 18, 2018, and April 19, 2019. You do not need to take action, other than making sure your address is current; if your address is wrong, contact Medicare immediately.

- The new card will not show your Social Security number; it will show your new Medicare number. This will not change any of your coverage or benefits.
- Once you receive this new card, please use the card and provide it to your medical doctors or facilities when receiving treatment.
    - This new number replaces your old number. Any future claims must include the new Medicare number for processing and payment of your medical claims and/or bills.
    - Medicare will provide your doctors and medical facilities a grace period until April 19, 2019 to comply with submitting your claims with the new identification number.
    - After April 19, 2019, any claims submitted with your old number will not be processed or paid.[9]

---

8 · See Social Security, https://www.ssa.gov/news/cola/.

9 · See Medicare & You 2018, https://www.medicare.gov/pubs/pdf/10050-Medicare-and-You.pdf, 2.

The Income-Related Adjustment Amount (IRMAA) and Modified Adjusted Gross Income (MAGI) are reduced for Tier 2 and above: IRMAA is the surcharge added to your monthly Medicare Part B premiums. The IRMAA will reduce the modified adjusted gross income (MAGI) on Tier 2 and up. Base level and Tier 1 will remain the same from your MAGI tax return of 2016. The changes are:

- Tier 2 for individuals MAGI went from $160,000 in 2017 to $133,500 for 2018, and for a married couple, modified adjusted gross income went from $320,000 in 2017 to $267,000 for 2018.
- Tier 3 for individuals MAGI went from $214,000 in 2017 to $160,000 for 2018, and for a married couple, MAGI went from $428,000 to $320,000 for 2018.
- Tier 4 for individuals MAGI went from above $214,000 in 2017 to above $160,000 for 2018, and for a married couple, the MAGI went from above $428,000 to above $320,000. Please refer to the table in chapter 4.

What this means is that individuals with a lower MAGI will now be put in a higher tier level, resulting in a higher IRMAA surcharge added on to the base cost of your premium for Medicare Part B. Consequently, it now takes far less income for a household to reach the top IRMAA tiers, shifting the majority of the cost of the Medicare Part B Premium to you.

Medicare Advantage Plans: Options for Medicare Advantage plans have been increasing across the country.

As a result, there will be more Medicare Advantage plans to choose from.

Medicare Part D Prescription Plans: Monthly charges for Medicare Part D prescription plans are expected to decrease slightly. Be advised that the cost of your plan may vary by location and the type of plan you choose. Of absolute importance is that you make sure your current plan still covers all your medications and compare costs before choosing a plan.

Medicare Coverage Gap Narrows: This Medicare coverage gap is known as the donut hole gap. This gap reflects the amount you and your insurance company have paid for your covered medications.

- In 2017, that amount was $3,700, which would then place you in the coverage gap. In 2018, that amount has increased to $3,750.
- In 2017, no more than 40 percent was paid of the plans' cost for covered brand-name prescription drugs. In 2018, amount paid has decreased to 35 percent of the plans' cost for covered brand-name prescription drugs.
- In 2017, generic prescription drugs paid no more than 51 percent of the cost. In 2018, this has decreased to no more than 44 percent of the cost for covered generic prescription drugs. The amount you pay toward your generic prescriptions will decrease each year until 2020, when it reaches 25 percent.

Surcharges for High Income: Some Medicare beneficiaries with a certain income level pay a higher premium for Medicare Part B and Medicare Part D.

- In 2018, the income threshold has changed, so more people will be subject to this income surcharge.
- For individuals who have earnings of $133,500 per year and couples with earnings of $267,000 per year, there will be a premium increase. Chapter 4 will further address these premiums by income bracket.[10]

---

10 · See Medicare Resources, https://www.medicareresources.org/faqs/what-kind-of-medicare-benefit-changes-can-i-expect-this-year/.

CHAPTER 3

Eligibility and Enrollments

This chapter breaks down the eligibility and different enrollments into basic categories that will make it easier to understand. Since there are a lot of categories, it can be quite confusing searching through the website. This should make it easier.

Who Is Eligible for Medicare Benefits?

- You become eligible at the age of sixty-five.
- You are eligible if you have a disability that qualifies and is approved for Medicare benefits. Certain disabilities qualify you for Medicare at a younger age, and you do not need to be sixty-five.
- You are eligible for Medicare benefits if you are diagnosed with a condition called end-stage renal disease, are on dialysis, or have had a transplant.
- You are eligible for Medicare benefits if you have been diagnosed with amyotrophic lateral sclerosis (ALS).[11]

It is not, however, as cut and dried as listed above; there are a number of specific rules and situations that determine what your Medicare benefits are, so let's start cutting through the red tape.

Eligibility Rules for Those Living outside the United States of America

To qualify, you must reside in the United States and file for Medicare Part B. The following apply:

---

11 See "Getting Started with Medicare," https://www.medicare.gov/people-like-me/new-to-medicare/getting-started-with-medicare.html.

- You must be a United States citizen.
- You must be sixty-five or older.
- You are eligible for Social Security or Railroad Retirement benefits.
- You were living in a foreign country when you became eligible at age sixty-five.

How to Enroll in Medicare after You Return to the United States

- You are eligible to enroll in Medicare Part B on the month you return to the United States and have established a new residence.
- You must enroll in Medicare Part B within three months from the time you return to the United States, to avoid a late-enrollment penalty of 10 percent on your monthly premium for as long as you have Medicare Part B.[12]

The Initial Enrollment Period

The Initial Enrollment Period for Social Security Retirement or Railroad Retirement Benefits

When you become eligible for Medicare at sixty-five years or older, you will automatically be notified by Medicare prior to your sixty-fifth birthday.

---

12 . "I'm Outside the US," https://www.medicare.gov/people-like-me/outside-us/signing-up-for-part-b-outside-us.html.

- You will receive a package in the mail from the Social Security Administration three months prior to your sixty-fifth birthday. The package will contain your Medicare card and a letter stating you are automatically enrolled.
    - This letter will explain how your Medicare plan works.
    - If you are receiving retirement benefits from the railroad, you will also receive the same package and your Medicare card from the Railroad Retirement Board.
- You will be automatically enrolled for Medicare Part A and Part B benefits only if you are receiving Social Security retirement benefits or railroad retirement benefits.
    - **It is important to know** that you will be penalized if you are eligible and wait a full twelve months to enroll. A 10 percent penalty will be assessed to your premiums as long as you have Medicare.
    - This penalty will increase by 10 percent every twelve months that you have delayed enrolling into the Medicare plan, and that penalty **will never be removed**.

The Initial Enrollment Period for Federal Employee Retirement Annuity, Union, or Other Pension Retirement Benefits

If you are not receiving your retirement benefits from Social Security or a railroad retirement benefit, you will then receive a letter three months prior to your sixty-fifth birthday.

- You then have three months prior to your sixty-fifth birthday to enroll, either in your birthday month or three months following your birthday. You can sign up at any time during the seven-month period.
- **It is important to know** that if you are eligible and wait a full twelve months to enroll, there will be a **penalty** of 10 percent added to your premiums as long as you have Medicare. This penalty will increase 10 percent every twelve months that you have delayed to enroll into the Medicare plan and **those penalties will never be removed**.

If You Are Not Automatically Enrolled in Medicare Part A or Part B Benefits:

- You can sign up at any time after your initial enrollment period starts.
- If you wait until your sixty-fifth birthday or anytime during the three months after your birthday, the Part A and Part B coverage will be delayed, and there will be a gap in your health care coverage.
    - Sign up in the month you turn sixty-five, and the Part A and/or Part B will be effective one month after signup.
    - Sign up in one month after you turn sixty-five, and your benefits will be effective two months after signup.
    - Sign up in two months after you turn sixty-five, and your benefits will be effective three months after signup.

- ○ Sign up three months after you turn sixty-five, and your benefits will be effective three months after signup.[13]

If You Are Divorced:
You can actually get Social Security and Medicare benefits from your ex-spouse's qualifying quarters earned, even if you are divorced, as long as you have been married to your ex-spouse for ten years or more. Time is measured from the date that the divorce was final. You can receive Social Security and Medicare benefits under your ex-spouse's work record, even if he or she has remarried.

If you are a widow or widower, you have to have been married at least one year before the date of your spouse's death. You can qualify for Social Security and Medicare benefits under your deceased spouse.
To meet these qualifications for Social Security and Medicare benefits, the following must apply:

- You must be unmarried as listed above.
- There is an age requirement for you, which is sixty-two years or older for securing Social Security benefits. To obtain Medicare benefits, you have to be sixty-five years old to qualify for spouse's benefits.
- Your ex-spouse must be entitled to Social Security retirement or disability benefits before you can qualify for them.

---

13 . "How to get Part A & Part B," https://www.medicare.gov/sign-up-change-plans/get-parts-a-and-b/when-sign-up-parts-a-and-b/when-sign-up-parts-a-and-b.html.

- Your benefits are based on your work quarters and are less than the benefits you would receive under your ex-spouse's work quarters.
- If you are eligible for both retirement benefits on your own work quarters as well as your ex-spouse's Social Security benefits, you will receive your benefits first. If it is determined that your ex-spouse's record is higher, then you will receive an additional amount on your ex-spouse's work record, resulting in the combination of benefits, which will equal the higher amount.

If you remarry, you cannot qualify to collect benefits further on your ex-spouse's records.[14]

Lack of Employment Quarters:

What does it mean if you have not worked enough quarters to qualify for premium-free Part A coverage?
The Social Security Administration uses your employment quarters to calculate your Social Security or Railroad Retirement Board benefits. These quarters are also known as credits and are based on your total income during the year. The year is divided into four employment credits.

- For those born in or after 1929, the requirement for Social Security or Railroad Board Benefits is forty quarters, which equates to ten years of work to be eligible.

---

[14] See Medicare.com, https://medicare.com/resources/medicare-and-divorce/.

- For those under the Railroad Retirement Board, your benefits are calculated by total calendar months, with a minimum of 360 months of railroad service to qualify you for a retirement annuity. With these minimum qualifications, you may qualify for premium-free Medicare Part A.
- If you do not have enough quarters, you could qualify under your spouse's work history, deceased or alive. To qualify, you would have to be sixty-five years of age. Furthermore, your spouse would have to have worked and earned forty quarters (equivalent to ten years of work). This will qualify for premium-free Part A; however, Parts B and D will always have a premium. If you wait to enroll until after you are eligible, you will be charged the 10 percent penalty for every twelve full months you delayed.[15]

General Enrollment Period:

If you opted out of enrolling during the initial enrollment, then you can sign up for Medicare Part A and/or Part B during the general enrollment period, which is offered January 1 through March 31 of each year.

- Your benefits will not be effective until July 1.
- If your general enrollment falls after a full twelve months, you may have to pay a higher premium for Medicare Part B.

---

15 . See Social Security Administration, https://www.ssa.gov/planners/credits.html.

    - Additionally, a 10 percent penalty will be added to your monthly premium for Medicare Part B forever.
    - The only exception to this penalty is if you should be eligible for a special enrollment period.

If you have to buy Parts A and B, you can only sign up during the valid enrollment period of January 1 to March 31. Your plan will not be effective until July 1.

Special Enrollment Period (SEP):

This enrollment period only applies to individuals covered by a group health plan. It is based on your current employment and if you were Medicare eligible during the time you were covered by your group health plan and did not sign up during your initial enrollment. The following applies to the SEP:

- You or your spouse is currently working and is covered by a group health plan through your employer or union containing more than twenty employees.
    - You can wait to enroll in both Medicare Part A and Part B.
    - You need to verify with your group plan and double check if you can wait to enroll in Medicare.

  - Be advised that if your employer has nineteen or fewer employees, then Medicare would be your primary insurance, and you should enroll in Medicare benefits when you are first eligible, to avoid the 10 percent penalty in Medicare Part B premiums.
- You will be given an eight-month SEP to sign up for your Medicare Part A and/or Part B, starting the month after your employment ends or your current group health plan terminates.
- This rule does not include COBRA insurance. If you have COBRA coverage and become Medicare eligible, the SEP does not apply.
  - You should enroll in Medicare when you are first eligible, to avoid the 10 percent penalty with your Medicare Part B premium.[16]

Delaying Enrollment in Medicare, if There Are Special Circumstances

There are probably many times when you are unsure if you should enroll in Medicare Part A and Part B. Listed below are some brief scenarios that may help you make a decision to enroll in Medicare Part A and Part B. It is always recommended that you enroll in Medicare Part A (hospital insurance) when you are first eligible. There may be special

---

16 . "How to Get Part A & Part B," https://www.medicare.gov/sign-up-change-plans/get-parts-a-and-b/when-sign-up-parts-a-and-b/when-sign-up-parts-a-and-b.html.

circumstances, and you may not be sure if you can delay the Part B benefits.

- **You are working and have a group health plan with nineteen or fewer employees:** If you are still working and you have insurance under your current job and have a group health plan through that employer:
    - If your company has nineteen or fewer employees, then you should sign up for Medicare Part A and B. Medicare would be your primary insurance, and your employer-based insurance would be your secondary.
    - If you don't sign up when you are first eligible, then the penalty of 10 percent for every full twelve months applies on your Part B premiums for as long as you have coverage.
- **You are working and have a group health plan with twenty or more employees**:
    - Check with your company's human resource department or whoever handles your company's group health insurance and verify that your company's health plan meets the IRS definition of a group health plan.
    - If it does meet IRS guidelines, then you can delay your Part A and Part B benefits and not be penalized by the 10 percent lifetime late-enrollment penalty on your Part B benefits.

- If your group plan terminates, you will have to enroll in Medicare Part A or Part B or both within eight months during the special enrollment period. Enrollment must be from the date your group health plan terminates or your employment terminates, whichever date comes first.
    1. If you wait past the eight months, then you will have the 10 percent penalty for every full twelve months that you have delayed in enrolling for Part B premiums.
    2. You could be eligible for COBRA, which is essentially continued health coverage, obtained through your current group plan, which covers up to eighteen months, with a higher premium attached.
        - You still need to sign up for your Part B benefits as soon as your employment ends, to avoid lifelong penalties, like the 10 percent penalty in perpetuity if you delay enrollment.
        - You have eight months to enroll, but this is based on the date your employment or your health plan ended, whichever happened first, despite signing up for COBRA insurance.

- **You are eligible for Part A, currently employed, and have a group health plan**

  - You are eligible for premium-free Part A and can enroll anytime you are first eligible. The coverage will become active six months from the date you sign up but not earlier than the first month you were eligible for Medicare benefits.
  - It is important to know that if you are contributing to a health savings account (HSA), you should stop contributing to it at least six months before you enroll in Medicare.
  - This will help you avoid any tax penalties.
  - You cannot contribute to the HSA when you are enrolled in Medicare, but you can withdraw from this fund to help pay for your medical expenses.
  - If you are not eligible for premium-free Part A benefits and elect not to buy it when you are first eligible, you may have to pay a penalty.
- **You are a dependent and your spouse is working and has a group health plan**
  - You are covered through your spouse's current insurance obtained through his or her current workplace.
  - If your spouse's company has nineteen or fewer employees, you should sign up for Medicare Part A and Part B. Due to the number of employees, your Medicare would be the primary insurance and your spouse's employer-based health insurance would be your secondary plan.

  - If you do not sign up when you are first eligible, you may have that 10 percent penalty for every full twelve months you wait to enroll.
  - Make sure your spouse checks with his or her employer's human resource department or the department that handles the group insurance, to make sure it meets the definition by the IRS as a group health care plan.
  - If it does comply with the IRS guidelines, depending on the situation, you can delay benefits and not be penalized by the lifetime late-enrollment penalty on your Part B benefits.
- **You are receiving Social Security, Railroad Retirement, or annuity benefits and are Medicare eligible**
  - If you are receiving your benefits from any of the above and you are sixty-five, you will automatically get Part A and Part B.
  - A package with instructions will be sent in the mail with your Medicare card, which will be mailed to you three months before your sixty-fifth birthday.
  - If you elect not to have Part B, then refer to the instructions that came with the card. Be advised if you keep the card, then Medicare will assume you want to keep your Part B benefits, and you will be charged the Part B premiums.
- **You are not receiving Social Security, Railroad Retirement, or annuity benefits and are Medicare eligible**

- If you are not getting benefits from Social Security, Railroad Retirement, or annuity, you can sign up during the seven-month initial eligibility: three months prior to your sixty-fifth birthday, the month of your birthday, and three months following your sixty-fifth birthday.
- If you are eligible for premium-free Part A and you are still employed with a group plan through your employer, you can enroll in Part A anytime after you first become eligible.
- The coverage will become active six months from the date you sign up, but not earlier than the first month you were eligible for Medicare benefits.
- It is important to know that if you are contributing to a health savings account (HSA), you should stop contributing to it at least six months before you enroll in Medicare.
- This will help you avoid any tax penalties.
- You cannot contribute to the HSA when you are enrolled in Medicare, but you can withdraw from this fund to help pay for your medical expenses.
- If you are not eligible for premium-free Part A benefits and elect not to buy it when you are first eligible, then you may have to pay a penalty.

- You could be eligible for COBRA, which is continued health coverage through your current group plan for a time period up to eighteen months, with a higher premium attached.
- Even with COBRA, you still need to sign up for your Part B benefits as soon as your employment ends, to avoid that lifelong 10 percent penalty on your Part B premiums.
- Even with COBRA, you have eight months from the date your employment ends.

Retiree Plan:

It is very important to remember, if you or your spouse is covered under a retiree plan from a former employer or COBRA insurance, to sign up for Medicare Part A and B when you are first eligible. Delaying enrolling in Medicare Part B will only penalize you 10 percent every twelve full months that you wait to enroll, which will result in a lifetime cost on your Part B premiums.

- **For Tricare Retirees or Dependents Who Are Medicare Eligible:** If you have Tricare and are a retiree service member, spouse, or dependent child:
  - Immediately sign up for Medicare Part A; you *must* sign up for Medicare Part B when you first become eligible, to keep your Tricare coverage.
  - The 10 percent penalty still applies on the Part B benefits if you wait to enroll and it exceeds a full twelve months from your initial eligibility date.

- **For Tricare Active-Duty Soldiers or Dependents Who Are Medicare Eligible:** If you have Tricare and are an active-duty service member, spouse, or dependent child:
    - You do not have to enroll in Medicare Part B to keep your Tricare coverage, as long as the service member is on active duty.
    - Before the service member retires, enroll in the Medicare Part B plan, to avoid a lapse in insurance coverage.
    - You can enroll during the special enrollment period if you have Medicare, are sixty-five or older, or are disabled.
    - If you have end-stage renal disease (ESRD), enroll in Parts A and B when you are first eligible.
- **For Veterans with Veterans Administration (VA) Benefits Who Are Medicare Eligible:** If you have veterans' benefits, you need to enroll in Medicare Part A and Medicare Part B when you are first eligible.
    - Delays in enrollment after you become eligible will result in a 10 percent penalty every twelve full months on your Medicare Part B premiums.
    - With authorization, the VA will pay for your medical benefits outside a non-VA hospital, non-VA facility, or physician. The VA would have to authorize the services, and those facilities and physicians that are VA authorized or contracted with the VA would have to provide you those services.

  - Keep in mind, you can only use one or the other (VA or Medicare) to cover those services.
  - Medicare cannot pay for the same services that are covered by the VA. The same applies to the VA; they cannot pay for services covered by Medicare.
- **For Champva Recipients Who Are Medicare Eligible:** If you have Champva, which is a benefit for dependents of qualifying veterans:
  - You must enroll in your Part B benefits to keep your Champva.
  - You must enroll when you are first eligible.
  - Delay in enrollment will cost you a 10 percent penalty on your Medicare Part B premiums and loss of your Champva benefits.
- **For End-Stage Renal Disease (ESRD) Patients Who Are Medicare Eligible:** Once you qualify after three months of dialysis for Part A, you can enroll in Part B.
  - You have a choice to enroll or not to enroll in Medicare Part B.
  - Keep in mind, to get the full benefit of Medicare, it is in your best interests to enroll in Medicare Part A and Medicare Part B to cover dialysis and a kidney transplant if given.
  - Once you are approved for Medicare under ESRD, if you were paying any penalty fee for late enrollment or delaying in Medicare Part B, this penalty will be removed when you become eligible at the age of sixty-five.

- **For those with Marketplace Insurance Who Are Medicare Eligible:** Marketplace insurance plans are a little tricky. If you are eligible for premium-free Part A, you can enroll in both when you are first eligible.
    - If you are the main or only policyholder for a family plan, contact the Marketplace insurance agent and change the household contact from just you to include your family member(s), to prevent the whole policy from being canceled for your family.
    - Do not do it online, but rather by phone. This will protect the premium tax credit for your family members.
    - If you are eligible and automatically enrolled in Medicare Part A, then you will lose any premium tax credits you are receiving, and you will be responsible for 100 percent of the premium cost for the Marketplace insurance once your Medicare part A is effective.
    - If you are still receiving this credit after your Medicare Part A is effective, then you will have to pay back these credits when you file your income tax return.
    - Always remember, delaying your enrollment in Medicare Part B after your initial eligibility will result in a 10 percent penalty in your Part B premiums for every twelve full months you delay.

For Those Who Do Not Want Medicare Part B Benefits:

- If you decide you don't want Medicare Part B coverage, even after receiving the package with your Medicare card, and if your Medicare is not yet effective, you can drop coverage. Simply return the card that you received in the mail and follow the instructions provided.
    - You will receive this card if you are automatically enrolled in both Part A and Part B.
    - Remember, if you keep the card, you will be required to pay the Part B premiums.
- If you signed up for your Medicare through Social Security, contact the Social Security Administration and drop that coverage.
    - If you decide later that you want Part B, you do have to wait for the general enrollment period of January 1 through March 31. You will have a 10 percent penalty on your Part B premiums for every twelve full months you have waited. So, if you wait twenty-four months to enroll, then you will have a 20 percent increase in your premiums. If you wait three years (thirty-six months), you will have a 30 percent increase in your monthly Part B premiums, and so on.
- If your Medicare is already effective and you want to drop the Part B coverage:
    - You will have to contact Social Security to advise you on how to send a signed request.

- ○ Once they receive it, then the Part B coverage will terminate on the first day of the month after the request is received.[17]

[17] "Should I Get Parts A & B?", https://www.medicare.gov/sign-up-change-plans/get-parts-a-and-b/should-you-get-part-b/should-i-get-part-b.html.

Disability:

Disability coverage can be a little more complicated. Below is a breakdown of the process to simplify how Medicare benefits and disability work. Everyone who is eligible and approved for Social Security Disability becomes eligible for Medicare after a twenty-four-month waiting period. There are three types of disability conditions that Social Security considers for determining coverage:

- Is your medical condition expected to improve?
- Does your medical condition have a possibility to improve?
- Is your medical condition not expected to improve?

Why are these condition considerations important?
These condition categories are important because the Social Security Administration will evaluate each and determine if you are likely to improve and go back to work. The following explains how these evaluations work with each of the categories.

How does your disability affect your Medicare Benefits?
As long as you suffer from a severe and permanent disability, there is no expiration date on your Social Security Disability benefits or your Medicare.

- You will typically continue to receive your disability benefits until you reach your retirement age.
- Your benefits will change once you reach your retirement benefits and are payable until you pass away.

- Your medical coverage with Medicare will usually continue without interruptions in your plan.

What happens if you recover from your disability?
If you recover from your disability that made you Medicare eligible, you will no longer be eligible to receive Medicare disability benefits.

- You will receive a letter from Medicare, and your Medicare coverage will end the month after you receive the notice.

How will you be notified when you are eligible for Medicare after the twenty-four-month waiting period?

- You will receive both a letter and a package that contains your new Medicare card and will be automatically enrolled for both Medicare Part A and Part B benefits.
- If you get your disability from the railroad, then your package and card will come from the Railroad Retirement Board.
    - In both cases, the letter will give you your monthly Part A cost; if you did not pay enough work quarters to qualify you for premium-free Part A, then you will have a premium.
    - The work quarters consist of forty quarters, equivalent to ten years for a job paying the FICA taxes.
    - If you have paid forty quarters, then you will qualify for premium-free Part A benefits. There is always a Part B premium. This amount will also be given on this letter.

    - These premiums will automatically be deducted from your social security check or your railroad disability annuity check, starting the month your coverage begins. You do have the option to turn down Part B.
- Keep in mind, if you turn down Medicare Part B benefit, you will be charged a penalty of 10 percent for every twelve full months you have not signed up for the Part B benefits.
- When you turn sixty-five, the penalty will no longer exist. If you were paying the penalty, then you will no longer pay that penalty on your premium.
- If you didn't sign up for Part B benefits during your disability period, then you can enroll when you are eligible by age and not have the penalty, but the rule still applies that if you delay enrollment by twelve full months, then the 10 percent penalty on your premium will start for every twelve full months you wait.
- If you wait twenty-four months, there will be an increase of 20 percent on your premium that has been calculated based on your income.

End-Stage Renal Disease:

What Is End-Stage Renal Disease?

End-Stage Renal Disease (ESRD) is a condition that is medically diagnosed when your kidneys are no longer functioning on a permanent basis. This condition requires a regular course of long-term dialysis treatment to maintain your life. You may qualify for a kidney transplant in lieu of your kidney-dialysis treatment.

ESRD and Medicare Eligibility:

You can qualify for Medicare under ESRD or a kidney transplant when you are diagnosed with this condition.

- When you enroll in Medicare for the ESRD condition, your Medicare will begin on the fourth month of dialysis, only if you receive dialysis treatments at a dialysis facility.

Can You Get Coverage Earlier than the Fourth Month?

- You can qualify for Medicare as early as the first month of dialysis if you participate in a home dialysis training program. This training program must be performed in a Medicare-approved training facility to learn how to do self-dialysis at home.
- To qualify, you would have to begin the training before the third month of your dialysis. You need to finish the training and give self-dialysis treatments.

For a Kidney Transplant, How and What Will Medicare Cover?

There are two ways Medicare will cover a kidney transplant:

1. Medicare eligibility and coverage will start the month you are admitted for a kidney transplant at a Medicare-approved hospital and includes any health care services performed that are needed for the transplant. The transplant needs to be performed within the same month of the kidney transplant admission.

2. Medicare eligibility and coverage can start up to two months prior to the kidney transplant. This applies only if the transplant was delayed two months after the admission for that transplant and the delay is due to health care–related services that were required prior to the transplant.

Does Medicare Terminate after a Transplant?

- If your only qualification for Medicare was based solely on having an ESRD medical condition, then yes, after you have a transplant, Medicare will end. This only applies if you are currently not eligible for Medicare due to your age.
- If you discontinue your dialysis treatments, then Medicare will end twelve months after the month you discontinue your treatments.
- If you have a kidney transplant, then Medicare will end thirty-six months after the month you have your transplant.
    - There is a thirty-month separate coordination period each time you enroll in Medicare for an ESRD condition.
    - In the event that you need to be placed back on dialysis thirty-six months after a kidney transplant, due to kidney failure, then your Medicare coverage will start immediately.
    - You do not have to wait the three months as you did initially to be eligible for Medicare to start dialysis. This also includes receiving another transplant.

Amyotrophic Lateral Sclerosis (ALS):

What Is Amyotrophic Lateral Sclerosis (ALS)?

Amyotrophic lateral sclerosis (ALS), also known as Lou Gehrig's disease, is a progressive neurodegenerative disease. It affects the nerve cells in the brain and spinal cord. This disease causes muscle weakness. Muscle deterioration can affect swallowing and breathing and can progress in later stages to paralysis. Unfortunately, this will eventually lead to death.

How Do I Qualify for Medicare if I Am Diagnosed with This Condition?

If you are diagnosed with ALS, you can qualify for the Social Security Administration's Compassionate Allowance Program.

- You can apply for this program with either the Social Security Administration or the Railroad Retirement Board as soon as you get diagnosed with ALS by your doctor.
- Your claim will be fast-tracked through the system for immediate approval of your Social Security Disability benefits or Railroad Retirement Board Disability. Make sure all your paperwork is completed and your medical records validate the diagnosis of ALS, including the neurological findings from your physician that he or she used to make this diagnosis.
- The twenty-four-month waiting period to get Medicare is waived, and you will automatically get Medicare Part A and Part B the month your disability begins.

Do I Get Premium-Free Medicare Part A Benefits and Premium-Free Part B Benefits?

The rule still applies on the Medicare premium-free Part A benefits.

- If you did not pay enough work quarters to qualify for premium-free Part A, you will have to pay a premium.
- The work quarters consist of forty quarters, equivalent to ten years in a job paying the FICA taxes.
- If you have paid forty quarters, then you will qualify for premium-free Part A benefits. You will always pay a Part B premium. This amount will also be determined and provided in a letter.
- These premiums will automatically be deducted from your social security check or your railroad disability annuity check, beginning on the month that your coverage begins.
- You do have the option to turn down Medicare Part B.
- Be advised, if you decide to turn down Medicare Part B benefits, you will be charged a penalty of 10 percent for every twelve full months you have not elected to sign up for Part B benefits.[18]

---

18 . "I Have a Disability," https://www.medicare.gov/people-like-me/disability/getting-medicare-disability.html.

CHAPTER 4

Medicare Premiums and Cost

Medicare Premiums and Assistance:

Your premiums are based on your modified adjusted gross income (MAGI), as reported to the IRS via your tax return, going back two years. For example, 2018 premiums are based on your 2016 tax return. You will receive a letter notifying you that you will have to pay a higher premium and will have an explanation as to why your premiums are higher.

How are the premiums determined by the federal government?

- The Medicare Part A premiums are covered 100 percent by the federal government only if you paid your forty quarters, equivalent to ten years of working and paying FICA (Federal Insurance Contribution Act) taxes.
    - If you worked thirty to thirty-nine quarters, your 2018 premium will cost you $232 per month for Medicare Part A.
    - If you worked less than thirty quarters, then your 2018 premium will cost you $422 per month for Medicare Part A.
- Medicare Part B premiums consist of the federal government paying 75 percent of the cost, leaving you to pay 25 percent of the cost of your premiums.
    - You would have had to pay forty quarters, equivalent to ten years of working and paying FICA taxes, to qualify for this.
    - Most people will qualify for the base-level 2018 premium of $134 for the Part B benefi t or less, depending on income level.

- Other people will pay more for their Part B premiums, based on their modified adjusted gross income from 2016.
    - This is determined by the income level they fall under, which will put most of the cost on you and not on the federal government.

There are five income tier levels, and your modified adjusted gross income from 2016 will determine your 2018 premiums.

- If your income exceeds by just one cent the amount listed in the income tier level, you will be moved to the next higher tier level.
- For each increase in the tier levels, the percentage of the cost of your Part B premiums will be adjusted to put most of the cost on you and less on the federal government.
- This is determined by using an income-related monthly-adjustment-amount sliding scale known as the IRMAA.
    - This law was enacted through the Affordable Care Act that requires individuals with a higher income to pay a higher premium for their Part B and Part D benefits.
    - This takes into account your tax-filing status, the modified adjusted gross income, and the income-related monthly adjustment amount (IRMAA sliding scale), which is a set percentage for each income level.
    - See the following table to determine what your Medicare Part B and Part D premiums will cost you.

Table 1: Baseline and Tier Level 1–4

Baseline If You Filed as Individual or Jointly as a Married Couple	**Monthly Premium Part B Amount**	**Monthly Premium Part D Prescription Amount**	**Premium Cost Percent Divided by the Government and You**
File as an individual with modified adjusted gross income of ***$85,000 or less***	2018 premium ***$134.00***	2018 plan premium: ***monthly***	Federal government will pay **75 percent** of the Part B premium and leave you to pay **25 percent** of the cost
File as a married couple with modified ad-justed gross income of ***$170,000*** or less	2018 premium ***$134.00*** per individual	2018 plan premium per individual: ***monthly***	
File as married and a separate tax return with modified adjusted gross income of ***$85,000*** or less	2018 premium ***$134.00*** per individual	2018 plan premium: premium per indi-vidual: ***monthly***	
Tier 1 If You Filed as Individual or Jointly as a Married Couple	**Monthly Premium Part B Amount**	**Monthly Premium Part D Prescription Amount**	**Premium Cost Percent Divided by the Government and You**
File as an individual and your modified adjusted gross income is ***$85,000*** to ***$107,000***	2018 premium ***$134.00*** plus ***$53.50***. Monthly total: ***$187.50***	2018 plan pre-mium plus ***$13.00*** monthly	Federal government will pay **65 percent** of the Part B premium and leave you to pay **35 percent** of the cost
File as a married couple with a modified adjusted gross income above ***$170,000*** to ***$214,000***	2018 premium ***$134.00*** plus ***$53.50*** per individual Monthly total per individual: ***$187.50***	2018 plan premium plus ***$13.00*** per Individual monthly	
File as married with a separate tax return and with a modified adjusted gross income above ***$85,000***	2018 premium ***$134.00*** plus $294.60 Monthly total: ***$428.60***	2018 plan premium and ***$74.80*** per individual monthly	Federal government pays **20 percent** of the Part B premium, leaving **20 percent** to you.

Tier 2 **If You Filed as Individual or Jointly as a Married Couple**	**Monthly Premium Part B Amount**	**Monthly Premium Part D Prescription Amount**	**Premium Cost Percent Divided by the Government and You**
File as an individual with your modified adjusted gross income above ***$107,000*** to ***$133,500***	2018 premium ***$134.00*** plus ***$133.90;*** total ***$267.90*** monthly	2018 plan premium plus ***$33.60*** monthly	Federal government will pay **50 percent** of the Part B premium and leave you to pay **50 percent** of the cost.
File as married couple with your modified adjusted gross income above ***$214,000*** to ***$267,000***	2018 premium ***$134.00*** plus ***$133.90*** per individual; total ***$267.90*** per individual monthly	2018 plan premium plus ***$33.60*** per individual monthly	
File as married and a separate tax return with modified adjusted Gross income above ***$85,000***	2018 premium ***$134.00*** plus ***$294.60;*** total ***$428.60*** monthly	2018 plan premium and ***$74.80*** per individual monthly	Federal government pays **20 percent** of the Part B premium, leaving **20 percent** to you.
Tier 3 If You Filed as Individual or Jointly as a Married Couple	**Monthly Premium Part B Amount**	**Monthly Premium Part D Prescription Amount**	**Premium Cost Percent Divided by the Government and You**
File as an individual with your modified adjusted gross income above ***$133,500*** to ***$160,000***	2018 premium ***$134.00*** plus ***$214.30;*** total *$348.30* monthly	2018 plan premium plus ***$54.20*** monthly	Federal government will pay **35 percent** of the Part B premium and leave you to pay 65 percent of the cost.
File as a married couple with your modified adjusted gross income above ***$267,000*** to ***$320,000***	2018 premium ***$134.00*** plus ***$214.30*** per individual; total ***$348.30*** per individual monthly	2018 plan premium plus ***$54.20*** per individual monthly	
File as married and a separate tax return with modified adjusted gross income above ***$85,000***	2018 premium ***$134.00*** plus ***$294.60;*** total ***$428.60*** monthly	2018 plan premium and ***$74.80*** per individual	Federal government pays **20 percent** Part B premium, leaving **20 percent** to you.

Tier 4 If You Filed as Individual or Jointly as a Married Couple	**Monthly Premium Part B Amount**	**Monthly Premium Part D Prescription Amount**	**Premium Cost Percent Divided by the Government and You**
File as an individual with your modified adjusted gross income above ***$160,000***	2018 premium ***$134.00*** plus ***$294.60;*** total ***$428.60*** monthly	2018 plan premium plus ***$74.80*** monthly	Federal government will pay **20 percent** of the Part B premium and leave you to pay **80 percent** of the cost.
File as a married couple with your modified adjusted gross income above ***$320,000***	2018 premium ***$134.00*** plus ***$294.60*** per individual; total ***$428.60*** per individual monthly	2018 plan premium plus ***$74.80*** per individual monthly	
File as married and a separate tax return with modified adjusted gross income above ***$85,000***	2018 premium ***$134.00*** plus ***$294.60*** per individual; total ***$428.60*** monthly	2018 plan premium and ***$74.80*** per individual monthly	Federal government pays **20 percent** Part B premium, leaving **20 percent** to you.

What can you do to plan ahead to keep your MAGI under the threshold for the Medicare premium surcharges?

- It is very important to remember that the IRMAA premium surcharge is based on your MAGI from your tax return of two years prior.
    - For 2018, the MAGI will be from your 2016 tax return.
- As you are getting closer to retirement age, before the two years prior to your Medicare eligibility, it is best to plan ahead and speak with a tax advisor or CPA. These advisors can assist you with your Roth or tax-deferred 401(k) plans. Talk with them about the restrictions and penalties that are applied to these accounts.

  - Roth contributions are currently taxed. This amount is added to your total current income now. For withdrawals after age 59½, where the Roth has been established for five years, your contributions and earnings are not taxed or considered part of your income.
  - Tax-deferred 401(k)s are currently not taxed. This is not added to your total current income. For withdrawal over the age of 59½, your contributions and earnings are taxed and considered part of your income.
- If you are a new retiree sixty-five years or over, please file form **SSA-44** to report that you have stopped working and your income is no longer what your MAGI shows on your tax return from the past two years.
  - This may help you avoid the first year of Medicare IRMAA surcharges.
  - This form is submitted to the Social Security Administration.
  - SSA-44 form can also be filed if there is a life-changing event that has lowered you MAGI from your reported tax return of two years prior. These life-changing events can include:
    1. You were single and are now married.
    2. You are now divorced and/or had an annulment.
    3. You are now a widow(er) due to the death of your spouse.

4. You are no longer employed due to retirement or being laid off.
5. Your work hours have been reduced.
6. You have experienced a loss of income-producing property due to a disaster or a similar circumstance.
7. You have experienced a loss of your pension income. This could be due to a pension default, etc.
8. You receive an employer settlement payment due to bankruptcy or reorganization of your employer.

- If you do not meet the life-changing events in form **SSA-44** then you can file form **SSA-561-U2** to formally appeal the IRMAA surcharge.
    - This is considered a "Request for Reconsideration."
    - Keep in mind that changes in your investment income, retirement withdrawals are not considered an exception on IRMAA surcharge.[19]

I recommend that you have a tax advisor or CPA look at your income and determine if it is better to have a higher income now or at retirement. This can determine if you stay below the threshold of the income tier level.

---

[19] See Social Security, "Medicare Premiums: Rules for Higher-Income Beneficiaries," https://faq.ssa.gov/link/portal/34011/34019/Article/3780/What-is-the-monthly-premium-for-Medicare-Part-B.

How Is Medicare Billing Done?

Social Security Benefits: If you get Social Security benefits, then your Medicare Part B premium will get deducted from your Social Security benefit payment.

Railroad Retirement: If you get Railroad Retirement Board benefits, then you Medicare Part B premium will get deducted from your Railroad Board benefit payment.

Civil Service Retiree: If you are a Civil Service retiree and you are not entitled to Social Security, your premiums will be deducted from your Civil Service annuity.

If You Do Not Get Social Security, Railroad Retirement, or Civil Service Benefits: You will receive a bill called a Medicare premium bill, which includes either a Part A, B, or D premium and also will include the Part B and Part D IRMAA surcharge if applicable. This bill is due on the tenth of the month.

Payment Options Regarding Your Bill:

- You can pay directly from your bank account after you set this up though your bank.
- ***Medicare Easy Pay*** is free, and you can set this up online through the Medicare website. Keep in mind that the deduction for your premiums will occur on the twentieth of the month from your checking or savings account, depending on which account you have set up for the withdrawal.

- You can pay by mail with a check or money order with the coupon from your bill.
- You can pay by credit card or debit card. You will just need to provide the information on your payment coupon from your Medicare bill. Do not forget to sign it and mail it back to the following address:

Medicare Premium Collection Center
P.O. Box 790355
St Louis, MO 63179-0355

For bills from Railroad Retirement Board, premium payments must be mailed to:

RRB, Medicare Premium Payments
P.O. Box 979024
St Louis, Mo 63194-9000

Types of Medicare Premium Bills You May Receive: There are different types of bills you may receive. Here are some tips for you to identify and determine if this is a bill or just a notification.

- Always locate the box in the upper-right corner and see what is printed. If it states:
    - **THIS IS NOT A BILL** – Your premium payment will be automatically deducted from your bank account each month. You do not need to do anything.

- **FIRST BILL** – This is your very first bill or you have paid your last bill in full. Make sure you send in a payment for the total amount shown by the monthly due date on the twenty-fifth. If you receive the bill after that date, the payment is due on the twenty-fifth of the next month.
- **SECOND BILL** – Your payment was not received by the twenty-fifth of the month. Send in your payment with the total amount due by the twenty-fifth of the next month.
- **DELINQUENT BILL** – Your payment was not received by the date of the second bill. Pay the total amount by the twenty-fifth of the next month to avoid losing your Medicare benefits.

Call the Social Security Office at 1-800-772-1213 or TTY: 1-800-325-0778 if you have any questions about the bill you received or if your benefits are still active.[20]

---

20 . "Pay Part A & Part B Premiums," https://www.medicare.gov/your-medicare-costs/paying-parts-a-and-b/pay-parts-a-and-b-premiums.html.

CHAPTER 5

Medicare Savings Programs/State Assistance Programs

State Assistance Programs:

There are state Medicare savings programs available to help pay or assist you with the cost of your Part A and B benefits. You are highly encouraged to apply, even if you do not think you will qualify. The information listed below is what is valid as of January 1, 2018 but may change periodically throughout the year. You can apply or call your state Medicaid program to apply for the Medicare savings programs listed below.

Qualified Medicare Beneficiary Program, Known as QMB:

This program will help pay for your Part A and Part B premiums, deductibles, coinsurance, and copayments.

- When you are on this program, Medicare providers cannot bill you for the deductible or coinsurance that Medicare does not cover.
- You must see a physician who is contracted and accepts assignment with Medicare for this program.
- There is an exception to this program: outpatient prescription drugs.
    - Your pharmacist may and can charge you up to the limited amount of your prescriptions but no more than $3.70 in 2018 for any prescription drugs covered by Medicare Part D.

How Do You Qualify for This Program?

The QMB income and resource limit for 2018 is based on your income being below the 2018 federal poverty level at 135 percent. The income level is different in Alaska and Hawaii and is determined by your family size:

- For 2018, the monthly income limit for an individual is $1,025.
- If you are married, the monthly income limit is $1,374.
- For 2018, for an individual the resource limit is $7,390.
- If married, the resource limit is $11,000.

What is considered in the resource limit?

- Checking or savings account balances
- Any stocks or bonds you have

What is not included in the resource limit?

- Your house or home
- One vehicle you own
- Your burial plot
- Up to $1,500 of money saved for a burial expense
- Any furniture you own
- Any other household and personal items you have

Specified Low-Income Medicare Beneficiary Program, Known as SLMB:

This program helps pay for Medicare Part B premiums only, not the Medicare Part A premiums.

How do you qualify for this program?

- For 2018, the SLMB qualifying monthly income for an individual is $1,226.
- If you are married, the monthly income limit is $1,644.

- For 2018, the individual resource limit is $7,390.
- If married, the resource limit is $11.090.

What is considered in the resource limit?

- Checking or savings account balances
- Any stocks or bonds you have

What is not included in the resource limit?

- Your house or home
- One vehicle you own
- Your burial plot
- Up to $1,500 of money saved for a burial expense
- Any furniture you own
- Any other household and personal items you have

Qualifying Individual Program, Known as QI:
This program help pays for Medicare Part B premiums only, not the Medicare Part A premiums.

How do you qualify for this program?
To qualify for this program, you must apply every year. Individuals that have qualified for this program are prioritized to be approved before new and first-time applicants. This program evaluates applications on a first come, first served basis. If you qualified for Medicaid, you cannot get this QI benefits.

How do you qualify for this program?

- For 2018, QI monthly income for an individual is $1,377.
- If you are married, the monthly income is $1,847.

- For 2018, the individual resource limit is $7,390.
- If you are married, the resource limit is $11,090.

What is considered in the resource limit?

- Checking or savings account balances
- Any stocks or bonds you have

What is not included in the resource limit?

- Your house or home
- One vehicle you own
- Your burial plot
- Up to $1,500 of money saved for a burial expense
- Any furniture you own
- Any other household and personal items you have

Qualified Disabled and Working Individuals Program (QDWI):

This program helps pay for the Medicare Part A premiums only, not the Medicare Part B premiums.

How do you qualify for this program?

- You are under the age of sixty-five and are disabled but currently working.
- You went back to work and lost your premium-free Part A benefit.
- You are not currently getting state medical assistance of any kind.
- You meet the 2018 individual monthly income of $4,105 or the married couple monthly income of $5,499.

- You also meet the 2018 individual resource limit of $4,000 or the married couple resource limit of $6,000.

What is considered in the resource limit?

- Checking or savings account balances
- Any stocks or bonds you have

What is not included in the resource limit?

- Your house or home
- One vehicle you own
- Your burial plot
- Up to $1,500 of money saved for a burial expense
- Any furniture you own
- Any other household and personal items you have

Program of All-Inclusive Care (PACE):

This is a Medicare and Medicaid program that only available in some states that offer this program under Medicaid for long term care.

- You can leave PACE at any time.
- This program helps organize and provide care services in your home, the healthcare community and at the PACE center. This program helps individuals with their health care needs, and is an alternative to going to a nursing home or other facility. You must use PACE preferred doctors, specialists or other providers in your community. PACE centers have to meet the state and federal requirements, and this place is usually where you will receive your care.

How do I apply?

To apply for PACE, you can contact your local Medicaid office or search online via their website for a PACE program near you.

How much does this program cost?

- The cost of PACE depends on your financial situation. If you are already approved for Medicaid, then you will not pay a monthly premium for your long-term-care portion of the PACE benefits.
- You do not need to be enrolled in Part D prescription services. You will get your necessary medications from your PACE program. Keep in mind, if you enroll in a separate prescription drug plan, you will be disenrolled from your PACE program and drug plan through PACE. There is no deductible or copayment for any medications, services, or any care approved by your PACE health care team.
- If you **did not get approved** or qualify for Medicaid but you have Original Medicare, then you will have a monthly premium for the long-term-care portion and the Medicare Part D drug portion associated with the PACE benefit. There is no deductible or copayment for any medications, services, or any care approved by your PACE health care team.
- PACE can be purchased if you do not have Medicare or Medicaid.

Extra Help Program:

Extra Help is a program to help people with limited income resources in paying for Medicare Part D prescription plan premiums, deductibles, and coinsurance.

- You can qualify for Extra Help for your Medicare Part D prescription drug coverage if you qualify for the QMB, SLMB or QI program.
- You can contact the Social Security office at 1-800-772-1213 to apply for this program.[21]

[21] "Medicare Savings Programs," https://www.medicare.gov/your-medicare-costs/help-paying-costs/medicare-savings-program/medicare-savings-programs.html.

CHAPTER 6

Medicare Part A and Coverage

Medicare Part A benefits and coverage can be complex. The following coverage breakdown will make it easier to understand the various forms of coverage. Medicare Part A benefits cover inpatient hospital care, which includes admission to a hospital where you have stayed twenty-four hours of more.

- This includes admission to inpatient rehabilitation facilities, long-term care hospitals, inpatient mental health care, skilled nursing facility care, nursing home care, hospice, and home health services.

What is the deductible for Medicare Part A?

For 2018, the Medicare Part A deductible is $1,340. This deductible is subject to change every year.

- Medicare considers each inpatient admission a **benefit period**. Each admission requires you to pay a $1,340 deductible. For example, if you are admitted to any of the above facilities four times in the year. You will pay the deductible of $1,340 individually for each of the four admissions, for a total of $5,360.

Below breaks down inpatient admission coverage:

- The $1,340 deductible is your cost per each inpatient benefit admission.
- For days 1–60 in the inpatient facility, you will pay a $0 coinsurance for each benefit period. Medicare will **100 percent** cover the cost for those days after you pay the $1,340 deductible.

- For days 61–90, you will pay $335 coinsurance per day for each benefit period. Anything over the $335 per day Medicare will cover. Keep in mind, you are still responsible for the $1,340 deductible.
- For day 91 and beyond, you are responsible for 100 percent of the cost for this benefit admission. Medicare pays nothing. You can choose to use your sixty lifetime reserve days.

What are Medicare reserve days, and how does this work?
Medicare gives you an additional sixty reserve days that you can use during your lifetime.

  - If you elect to use these days, then you pay $670 per reserve day, and Medicare will cover the rest.
  - Once the reserve days are used up, you are responsible for 100 percent of the cost.
  - These reserve days do not restart with a new benefit admission.
  - If you do not want to use your reserve days on an admission, you must notify the hospital ninety days prior to your being discharged from the inpatient facility.
- There must be sixty days between a discharge and admission to be considered a new benefit admission.

Here is an easy way to remember this benefit coverage:

- Sixty days – Medicare will pay 100 percent of inpatient coverage after you pay the $1,340 deductible for each benefit admission.

- Sixty days – It must be sixty days between a discharge and an admission to be considered a new benefit admission. The deductible does apply for each benefit admission.
- Sixty days – The total number of reserve days that you can use for your lifetime. These do not renew once they have been used.

When selecting a Medigap or a Medicare Advantage plan, review the insurance policy and see how they cover inpatient deductibles, daily coinsurance, and reserve days.

Mental Health:

Medicare covers mental health benefits for admission into an inpatient freestanding psychiatric hospital or a general hospital that treats mental health conditions. The difference between the inpatient hospital admissions and a freestanding psychiatric hospital is that if you are admitted into a freestanding psychiatric hospital, there are 190 days per lifetime limitation that Medicare Part A will pay.

Here Is How Mental Health Inpatient Coverage Is Broken Down:

- **The $1,340 deductible** is for each inpatient mental health benefit admission.
- **For days 1–60** in the inpatient facility, you will pay a $0 coinsurance for each benefit period.

    - Medicare will cover 100 percent of the costs for those days after you have paid the $1,340 deductible.
- **For days 61–90**, you will pay $335 coinsurance per day for each benefit period.
    - Medicare will cover anything over $335 per day.
    - Keep in mind, you are still responsible for the $1,340 deductible.
- **For day 91 and beyond**, you are responsible for 100 percent of the cost for this benefit admission.
    - Medicare pays nothing. You can choose to use your sixty lifetime reserve days
- **What are Medicare reserve days, and how does this work?** Medicare gives you an additional sixty reserve days that you can use in a lifetime.
    - If you use the reserve days, you pay $670 per reserve day, and Medicare will cover the rest.
    - Once the reserve days are used up, you are responsible for 100 percent of the cost.
    - These reserve days do not restart with a new benefit admission.
    - If you do not want to use your reserve days on an admission, you must notify the hospital ninety days prior to your discharge from the mental health inpatient facility.
- Lastly, Medicare will cover 80 percent of the cost for care provided by your doctors or providers while you were in the hospital. You will be responsible for 20 percent of the Medicare-approved cost.

There is no limit on the number of inpatient admission benefits you have per year in a general hospital that treats mental health conditions. The only restriction is the lifetime limit of 190 days in a freestanding psychiatric hospital.

Skilled Nursing:

Medicare Part A will cover for a limited time, skilled nursing care in a skilled nursing facility (SNF) for certain conditions you may have. This benefit can be used for a short-term rehabilitation or a long-term stay. Each benefit period has one hundred days, but there are rules that dictate when you can restart the benefit period.

How do I qualify for skilled nursing?

- You must be admitted in an inpatient facility for three consecutive days. This includes the day you are admitted but not the day you leave the hospital.
- Your doctor has put in an order that documents your condition requiring you to be in a skilled nursing facility. This will require care from a licensed medical professional. This includes a registered nurse, physical therapist, occupational therapist, speech therapist, and audiologist who provide the care or are under the supervision of these skilled individuals.

- You require this type of skilled care on a daily basis and it is needed in a skilled nursing facility. In the instance of therapy, if you are in this facility for a specific therapy and receive the services five or six times a week and not daily, the care is categorized as daily and will be covered.
- You have an ongoing condition that was treated during your inpatient three-day hospital stay. This condition does not have to be the one that got you admitted to the hospital but the one that requires skilled care. It will be covered by Medicare.
- If a new condition arises while you are in the skilled nursing facility, Medicare **may cover** that condition.
- These services at the skilled nursing facility must be what Medicare calls "reasonable and necessary" treatment for your medical condition. Medicare determines if they will cover the cost or not.
- Lastly, you must get these services at a Medicare-certified skilled nursing facility. That means they must be contracted with Medicare and accept assignment.

How does Medicare cover skilled nursing facility?

- Medicare coverage begins the day you start getting treatment at a skilled nursing facility.
    - Medicare will cover up to one hundred days per benefit admission.
    - If you use all your one hundred days, then your benefit must end before you can start a new benefit period.

- If your treatment at the skilled nursing facility ends and is less than thirty days, you do not need a qualifying three-day admission if you should require additional skilled nursing care.
    - Since the gap between the SNF care is less than sixty days in a row, it is considered the same benefit period.
    - The maximum coverage would be the amount of unused days from that original benefit period.
- If your care from the skilled nursing facility ends and is over thirty days but less than sixty, you would need to be admitted at an inpatient hospital, and a three-day qualifying stay is necessary to get the benefit again.
    - The admission condition does not have to be the same one as the last inpatient admission condition.
    - The hundred-day coverage would not restart, if the break from the skilled nursing facility is less than sixty days.
    - You would qualify for the current benefit admission and use the remainder of unused days from that benefit period.
- If your break is sixty days or more from a skilled nursing facility, you will need a qualifying three-day admission into a hospital, so your skilled nursing facility benefit can restart, and you will have one hundred days of coverage for this benefit.
- There has to be sixty days in between each benefit period in order for that benefit to restart with one hundred days.

How does Medicare cover the skilled nursing facility benefit?

- **For days 1–20**, there is no cost to you for each benefit period.
- **For days 21–100**, there is a $167.50 daily cost to you for each benefit period.
- **For days over 100**, you will be responsible for 100 percent of the cost of the benefit period.

There is no limit on how many benefit periods you can have. It is important to look at other resources for assistance in payment.

- Check with your state to see if you can qualify for benefits with Medicaid. Medicaid has a nursing home benefit or PACE (Programs of All-Inclusive Care for the Elderly).

If you have insurance coverage through your employer or spouse's employer or insurance through the union you belong to:

- Check with the health benefits administrator in your company's human resources department to verify what your insurance plan covers.
- If you have a Medigap supplement plan, make sure you check on coverage for days 21–100 for skilled nursing facilities coinsurance.
- If you want to enroll in a Medigap plan, please review the coverage on each plan to see which one provides the most coverage for skilled nursing facilities.

Home Health Services:

Medicare Part A and Part B will pay for a wide range of health benefits and social services that can be provided at home.

- These services will assist the patient with part-time or intermittent skilled nursing care.
- These services include medical assistance to people with disabilities, nursing services, social services, physical therapy, occupational therapy, speech therapy, injectable osteoporosis drugs, and help with essential activities for everyday living.

How do you qualify for home health services?

- You have to be homebound.
  - Homebound means your doctor has determined that leaving your home will be harmful to your health.
  - Furthermore, you also need assistance from a person or from a device like a wheelchair, walker, or any other equipment. This makes it highly difficult or impossible to leave your home unassisted.
- You require skilled care on a part-time or intermittent basis, not just for having your blood drawn.
  - If you require care on a full-time basis, then you do not qualify for home health.
  - This care can include skilled nursing on an ongoing or intermittent timeframe.
  - It can be once a day, two to four times per week, or once every sixty days.

  - Medicare can cover services up to seven days a week, but no more than eight hours per day and twenty-eight hours per week.
  - You may need physical, occupational, or speech therapy by a licensed therapist.
  - This treatment has to have an expectation of improvement in a reasonable timeframe.
- Your doctor will have to sign paperwork for home health that certifies that you are homebound and require intermittent skilled medical care.
  - The paperwork that your doctor is signing outlines his or her plan of care, which the doctor is required to review and validate on a regular basis.
  - Homebound diagnosis, doctor's treatment plan, and certification can all be included in one certification form with your doctor's signature, to be forwarded to Medicare.
- Medicare requires you to do a face-to-face meeting with your doctor, nurse practitioner, or physician's assistant.
  - The face-to-face meeting has to be done within ninety days of starting home health services.
  - It can also be done within thirty days of starting home health services.
  - The documentation needed on this face-to-face visit has to state and confirm that you are homebound and require skilled care and meet the qualifications for this service.

- A certified Medicare home health agency must be used to receive your home health services for Medicare to cover.
- Occupational therapy alone will not qualify you for home health services. It will have to be combined with another condition to be covered.
- Certain medical supplies used by a Medicare-certified home health agency can be 100 percent covered, such as catheters and dressings.
    - If you need a wheelchair or walker, you will be responsible for 20 percent of the cost.
- Medicare usually covers 100 percent of home health services, if you meet the qualifications. Exceptions are durable medical equipment, which requires you to cover 20 percent of the cost for that equipment.

Hospice Care:

Hospice care is a program for terminally ill people, to assist them in living comfortably. This care is provided in the home by specially trained professionals and caregivers.

- This care includes counseling, physical care, medications and drugs, equipment and supplies related to the terminal illness, and conditions that are related to that illness.
- Hospice benefit allows you to have care for two ninety-day benefit periods.
- After that, you can continue with unlimited sixty-day benefit periods.

- The first ninety-day period includes an evaluation by your hospice doctor, who will certify that your condition is terminal and you have six months or less to live.
- At the start of your ninety-day or sixty-day period, you will have to be recertified again that your condition is terminal and you have six months or less to live.
- Each benefit period begins with the date you start hospice and ends on your ninety-day or sixty-day period.
- You can switch your hospice provider once during any of your benefit periods.
- Your hospice doctor and nurse are available twenty-four hours a day, and seven days a week for you and your family.

How do I qualify for hospice?

- You qualify for this benefit if your hospice doctor, medical doctor, or nurse practitioner certify that your condition is terminal and you have six months or less to live.
- You accept the hospice care and reject any care to cure your illness.
- You sign a document or statement that you have chosen hospice instead of any other covered treatments for that terminal condition. The terminal condition must be approved and defined by Medicare as a terminal condition that qualifies for hospice benefits.

What does Medicare cover?

- Medicare will cover a one-time hospice consultation with a hospice doctor or a hospice medical director. This is a one-time consultation that is covered even if you do not get hospice care.
- Medicare will cover everything related to your terminal condition, but the care has to be from your Medicare-approved hospice provider.
    - Hospice is covered in the home as well as in an inpatient hospice facility depending on your terminal illness. Your hospice team will create a care plan that will include part or all of the following:
        - Hospice doctor services provided
        - Any nursing care ordered by your hospice team
        - Medical equipment, including wheelchairs or walkers that are ordered for your terminal condition
        - Medical supplies used for your hospice care for your terminal condition
        - Prescriptions or drugs needed for your pain and symptoms of your terminal condition
        - A hospice aide and/or homemaker services ordered by your Hospice team for your terminal condition
        - Physical and occupational therapy for your terminal condition
        - Speech language services for your terminal condition

    - Social worker services for you and your family
    - Dietary counseling related to your terminal condition
    - Counseling for you and your family for grief and loss
- **Short-term inpatient care** is for pain and symptom control for your terminal condition, which is arranged by your hospice team.
- **Short-term respite care** is interim care for you while your caregiver is taking time to go home and rest.
    - Medicare will pay for you to go to a Medicare-approved hospice facility while your caregiver is resting. This can include a hospital or nursing home.
    - Your hospice doctors will have to arrange for Medicare to pay.
    - Short-term respite care admission gives you up to five days of coverage.
    - You can use this benefit on an occasional basis.
    - You will have to pay a small cost for this.

What will Medicare *not* cover?

- Any treatment used to cure your terminal condition or any related illness
    - That doesn't mean you don't have the option to stop hospice.
    - If you decide later that you want treatment, be sure to advise your hospice doctor, so he or she can terminate your hospice care.

- Any prescription drugs not used for pain management and/or controlling your symptoms for your terminal condition
- Any care received by any provider or doctor not approved or arranged by your hospice team
- Room and board
    - Unless your hospice team decides you require a short-term inpatient stay or respite care.
    - Your hospice team will have to arrange this in order for Medicare to pay.
- Any outpatient care, including emergency room, admission to a hospital, ambulance transportation that has not been prearranged by your hospice team
    - If these are unrelated to your terminal condition or anything related to that condition, Medicare will not cover it. You will be responsible for the entire cost.
    - Always talk with your hospice team to arrange any services that you feel you need for your terminal condition.

What will Medicare pay, and what will I pay?

- Medicare will pay your hospice provider and waive the deductible.
- You will still have to pay your Medicare Part A and Part B premiums.
- You will pay a copayment up to five dollars per prescription for medication to control your pain and to manage your symptoms related to your terminal illness.

    - There may be an instance when Medicare may not cover a drug, but your hospice provider can contact your Medicare drug plan for coverage through Part D (if you are enrolled) to see if that plan will pay for that medication.
- Medicare will pay 95 percent of inpatient respite care in a Medicare-approved hospice facility, leaving you to pay the remaining 5 percent of the cost.
- Medicare will cover services for conditions unrelated to your terminal illness, but you will be responsible for the deductible and coinsurance.

Can I stop hospice care?

You will always have the option to stop hospice care at any time.

- Speak to your hospice team, and they will require you to sign a form that identifies the date your hospice care terminates.
- If your terminal condition goes into remission, your hospice doctor may stop your hospice care.
- If your condition worsens, your hospice doctor can recertify you with the above qualifications.[22]

[22] "What Part A Covers," https://www.medicare.gov/what-medicare-covers/part-a/what-part-a-covers.html.

CHAPTER 7

Medicare Part B and Coverage

What is Medicare Part B?

Medicare Part B benefits cover medical care performed in an outpatient setting and not as an inpatient hospitalization.

- The outpatient setting includes doctor visits, twenty-three-hour observation admission to a hospital, emergency room, X-rays, laboratory, physical therapy, occupational therapy, speech therapy, durable medical equipment, ambulance services, mental health services, mental health partial hospitalization, and some prescription drugs administered and performed by a health care professional.
- There is a yearly deductible for your Medicare Part B benefits. For 2018, the deductible is $183. Medicare requires you to pay the first $183 out of pocket before Medicare will pay 80 percent of the cost of Medicare-approved services, leaving you with 20 percent of the cost.
- You must see a physician or provider that is contracted with Medicare and accepts assignment.

There are two groups of services that your Medicare Part B covers:

- Medical services or supplies necessary to diagnose and treat your medical condition. They should meet the medical standard practices required by Medicare.
- Preventive services to prevent illness or detect a condition in the early stages. Treatment is more successful when conditions are caught in the early stages.

Preventive services are covered by Medicare 100 percent as long as you see a doctor or provider that is contracted with Medicare and accepts assignment. There are specific guidelines for these preventive services in order for Medicare to cover them 100 percent. I will go into more detail in chapter 8 on how to maximize your coverage.

Clinical Research Studies:

Does Medicare cover clinical research studies?

- Medicare Part A and Part B will cover **some** of the costs, but not all, if you are part of a covered clinical research study. Your deductible of $183 still applies, and the 20 percent coinsurance is your cost.
- Medicare will cover services related to the research study including room and board in an inpatient admission. This would be covered regardless if you were in a research study or not.
- Medicare will cover the implantation of a device or item being tested if that implant is part of the research study.
- Medicare will cover any treatment required for any side effects or complications that are due from participation in the research study.

What will Medicare *not* cover in a clinical research study?

- Medicare will not cover a new item or service that the research study is testing. The exception would be if it is a certain medical device that Medicare would have covered if you were not in a research study.

- Medicare will not cover any free treatment that the study offers.
- Medicare will not cover any testing used to collect data. This type of testing is not used for your direct health care needs. Your deductible and coinsurance will apply to this service.

Ambulance Services:

How are ambulance services covered under Medicare?
Medicare Part B will cover ambulance transportation if your medical health is in danger by utilizing a car or any other mode of transportation to or from a hospital, critical access hospital (CAH), or skilled nursing facility (SNF). If your health may be compromised using other forms of transportation, then ambulance transportation is needed.

- You will be responsible for the Medicare Part B deductible of $183 and the 20 percent coinsurance cost of the medically approved services.
- Medicare will only cover transportation to the nearest facility available to provide you the care you need.
- If you choose to go to a different facility that is farther than the closest facility, Medicare will base their payment on the closest appropriate facility, and you will be responsible for paying the difference.
- If the nearest facility cannot handle or treat your medical needs, Medicare will pay for ambulance transportation to the nearest hospital or facility outside the area that can provide you the medically necessary care you require.

There are different types of ambulance transportation that you need to be aware of:

Emergency ambulance transportation consists of a sudden medical emergency, not something that was planned.

- Your health must be endangered and at risk if you are transported by using a car, taxi, or bus or other means of transportation.
- This emergency requires that you would need skilled medical personnel during this type of transportation.
    - Medicare will review the claim and see if it was medically necessary to utilize ambulance transportation and determine if it will be covered.

Ambulance by air transportation, which involves an airplane or helicopter.

- This may be paid by Medicare if your condition requires immediate and fast transportation and ground transportation would endanger your life because of time restraints. Other reasons to use this type of transportation are if you are unable to easily reach the hospital due to complications or delays like traffic that prevents you getting the rapid treatment your medical condition requires.

Nonemergency ambulance transportation can be covered by Medicare if your doctor writes an order specifying it is medically necessary to use an ambulance for transporting you for your medical care because of your medical condition.

Durable Medical Equipment (DME):

Durable medical equipment can be covered by Medicare.

- You must use a supplier contracted with Medicare.
- Your doctor who is writing the order for the equipment must also be contracted with Medicare to be paid by Medicare.
- **Only your doctor** can prescribe the medical equipment to be used in your home for your condition.
    - Your cost for DME will fall under the Medicare Part B deductible of $183 plus the 20 percent of the cost after you have paid the deductible.

You cannot just get any kind of durable medical equipment.

- Equipment must be durable and last longer because the equipment needs to be able to withstand repeated use.
- It has to be used for a medical reason and cannot be useful for someone else who is not ill or injured.
- It has to be able to last at least three years.

Which type of DME will Medicare cover?

- Medicare will cover rented **air-fluidized beds or other supported surfaces**. Medicare will only cover rental, not purchasing.
- Medicare may cover **any blood sugar monitors** including your **blood sugar test strips** and other supplies.
- Medicare may cover **canes** to help you walk, but Medicare **will not** cover the white canes that are used for the blind.
- Medicare may cover **commode chairs**.
- Medicare may cover **continuous passive motion (CPM) machines**.
- Medicare may cover **crutches**.
- Medicare may cover **hospital beds**.
- Medicare may cover **infusion pumps and supplies** based on the medical necessity to administer certain drugs.
- Medicare may cover both **manual wheelchairs and power wheelchairs or power mobility devices** like scooters. Power wheelchairs have to be medically necessary and do require a prior authorization in order for Medicare to pay their portion of the cost.
- Medicare may cover **nebulizers,** including the **medication** for the nebulizer machine.
- Medicare may cover **oxygen equipment** and any **accessories** that are needed.
- Medicare may cover **patient lift devices**.

- Medicare may cover the **continuous positive airway pressure (CPAP) devices** and **accessories** to treat your sleep apnea.
- Medicare may cover **suction pumps**.
- Medicare may cover **traction equipment**.
- Medicare may cover **walkers.**

Mental Health Services:

Medicare Part B will cover your mental health services and visits with a psychiatrist or a doctor.

- This includes a clinical professional like a psychologist, a social worker, a nurse specialist, a nurse practitioner, or a physician assistant.
- Counseling or therapy must be provided by a health care provider contracted with Medicare who accepts assignment, in order for Medicare to cover these types of visits.

How does Medicare cover outpatient mental health?
Medicare Part B covers outpatient mental health services provided in an outpatient office by a doctor or other health care provider.

- This includes treatment performed in a hospital outpatient department or a community mental health center.

What does Medicare cover?

- Medicare does cover a portion of the treatment for **alcohol and drug use.**

- Medicare does cover one **depression screening** per year at 100 percent, as long as it is done at your primary-care doctor's office or a primary-care clinic that will provide you with follow-up treatments and/or referrals required for your treatment. The deductible of $183 and the 20 percent coinsurance to you does not apply to this service if the Medicare guidelines are followed.
- If allowed by your state, Medicare does cover a portion of **individual and/or group psychotherapy** administered by a doctor or certain other licensed professionals.
- Medicare does cover a portion of **family counseling** only if the primary reason is to help you with your treatment.
- Medicare does cover a portion of **ordered testing** if it helps evaluate your current treatment and see if the treatment is working.
- Medicare does cover a portion of **psychiatric evaluations**.
- Medicare does cover a portion of **medication management**.
- Medicare does cover a portion of **prescription drugs** that you cannot take on your own—for example, injections or infusions.
- Medicare does cover a portion of a **diagnostic test**. Diagnostic tests include labs and/or X-rays required for the treatment for your condition.
- Medicare does cover a portion of your **partial hospitalization** if it is medically necessary.

- This is an outpatient psychiatric facility with a more structural program available in a hospital outpatient department or community mental health center.
- The treatment at this facility is more intensive than the care you could get in your doctor's or therapist's offices.
- The program take place during the day, and you do not have to stay in the hospital overnight.
- Medicare may cover occupational therapy, patient training, and education related to your condition as part of your mental health treatment.
- You must receive this care in a partial hospitalization program that is contracted with Medicare and accepts assignment.

Just remember that these services are covered under your yearly deductible of $183, and your share is 20 percent of the cost after you have paid the deductible, with the exception of the one depression screening per year that is covered.

Preventive services: There are services that Medicare reviews and might cover at 100 percent. Pay very close attention to your "yearly Medicare wellness visit." These are broken down in detail in **chapter 8.**

Surgeries and second opinions are only covered by Medicare Part B if the surgery is medically necessary.

- If the surgery is medically necessary, then Medicare will cover a second opinion or a third opinion.
- If the surgery or procedure (for example cosmetic surgery) is not medically necessary, then Medicare will not cover it or the second opinion.
- Your Medicare Part B deductible of $183 and your 20 percent coinsurance will apply.

Limited outpatient prescription drug coverage is for medication used in your doctor's office, hospital outpatient, or outpatient facility.

- Medicare Part B generally doesn't cover medications that you use at home.
- Some medications used in these facilities may not be covered under the Medicare Part B benefit but may be covered under your Medicare Part D coverage.
- You can always check the formulary of your selected Medicare Part D plan if a certain medication is not covered under your Medicare Part B.
- Your doctor can still bill Medicare for the administration, but the medication would need to be purchased and paid by you and then mailed to your doctor or provider's office or hand carried to your appointment. Your pharmacy may require some medications to be mailed only to your provider.
    - If there is a temperature requirement for your medication due to refrigeration, it may be better for you to have it mailed to your doctor's or provider's office, to have them store it and ensure the medication does not go bad.

    - You always have to check with your doctor's or provider's office if this is an option for you. It is at their discretion to agree or not to accept responsibility for your medication.
- If you are signed up for Medicare Part C (Medicare Advantage Plan) and have a prescription plan, these medications may be covered under this plan.
    - Keep in mind, Medicare may cover all or part of these drugs.
    - There may be a cost on your part for these outpatient drugs.

Medicare Part B may help cover the following outpatient medications:

Medication used with durable medical equipment. This includes medications used in your nebulizer or the medication infused through an infusion pump.

Medicare will cover antigens prepared by your doctor and administered by a properly trained individual under appropriate supervision. The patient can administer the antigen if properly trained.

Osteoporosis injectable drugs can be partially covered by Medicare if administered by a home health care nurse or aide, only if the patient meets the specific home health criteria.

- The patient's doctor or provider would have to document that the patient has a bone fracture related to postmenopausal osteoporosis and describe the specific reason why the patient is unable to learn or inject herself with the drug.
- All other options must be exhausted, including that the family and/or caregiver are unwilling to give the injection to the patient.

Erythropoiesis stimulating agents are partially covered by Medicare if you have end-stage renal disease.

- If you have anemia and need this drug to treat the Medicare-approved criteria for certain conditions, Medicare will cover the injection of erythropoietin.

Blood-clotting factors are partially covered, if you have the condition **hemophilia**.

- Medicare will help cover the cost for blood-clotting factors that you self-inject.

Injected or infused medication: Medicare will partially cover most drugs injected and/or infused by a licensed medical provider.

End-stage renal disease (ESRD) drugs taken by mouth: Medicare will partially pay for some oral medication if it is available in injection form.

- It does cover medication for intravenous use.

- Effective January 1, 2018, Medicare will now cover **Calcimimetic** medications. This includes **Parsabiv Intravenous** medication and **Sensipa**r medication taken by mouth.
- Medicare Part B already covers the oral form of this medication, but the cost changed in January 2018.
- These medications will have to be given to you by your ESRD facility or a pharmacy they work with.
- Your ESRD facility and doctor can advise you how this medication can be obtained and the cost to you.

Intravenous and tube feeding, also known as parenteral and enteral nutrition:

- Medicare Part B may partially pay for certain nutrients given intravenously or through a feeding tube for people who cannot absorb nutrients through their intestinal tract or are unable to eat food by mouth.

IVIG, known as intravenous immune globulin, administered in your home is partially covered by Medicare if you have a primary diagnosis of immune deficiency disease.

- Your doctor or provider must render a decision that it is medically necessary for IVIG to be administered in your home.
- **Very Important:** Medicare Part B will cover the IVIG alone, but the services or items needed for you to have this infusion administered will not be covered.

Immunizations, shots, vaccinations: Most are covered by Medicare Part B, based on the recommended guidelines by the Centers for Disease Control (CDC) and may be covered 100 percent.

- If you are required to have these shots outside the CDC recommendations, you may have a cost associated with the shots. There may be other vaccines that Medicare may help pay for, if it is directly related to an injury or illness that requires vaccines for the treatment of those conditions.
  - **Flu shots** are usually covered 100 percent if administered one per flu season and by a doctor or health care provider contracted with Medicare who accepts assignment.
  - **Pneumococcal shots** (to prevent pneumonia) are usually covered 100 percent if administered by a doctor or health care provider contracted with Medicare who accepts assignment. You will need to meet the guidelines for this type of shot. Medicare may cover the first shot and the second shot one year later if it is required by your doctor.[23]
  - **There are two types of pneumococcal shots** listed below with the guidelines recommended by the Centers for Disease Control:

23 . "What Part B Covers," https://www.medicare.gov/what-medicare-covers/part-b/what-medicare-part-b-covers.html.

- **Pneumococcal conjugate vaccine:**
  - This is recommended for children under the age of two, anyone sixty-five years or older, or anyone age two to sixty-four with specific medical conditions.
  - Your doctor can advise you if you have those medical conditions that require you to receive this shot between the ages of two and sixty-four.
- **Pneumococcal polysaccharide vaccine**:
  - This is recommended for anyone sixty-five years of age and older and anyone age two to sixty-four with specific medical conditions.
  - Recommended for anyone age nineteen to sixty-four who smokes cigarettes.[24]
- **Hepatitis B shots** may be covered 100 percent if you fall under a high or medium risk for hepatitis B due to your body having a lower resistance to infection.
  - These conditions can include hemophilia, end-stage renal disease (ESRD), diabetes, or other conditions that cause your body's immune system to be lowered.

---

[24] See Centers for Disease Control and Prevention, https://www.cdc.gov/vaccines/vpd/pneumo/index.html.

        - Your doctor or health care provider can advise you if you fall into these risk factors.
        - As long as your doctor and health care provider are contracted with Medicare and accept assignment, then Medicare will most likely cover 100 percent of the cost.

Transplant drugs (medications known as immunosuppressive drugs) can be partially covered by Medicare within certain guidelines.

- If Medicare helps pay for your organ transplant, then Medicare may cover your transplant drug therapy.
- Keep in mind, not all the medications will be covered under the Part B benefit. Medicare Part D prescription plan may cover these medications, even if Medicare Part B didn't cover any part of the organ transplant.
    - If you got Medicare because of ESRD, known as permanent kidney failure, and received a transplant, Medicare coverage will end thirty-six months after the month you received the transplanted organ.
        - Medicare will not cover anything after the termination of your Medicare plan.

- If you got Medicare because of your age or disability and then developed ESRD (permanent kidney failure) and then received a transplant paid by Medicare as the primary or as a secondary insurance to a private insurance, then Medicare will help cover the costs of your transplant drugs through your Part B coverage or Part D if not covered by Part B benefit.
- Keep in mind, the transplant had to be performed in a Medicare-contracted facility/hospital. There is no time limit on the coverage.

Cancer drugs taken orally can be covered by Medicare. Not all drugs are covered.

- The drugs that may be covered include drugs taken by mouth only if it is available in an injection form or is a prodrug of the injectable medication.
- A prodrug is a drug that, when taken by mouth, will break down to the same active ingredients as the injectable type of that drug.

Oral Antinausea drugs in part with chemotherapy for an anticancer chemotherapeutic regimen may be covered by Medicare.

- This is a therapeutic replacement for an intravenous antinausea drug to be given by mouth immediately before or within forty-eight hours of your chemotherapy.

Self-administered drugs in an outpatient Medicare-contracted facility may be covered by Medicare Part B.

- These drugs are given intravenously, intramuscular, or subcutaneously and are needed for the outpatient services you are receiving for an acute medical issue.

What is your cost?

Always check with your doctor or facility to make sure they are contracted with Medicare and accept assignment. Check the coverage and cost under your Medicare Part B, Medicare Part D, or Medicare Part C.

A quick tip: Medicare Part B **prescription drugs given by a doctor's office or a pharmacy** may be covered as long as they are contracted with Medicare and they accept assignment. This coverage falls under your deductible of $183, and once you have paid that deductible, you will be responsible for the remaining 20 percent cost.

Any Part B prescription drugs you get in a hospital outpatient setting will usually have a copayment. If these drugs are not covered by your Medicare Part B, you will be responsible for 100 percent of the cost. Your Part D or Part C prescription plan may cover these drugs, but the hospital has to be covered in their network.[25]

---

[25] "What Part B Covers," https://www.medicare.gov/what-medicare-covers/part-b/what-medicare-part-b-covers.html.

CHAPTER 8

Preventive Services/ Laboratory Testing Coverage

Preventive Services:

Medicare Part B covers 100 percent of preventive services based on certain conditions. Below are some specific guidelines for each screening to have the benefits paid at 100 percent.

- You must see a doctor, medical provider or utilize a facility that is contracted with Medicare and accepts assignment to get the benefit of coverage.
- Some of the preventive services may be covered 100 percent or may fall under your Medicare Part B deductible and 20 percent coinsurance.

Non-Preventive Services:

The following are considered non-preventive screening examples:

- Individuals exhibiting medical symptoms.
- Individuals who have been diagnosed with a medical condition requiring treatment or testing.
- Individuals requiring a doctor to diagnose symptoms or treat to control those symptoms.

Therefore, an additional charge is billed and Medicare Part B will process this extra charge and apply it to your deductible and/or your 20 percent coinsurance.

Note: You *cannot* include sudden illness symptoms (i.e., cough, cold, sore throat or other symptoms) or treatment of a chronic condition that requires testing, evaluation and medication management with your Medicare wellness visit.

- If you include these sudden illnesses or evaluation for an unstable chronic condition with this Wellness visit, then your doctor will bill an extra code and Medicare will not cover this extra charge 100 percent and will process this charge to your Medicare Part B deductible of $183 and/or your 20 percent coinsurance. This will be your financial responsibility if you do not have a secondary insurance to cover the balance.
- This is a common patient error, resulting in the receipt of a bill for the visit and not understanding why a wellness visit is not covered 100 percent. The wellness visit code is covered 100 percent but the additional code charged to Medicare went towards your Medicare Part B deductible of $183 and/or your 20 percent coinsurance for the sudden illness or unstable chronic condition that was treated along with your Medicare Wellness visit.

How does this happen?

- A lot patients don't want to make a second trip for two appointments so they want to bundle everything on this Medicare Wellness visit and by doing this, it is going to cost them money. Just remember to either change that Medicare Wellness visit to a sick visit or reschedule the Medicare Wellness visit.
- This will ensure that you maximize your coverage and take advantage of the 100 percent coverage that is offered by the Medicare Wellness visit. If you need to be treated for multiple issues at this appointment, just be aware that there may be an additional cost especially if you don't have a secondary insurance that covers the balance of Medicare.

Note: Do not expect your doctor to remind you of your coverage. They are in the business of taking care of your health concerns not your insurance. If you ask them to treat another problem, they will do so, per your request.

Listed below are the types of preventive coverage Medicare offers:

Welcome to Medicare Preventive Visit: This visit is not required to be eligible for the "Yearly Medicare Wellness Visit." Medicare will cover this visit only once, as a "Welcome to Medicare" preventive service. This visit is performed within the first twelve months you are enrolled in Medicare Part B. Medicare does not require you to use this visit.

- This initial evaluation with your doctor or provider includes a review of your medical history, social history, risk for depression, and your personal safety related to your health.
- You will get education and counseling on preventive services or screenings.
- A basic exam will be performed, including measurements of your height, weight, blood pressure, and a simple vision test. They review your immunizations and refer you for specific screening based on your risk evaluation.
- They will discuss, explain, or assist you in creating an advance directive. An advance directive is a document that names someone you trust to make a medical decision on your behalf if you are unable to do so.

Yearly Medicare Wellness Visit: Medicare will cover a yearly wellness visit. During this visit, you can update your doctor or provider on any changes in your mental health, so he or she can evaluate and track your changes annually. This is offered twelve months after you have had Medicare Part B, and then every twelve months after that. This service is covered 100 percent. This visit is to provide your doctor with your risk factors, so he or she can assist in the prevention of disease and/or disability. The key is finding this early enough to start treatment, for you to have a better result now rather than later.

- You and your doctor/provider will fill out a "Health Risk Assessment" together, so he or she can start this personalized preventive treatment plan to keep you healthy.
- During this visit, your doctor/provider will review your medical and family history with you to update your risk factors. Your provider will update your medication list and include a list of other doctors you are currently seeing for treatment and the medications they are prescribing.
- A basic exam will be done to update your height, weight, blood pressure, and any other routine measurements. You doctor/provider will check for any cognitive impairments, so he or she can monitor this yearly and catch any changes early for a better treatment result.

- Your doctor/provider will advise you of treatment options based on your risk factors and provide personalized health advice. You doctor/provider will schedule you for any screening services or immunizations you are due to receive.
- The provider will discuss, explain or assist you in creating an advance directive. An advance directive is a document that names someone you trust to make a medical decision on your behalf if you are unable to do so.

Medicare Screenings Offered:

Abdominal Aortic Aneurysm Screening: This test is to check for any widening or bulging of the blood vessel that runs from the lower heart to the mid abdomen.

- Medicare will cover this once (meaning one time only, not yearly) and may pay 100 percent as long as one of the following criteria is met: your doctor or medical practitioner has made a referral for the test, your provider and/or facility are contracted with Medicare and accept assignment:
    - You must have a family history of abdominal aortic aneurysms.
    - You must be a male aged sixty-five to seventy-five and who has smoked at least a hundred cigarettes in your lifetime.
    - If you are diagnosed with a condition, then this visit is no longer a screening.

Alcohol Misuse Screening and Counseling, Not Alcohol Dependent: This screening is offered once per year and may be covered 100 percent. To meet the coverage criteria, the following applies:

- Adults, even pregnant women, who misuse alcohol but do not meet the criteria for dependency can qualify for four brief face-to-face counseling sessions. The criteria are: if your primary doctor or primary care practitioner determines that you are misusing alcohol, are not alcohol dependent, and require this assistance.
- These visits must take place in your primary-care doctor's office by your primary-care doctor or practitioner. Your doctor or practitioner must be contracted with Medicare and accept assignment.
- You must be alert and competent during these visits.
- You cannot combine this visit with an illness, or it will not be covered 100 percent under preventive services.

Bone Density (Bone Mass Measurement/BMD): This test helps to see if you are at risk for bone breakage or fractures and is covered every twenty-four months and may be covered at 100 percent of the cost.

- This is for individuals who require this test due to medical necessity and a medication regimen for osteoporosis or any other condition. Medicare will consider payment if it is medically necessary and the BMD is coded to reflect that.

You are eligible if you meet one or more of the following criteria and you are at risk for osteoporosis:

- A doctor must determine by the medical history or findings that the individual is estrogen deficient and at risk for osteoporosis.
- X-rays show possible osteoporosis, osteopenia, or vertebral fractures.
- An individual is planning to start treatment or already taking steroid-type drugs like prednisone.
- An individual has a diagnosis with primary hyperparathyroidism.
- An individual is on osteoporosis drug therapy and required this test to monitor if this drug is improving or declining.
- You must have a referral written by a Medicare contract provider, and your test must be performed at a Medicare contracted office, facility, or outpatient hospital setting that accepts assignment.

Cardiovascular Disease Screening: These screenings detect conditions that may lead to a heart attack or a stroke, by running some blood tests to see if you are at risk.

- The blood test is a lipid profile; this includes your total cholesterol, triglyceride, HDL (good cholesterol) and LDL (bad cholesterol). This test is done every five years and may be covered 100 percent.

- You must have your laboratory test performed at an office, facility, or outpatient hospital that is contracted with Medicare and accepts assignment.
- If you are diagnosed with a condition, then this visit is no longer a screening.

Cardiovascular Disease Behavioral Counseling/Therapy: To help lower your risk of developing cardiovascular disease, Medicare Part B will cover one visit per year by your primary doctor or primary practitioner.

- The office visit will be performed in a primary-care setting, for counseling or tips on changing your diet to eat healthier.
- Your doctor or practitioner may talk with you about adding aspirin or other medications to your treatment plan and evaluate your blood pressure to help you lower your risk for cardiovascular disease. Medicare will pay 100 percent of the cost for this one yearly visit.
- Your doctor or practitioner must be contracted with Medicare and accept assignment.
- If you are diagnosed with a condition, then this visit is no longer a screening.
- You cannot combine this visit with an illness or it will not be covered 100 percent under preventive screening.

Cervical and Vaginal Cancer Screening: Medicare Part B may cover Pap test, Pap lab specimen, pelvic exam, and breast exam 100 percent for all women. These exams are to detect cervical, vaginal, and breast cancer. There are criteria that need to be met for Medicare Part B to cover these exams:

- Medicare Part B covers the Pap test, Pap lab specimen, pelvic exam, and breast exam for all women once every twenty-four months.
- If you are at high risk for cervical or vaginal cancer, are of childbearing age, or have had an abnormal Pap smear in the past thirty-six months, then Medicare Part B may cover 100 percent of the cost once every twelve months.
- Your doctor, practitioner, and laboratory facility must be contracted with Medicare and accept assignment.
- If you are diagnosed with a condition, then this visit is no longer a screening.
- You cannot combine this visit with an illness, or it will not be covered 100 percent under preventive screening.

Colorectal Cancer Screening: There are different types of colorectal cancer screenings used to find precancerous growths. If found early, treatment is more effective. There are different coverages applied to the different types of colorectal cancer screenings.

- **Barium Enema Screening:** This test would have to be a substitute for a flexible sigmoidoscopy or colonoscopy to be used for screening.

  - If you are fifty years of age or older, Medicare covers this test once every forty-eight months.
  - If you are at high risk for colorectal cancer, Medicare will cover once every twenty-four months.
  - Medicare will waive the deductible, but the 20 percent coinsurance applies to the doctor charges. You will have the 20 percent coinsurance and a copay for the hospital outpatient setting.
  - The doctor and facility must be contracted with Medicare and accept assignment.
  - If you are diagnosed with a condition, then this is no longer considered a screening.
- **Colonoscopy Screening:** Colonoscopy uses a thin, flexible tube with a camera at the end to look at the entire colon. You will be sedated for your colonoscopy.
  - If you are at **low risk** for colorectal cancer, Medicare will cover this test once every 120 months or 48 months after your previous flexible sigmoidoscopy.
  - If you are at **high risk** for colorectal cancer, then Medicare will pay for this test once every twenty-four months for screening.
  - If this is a screening colonoscopy, Medicare will cover 100 percent of the cost.

  - If the screening colonoscopy results in the doctor having to do a biopsy, a removal of a lesion, or removal of a growth during the screening colonoscopy, then this procedure turns from a screening to a diagnostic procedure. Medicare will waive the deductible, but the 20 percent coinsurance applies to the doctor charges. You will have the 20 percent coinsurance and a copay for the hospital outpatient setting.
  - The doctor and facility must be contracted with Medicare and accept assignment.
  - If you are diagnosed with a condition, then this is no longer considered a screening.
- **Fecal Occult Blood Test Screening:** If you are fifty years or older, Medicare will cover this lab test once every twelve months and may be covered 100 percent by Medicare.
  - The criteria for coverage is that you must have a referral from your doctor, physician assistant, nurse practitioner, or a clinical nurse specialist to qualify for the 100 percent coverage.
  - The doctor and laboratory facility must be contracted with Medicare and accept assignment.
  - If you are diagnosed with a condition, then this is no longer considered a screening.
- **Multi-Target Stool DNA Test:** This test is done at home, and Medicare may cover this every three years at 100 percent of the cost. You would have to meet all of these conditions:

- You have to be between the ages of fifty and eighty-five.
- You show no signs or symptoms of colorectal disease, including lower gastrointestinal pain, bloody stools, positive guaiacum fecal occult blood test, or a positive fecal immunochemical test and more.
- You are at an average risk for developing colorectal cancer. This means you have no personal history of adenomatous polyps, colorectal cancer, or inflammatory bowel disease, including Crohn's disease and ulcerative colitis.
- You have no family history of colorectal cancer or adenomatous polyps, familial adenomatous polyposis, or a hereditary nonpolyposis colorectal cancer.
- Medicare may cover 100 percent as long as a laboratory facility is contracted with Medicare and accepts assignment.
- If you are diagnosed with a condition, then this is no longer considered a screening.

• **Flexible Sigmoidoscopy Screening:** Sigmoidoscopy uses a thin, flexible tube with a camera at the end to look at the colon. This test is a partial exam that only views the left side of the colon. This test is easier on the individual than a full colonoscopy and sometimes does not require sedation.
  - For most individuals fifty years or older, Medicare will cover this test once every forty-eight months.

- ○ If you are not at high risk for colorectal cancer, then Medicare will cover this screening once every 120 months after your previous screening colonoscopy.
- ○ If this is a screening flexible sigmoidoscopy, then Medicare may pay 100 percent of the cost.
- ○ If the screening sigmoidoscopy results in the doctor having to do a biopsy or removal of a lesion or growth during the screening sigmoidoscopy, then this procedure turns from a screening to a diagnostic procedure. Medicare will waive the deductible, but the 20 percent coinsurance applies to the doctor charges. You will have the 20 percent coinsurance and a copay for the hospital outpatient setting.
- ○ The doctor and facility must be contracted with Medicare and accept assignment.
- ○ If you are diagnosed with a condition, then this is no longer considered a screening.

Depressive Screening: Medicare will cover one screening for depression per year. This visit may be covered 100 percent.

- The screening has to be performed in a primary setting like a doctor's office. This doctor needs to provide follow-up treatment and/or a referral for treatment.
- The doctor or provider must be contracted with Medicare and accept assignment.
- If you are diagnosed with a condition, then this is no longer considered a screening.

Diabetes Screening: Medicare may cover two diabetes screenings per year. Medicare may pay for blood tests to screen for diabetes, to see if you are at risk for diabetes, or to see if you have prediabetes. Medicare Part B may cover this test 100 percent. The diabetes screening test that is covered by Medicare is a fasting blood glucose test and/or a post glucose challenge test.

- The risk factors that make you eligible for Medicare to cover your laboratory testing for diabetes screenings are:
    - You have high blood pressure (hypertension).
    - You have dyslipidemia, which means abnormal cholesterol and triglyceride levels.
    - You have a prior blood test showing high sugar (glucose).
    - You are overweight (obese) showing a body mass index of thirty or more.
- If you have two or more of the following criteria, Medicare may cover the laboratory testing:
    - You are overweight (obese) with a body mass index between twenty-five and thirty.
    - You have family history of diabetes; this includes mother, father, brothers, and sisters.
    - You have a history of gestational diabetes, which means you developed diabetes when you were pregnant. You had a baby weighing over nine pounds.
    - You are sixty-five years of age or older.

- If you have been given a diagnosis of prediabetes, Medicare will cover two screening tests in a twelve-month period (calendar year). A prediabetes diagnosis exists when your blood sugar (glucose) levels are higher than normal but not high enough for your condition to be classified. These tests may be covered 100 percent as long as your condition is not diagnosed as diabetes.
- The doctor or practitioner ordering the test and the laboratory facility must be contracted with Medicare and accept assignment.
- If you are diagnosed with diabetes, then this is no longer considered a screening.

Diabetes Self-Management Training: This is training for individuals at risk for complications with diabetes.

- Your doctor or health care practitioner must write an order for this training.
- Medicare Part B may cover ten hours of initial diabetes self-management training (DSMT). This training is broken up into one hour of individual training and nine hours of group training.
- This training consists of teaching you how to handle, cope with, and manage your diabetes.
- This training assists you with tips to eat healthier, how to stay active, how to keep track of your blood sugar, how to take your medications, and how to reduce your risks.

- You may qualify with Medicare Part B for an additional two hours of follow-up training each year if it occurs in a calendar year after the year you received your initial training.

There are some exceptions that Medicare Part B will allow you to have individual training sessions:

- There are no group sessions available.
- You have special needs and your doctor/medical practitioner states an individual training session would be better for you based on that special need.
- If you reside in a rural area, you may be able to get this training from a registered dietician located in a different location. You would have to use a system called telehealth. Telehealth is a service using a two-way interactive telecommunication system (audio and video) with a health care practitioner.
- All providers, doctors, and facilities must be contracted with Medicare and accept assignment.
- Medicare Part B coverage for this training falls under the Medicare Part B deductible of $183. Once you have paid this amount, Medicare will pay 80 percent of the approved cost, leaving you the remaining 20 percent.

Glaucoma Testing: Medicare Part B may cover one glaucoma test every twelve months. This test is for individuals who are at high risk for glaucoma.

- A doctor who specializes in the eye has to do or supervise the test.
- He or she must be licensed and allowed to practice in your state. You are eligible for this testing if you are at high risk for glaucoma.

The high-risk criteria consist of:

- You have diabetes.
- You have a family history of glaucoma.
- You are fifty years or older and are African American.
- You are sixty-five years or older and are Hispanic.

Medicare coverage for this testing is as follows:

- Medicare Part B coverage for the glaucoma testing falls under the Medicare Part B deductible of $183; once you have paid this amount, then Medicare will pay 80 percent of the approved cost, leaving you the remaining 20 percent. If done in a hospital setting, then a copay will also apply.
- The doctor and facility must be contracted with Medicare and accept assignment.

Hepatitis C Screening: Medicare will cover one hepatitis screening test once a year if you meet certain criteria. Medicare may pay 100 percent of the cost. Your primary care doctor or medical practitioner must order this test.

The following criteria make you eligible for this test:

- You are at high risk due to current or past history of illicit injection drug use.
- You had a blood transfusion before 1992.
- You were born between 1945 and 1965.

- Your primary doctor or medical practitioner along with the laboratory facility must be contracted with Medicare and accept assignment.
- If you are diagnosed with the condition, then this is no longer considered a screening.

HIV Screening: HIV (human immunodeficiency virus) often leads to acquired immunodeficiency syndrome (AIDS).

- Medicare Part B will cover one test every twelve months for individuals who meet certain criteria.
- Medicare Part B will also cover the screening up to three times during your pregnancy.
- Medicare may cover this screening 100 percent if you are eligible.

The criteria that make you eligible are:

- You are between the ages of fifteen and sixty-five.
- There is an increased risk for individuals younger than fifteen years of age and older than sixty-five years of age.
- If you are pregnant. As stated above, Medicare Part B will cover up to three screening tests during your pregnancy.
- The doctor, medical practitioner, and laboratory facility must be contracted with Medicare and accept assignment.
- If you are diagnosed with the condition, then this is no longer considered a screening.

Lung Cancer Screening: Medicare Part B will cover one lung cancer screening per year after you have consulted with your doctor to see if this option is right for you.

- This screening would be done with a low-dose computed tomography (LDCT). A LDCT is a newer scan that takes several three-dimensional X-rays of the lungs.
    - These X-rays are very detailed and can pick up lung abnormalities the size of a grain of rice versus traditional X-rays that can only identify lung abnormalities the size of a dime.
    - The big difference is that the smaller the tumor is when it is first detected, the less likely for the cancer cells to spread to other parts of the body.
    - Your survival rate increases because there are more treatment options available to tackle your tumor. Medicare may cover this 100 percent.
- **You will have to meet all of these criteria:**
    - You are between the ages of fifty-five and seventy-seven.
    - You do not show any signs or symptoms of lung cancer.
    - You are a current smoker or have quit smoking within the last fifteen years.
    - You have a tobacco-smoking history of an average of one pack per day for thirty years.
    - You have a written order from your doctor.
    - The doctor and facility must be contracted with Medicare and accept assignment.

  - If you are diagnosed with a condition, then this is no longer considered a screening.

Mammogram Screening: Medicare Part B may pay 100 percent of the cost for one screening mammogram per year. A screening mammogram is defined as **not** having any symptoms or medical issues with your breast.

You are eligible for a screening mammogram:

- If you are a woman age forty or older. You can get a mammogram every twelve months.
- If you are a woman between thirty-five and thirty-nine years of age, you are eligible one baseline mammogram.
- The doctor and facility must be contracted with Medicare and accept assignment.

How is a mammogram covered by Medicare?

- Medicare may cover a **screening mammogram** 100 percent of the cost.
- Medicare may cover a **diagnostic mammogram**.
  - Your Medicare Part B deductible will apply along with your 20 percent coinsurance.
  - A diagnostic mammogram is when you have signs or symptoms with your breast; for example, a lump or pain in your breast.
  - The diagnostic mammogram is performed to rule out a condition based on your active symptoms.

Nutrition Therapy Services for Medical Health: Medicare Part B will cover medical nutrition therapy (MNT) services when ordered and referred by a doctor for these or other related services. The registered dietician or nutrition professional has to meet certain requirements by Medicare to provide you these services.

The MNT services may include the following:

- You will have an initial nutrition assessment.
- You will have an initial lifestyle assessment.
- You may have a one-to-one nutritional counseling.
- You may have more than one follow-up visit to monitor your progress and help manage your diet for better success.

You are eligible for these services if:

- You have a referral from your doctor or health care professional who is contracted with Medicare and accepts assignment.
- You have diabetes.
- You have kidney disease.
- You have received a kidney transplant in the last thirty-six months.

How are the nutrition therapy services covered by Medicare?

- Medicare may cover the nutrition therapy services 100 percent of the cost.
- The doctor, registered dietician, or nutrition professional must be contracted with Medicare and accept assignment.

Obesity Screening and Counseling: Medicare Part B may cover 100 percent of the cost for behavioral counseling sessions to assist you in losing weight.

- Your counseling has to be done in a primary-care setting, doctor's office.
- To qualify for this screening, you must have a body mass index (BMI) of thirty or more.
- The doctor must be contracted with Medicare and accept assignment.
- Medicare may cover the obesity screening and counseling at 100 percent of the cost.

Prostate Cancer Screening: Medicare Part B will cover one every twelve months for a prostate-specific antigen (PSA) blood test, a digital rectal exam once every twelve months.

- **Prostate-Specific Antigen (PSA):**
  - You must be a man over fifty years of age. This means one day after your fiftieth birthday will qualify you to have this test.
  - The cost of this test may be covered 100 percent.
  - The doctor and laboratory facility must be contracted with Medicare and accept assignment.
  - If you are diagnosed with a condition, then this is no longer considered a screening.
- **Digital Rectal Exam:**
  - You must be a man over fifty years of age. This means one day after your fiftieth birthday will qualify you to have this test.

- ○ Your yearly digital rectal exam along with your doctor services will be covered under the $183 deductible; once you have paid this deductible, Medicare will cover 80 percent of the cost and leave you the remaining 20 percent. If this test is done in a hospital outpatient setting, a copayment would also apply.
- ○ The doctor must be contracted with Medicare and accept assignment.

Sexually Transmitted Infections (STI) Screenings and Counseling: Medicare covers one screening every twelve months for sexually transmitted infections. This screening includes:

- Screenings for chlamydia, gonorrhea, syphilis, and hepatitis B.
    - ○ If you are diagnosed with the condition, then this is no longer considered a screening.
- If you are pregnant, Medicare will cover screenings for certain times during your pregnancy.
- Medicare will cover two high-intensity behavioral counseling sessions per twelve months.
    - ○ This counseling must be face to face and last twenty to thirty minutes.
    - ○ This counseling is for sexually active adolescents and adults who are at increased risk for getting sexually transmitted infections.
    - ○ This counseling has to be done in your primary-care doctor's office or primary-care clinic by your doctor.

- Your doctor will have to order this counseling, to be covered by Medicare Part B.
- The doctor, counselor, and facility will have to be contracted with Medicare and accept assignment.

You are eligible for these services if:

- You are pregnant and have Medicare Part B.
- You are at increased risk to get STI and your doctor has ordered the test to be done.
- You are at increased risk to get STI due to your sexual activity. This includes adults and adolescents. This group also will be eligible for behavioral counseling.

How is this screening and counseling covered by Medicare?

- Medicare Part B may cover STI screenings 100 percent of the cost.
- Medicare Part B may cover behavioral counseling sessions 100 percent of the cost as long as your doctor performs this counseling in the primary-care office or primary-care clinic and is contracted with Medicare and accepts assignment.
  It is important to note that if these counseling sessions take place in an inpatient or skilled nursing facility, then this will not be considered preventive.

Immunizations/Shots/Vaccinations: Medicare Part B may cover these services based on the recommended guidelines by the Centers for Disease Control (CDC) and may be covered 100 percent.

- If you are required to have these shots outside the recommendations, you may have a cost associated with that shot.
- There may be other vaccines that Medicare may help pay for if it is directly related to an injury or illness that requires vaccines for the treatment of those conditions.
    - **Flu shots** are usually covered 100 percent of the cost if done one per flu season and by a doctor or health care provider contracted with Medicare who accepts assignment.
    - **Pneumococcal shots** (to prevent pneumonia) may be covered 100 percent if done by a doctor or health care provider contracted with Medicare who accepts assignment. You will need to meet the guidelines for this type of shot. Medicare may cover the first shot and the second shot one year later if it is required by your doctor.
    - **There are two types of pneumococcal shots. Listed below** are the guidelines recommended by the Centers for Disease Control:
        - **Pneumococcal conjugate vaccine:**
            - This is recommended for children under the age of two, anyone sixty-five years or older, or anyone aged two to sixty-four with specific medical conditions.

  - ○ Your doctor can advise you if you have medical conditions that require you to receive this shot between the ages of two and sixty-four.
- ○ **Pneumococcal polysaccharide vaccine**:
  - ○ This is recommended for anyone sixty-five years of age and older or anyone aged two to sixty-four with specific medical conditions.
  - ○ Recommended for anyone aged nineteen to sixty-four who smokes cigarettes.
- ○ **Hepatitis B shots** may be covered 100 percent if you fall under a high or medium risk for hepatitis B due to your body having a lower resistance to infection.
  - ○ These conditions can include hemophilia, end-stage renal disease (ESRD), diabetes, or other conditions that cause your body's immune system to be lowered.
  - ○ Your doctor or health care provider can advise you if you fall into these risk factors.
  - ○ As long as your doctor and health care provider are contracted with Medicare and accept assignment, then Medicare will most likely cover 100 percent of the cost.

Smoking and Tobacco Use Cessation (counseling to stop smoking or using tobacco products): Medicare Part B will cover eight face-to-face visits done in a twelve-month period.

- These visits must be done by a qualified doctor or medical practitioner who is contracted with Medicare and accepts assignment.
- These visits may be covered 100 percent for all individuals with Part B who use tobacco.

If any of the screenings are done after you have already been diagnosed and undergoing treatment for a condition, then Medicare will not cover the services under preventive but instead cover under your Medicare Part B deductible and coinsurance.[26]

Laboratory Criteria and Restrictions:

Medicare will cover laboratory tests if they consider the service medically necessary and will review the criteria if done under preventive diagnosis. If you reviewed the preventive coverage above, there are a few laboratory tests that may be covered at 100 percent. I could only find a lipid profile every five years, a fasting glucose (sugar) maybe twice a year, PSA, HIV, and hepatitis C every year only if you meet the criteria. These tests are covered under the preventive coverage as long as you are not diagnosed with a condition. Even if your medical provider orders a group of laboratory tests and uses a preventive diagnosis code,

---

[26] . "Your Medicare Coverage," https://www.medicare.gov/coverage/preventive-and-screening-services.html.

Medicare will not cover all the tests because they are not listed as a preventive service. Medicare will only cover the tests that meet the criteria under the preventive services and will determine if those tests will be covered 100 percent. For all other laboratory tests performed, Medicare will review the claim to determine if it is reasonable and necessary for the treatment of the medical conditions and process the payment under your deductible of $183 and coinsurance.

The top reasons for Medicare to deny labs:

- The laboratory test was ordered for screening with a preventive diagnosis, but you already have a condition diagnosed and/or are being treated for that condition. Therefore, Medicare Part B will not cover this laboratory test under preventive. The Medicare Part B deductible and the 20 percent coinsurance will apply to you.
- Laboratory tests done for administrative purposes, including those required by insurance companies, business establishments, government agencies, and/or third party requests are not covered.
- The claim is denied by Medicare, and there was failure to provide the medical-necessity documentation to justify the relevant signs, symptoms, or abnormal findings needed for the medical necessity of ordering the test for the treatment of your condition.
- The test was not ordered by the treating doctor or a qualified nondoctor practitioner through documentation from the doctor's office.

- The diagnosis attached to the test and the claim sent to Medicare for processing is not listed as a Medicare-approved diagnosis for that test and is not considered reasonable and necessary. Medical documentation may be submitted for review to justify medical necessity for that test with the diagnosis.
- The test that is done exceeds the medical frequency that Medicare has set as the guideline to cover that specific test. Usually, you will be asked to sign an advance beneficiary notice (ABN), which explains that specific test that is not going to be covered. This document will list the test name, the reasons for denial, and the price of the test if you elect to have it done. You will be asked to read this document and select your option and sign the document.
    - **Option 1** – You want the test or service that may not be covered or paid by Medicare. Your provider or facility may ask you to pay for the test or service now, but you also want them to submit the claim to Medicare for consideration of payment. If Medicare denies the payment, then you are responsible for the cost or will not get a refund if you are required to pay now. By submitting the claim, you are entitled to appeal Medicare's decision.

- **Option 2** – You want the test or services that may not be covered or paid by Medicare. Your provider or facility may ask you to pay for the test or service now, but you do not want them to file a claim to Medicare. In this case, since a claim is not submitted to Medicare for denial, you cannot appeal Medicare's decision.
- **Option 3** – You do not want the test or services that may not be covered by Medicare. You are not responsible for payment nor will a claim be submitted to Medicare for consideration.[27]

If you select this option, then it is in your best interest that you contact your doctor and inform him or her that you have decided not to do the requested test or service due to Medicare's possible denial of payment.

It is very important to know that ABNs give you information to make an informed choice as to whether or not to receive the test or service. An ABN is not an official document of denial of the claim. Just remember that some of your secondary plans follow Medicare guidelines; if Medicare denies, then your secondary insurance will deny. Always check your secondary coverage to see if there is an option of coverage if Medicare denies.

27 · See Medicare National Coverage Determinations, https://www.cms.gov/Medicare/Coverage/.../Downloads/manual201701_ICD10.pdf.

CHAPTER 9

Medicare Part C (Medicare Advantage Plan) and Coverage

Medicare Advantage Plan Enrollment Period:

Medicare Advantage Plan and Medicare Part D prescription services enrollment can occur when you are first eligible for Medicare at the age of sixty-five or under sixty-five with a disability. The timeframe you first become eligible is called your **initial enrollment period**.

- You can enroll three months prior to your sixty-fifth birthday, during the month of your birthday, and also for three months after your birthday month.
    - If you have a **disability** and are under sixty-five years of age, you are eligible to sign up for Original Medicare after twenty-four months from the date your disability benefits started. You have until the twenty-eighth month after you get disability benefits to sign up for Original Medicare, Medicare Part C Advantage Plan, and/or Medicare Part D prescription plan.
- During the open enrollment period of October 15 through December 7 of each year, which will be effective January 1 of the next year. The following options apply:
    - You can switch from Original Medicare to a Medicare Advantage plan or conversely from a Medicare Advantage plan to Original Medicare.
    - You can switch from your Medicare Advantage Plan to another Medicare Advantage plan.
    - You can switch a Medicare Advantage Plan that does not offer a prescription plan coverage to a Medicare Advantage plan that does offer prescription coverage.

- ○ You can switch a Medicare Advantage plan that does offer a prescription plan coverage to a Medicare Advantage plan that does not offer a prescription plan coverage.
- ○ You can join a Medicare prescription plan.
- ○ You can switch from a Medicare prescription plan coverage to another Medicare prescription plan coverage.
- ○ You can drop your current Medicare prescription plan coverage completely.

Medicare Advantage Disenrollment Period:

Medicare Advantage disenrollment period, January 1 through February 14, is a period that you can only switch from a Medicare Advantage plan to Original Medicare. You have until February 14 to enroll in a Medicare Part D prescription plan. Your effective date on your coverage will begin on the first day of the month after your enrollment form is received.

What you should know about Medicare Part C (Medicare Advantage Plan)

- Medicare Part C is also called Medicare Advantage Plans.
- These are plans offered by private companies that contract with Medicare and are paid a fixed amount per person to provide Medicare benefits.

- This plans cover the Medicare Part A, Medicare Part B, and Medicare Part D (prescription) coverage. You have the option to opt in or opt out of the prescription coverage, depending on the plan you select.
- You still have Original Medicare, but once you sign up for these plans, you are covered under this plan. **You do not have two individual insurance coverages**.
    - Your Original Medicare is on hold unless you disenroll in the Medicare Advantage plan. The Medicare Advantage plan is the only insurance you will provide to your providers/facilities to file your claims for your services.
- If you have end-stage renal disease, you **will not** be able to enroll in this plan.
    - If you develop end-stage renal disease **after** you have enrolled in this plan, then you can keep the plan.
- If you have employer or union coverage plans, please check with your benefits administrator to have them advise you if you can enroll in the Medicare Advantage plan.
    - There is a risk if you join this plan that you could lose your coverage with the employer or union plans for yourself and your dependents.
    - If you drop your employer or union coverage, you may not be able to enroll back into this coverage.

    - Your retirement plan may switch to a Medicare Advantage plan; you must check the benefits on this plan to see if the coverage offered is what you need. Just remember, if you opt out of this option, it may drop you out of your employee retirement coverage.
- You will still have to pay your Medicare Part B premium and Part A if you are required to pay for Part A.
- You may have a premium in addition with your Medicare Advantage Plan, depending on the coverage.
- Your plan may have a copayment, deductible, or coinsurance cost related to treatment coverage.
- You may have a higher cost share for certain services like chemotherapy or dialysis and other services.
- These plans may provide coverage for vision, hearing, and dental care that Original Medicare does not cover.
- You may need a preauthorization for services such as high-cost infusions, injections, an MRI, or more that Original Medicare would not require.
- You may be covered only in the state where you reside. There may be no out-of-state coverage.
- You must choose to include a prescription plan in your coverage for a cost, if it is offered with the plan that you select.
    - There are plans that allow you to opt out of their prescription plan and enroll in a Medicare Part D freestanding plan.

  - There are plans that you are required to enroll in their prescription plan, or if you select a separate prescription drug plan, you will be disenrolled from your Medicare Advantage plan. You will be back to your Original Medicare. You will then be able to enroll in Medicare Part D benefits.
- This plan does have an out-of-pocket that can differ for each plan. Original Medicare does not offer an out-of-pocket benefit. This means if you meet an amount set by the plan that you have paid out of pocket, then the insurance will cover 100 percent until the end of the year.
- These plans may require you to get a referral from a designated primary-care provider for any services needed, such as a specialist. Original Medicare does not require a referral, but keep in mind, specialists may still require a referral, even though your insurance does not.

There Are Different Types of Medicare Advantage Plans Available:

Medicare Advantage Plan Health Maintenance Organization (HMO) is a plan that covers Part A, Part B, and Part D prescription services.

- You must enroll in this prescription portion with this plan. If you enroll in a prescription plan outside this plan, you can be disenrolled from the Medicare Advantage Plan.

- The plan requires you to select a primary-care physician in their network. This physician is the one who coordinates your care and decides to refer you to a specialist for treatment. Without your primary-care physician's permission, the insurance may not cover the cost.
- This plan only covers care from doctors, hospitals, and health care providers in the HMO network.
    - If you see or use doctors or facilities out of the HMO network, you will be responsible for 100 percent of the cost, with the exception of urgent care or emergency rooms.
    - You cannot use your Original Medicare to pay for these services. Please check and clarify the coverage for this before selecting this plan.
    - Your out-of-pocket coverage is usually $6,700 before your insurance will pay 100 percent of the cost.
    - This plan may have **point of service (POS)** options that may be available for you to use as an out-of-network provider that is not part of your plan's network of health care providers. This would help cover emergency care, out-of-area urgent care and/or out-of-area dialysis.
    - This option may allow you to have treatment without a referral or prior approval from your primary-care provider or the insurance.
    - The out-of-pocket limit may differ from the in-network coverage.

- ○ If your plan does not have POS benefits, you will have to pay the full cost going outside the network.
- ○ This plan cannot charge a higher cost for certain care than what Original Medicare would charge for treatment like chemotherapy, dialysis, and durable medical equipment.
- ○ This plan can charge you more for home health care, a skilled nursing facility, and inpatient hospital services.
- ○ It is important that you follow your plan's rules and get prior authorization for services that require them.

Medicare Advantage Plan Preferred Provider Organizations (PPO) cover Part A, Part B, and Part D prescription services.

- You must enroll in the prescription plan that is offered. If you enroll in a prescription plan outside this plan, you can be disenrolled from this Medicare Advantage Plan.
- If you see doctors or utilize facilities in the plan's network, it will cost you less. If you choose to utilize services in facilities outside the plan's network, it will cost you more. You do have the flexibility with this plan to select your providers or facilities. The difference is the cost to you.
- The plan does not require you to select a primary-care physician to coordinate or get permission for your care.

- You are not required to have a referral to see a specialist.
- It is cost-effective for you to use the doctors or health care providers in the PPO network.
    - These PPO plans must cover out-of-network services, but you may pay more if you go out of the plan's network.
- This plan is limited on how much they can charge you for your copays but can charge you more for some services such as home care and skilled nursing facility services.
- There are two different out-of-pocket limits for in-network and out-of-network services. These plans may not be available in all the states within the United States.
- These PPO plans may offer extra benefits beyond what Original Medicare would cover. There would be an extra cost for these benefits.

Medicare Advantage Plan Private Fee for Service (PFFS) covers Part A, Part B, and Part D but is not required to provide prescription services.

- If the plan does not include the Part D prescription portion, you can join a standalone Medicare drug plan to cover your prescriptions.
- Your plan is contracted with a network of doctors, health care providers, hospitals, and facilities.
- The plan does not require you to select a primary-care physician to coordinate or get permission for your care.

- You are not required to have a referral to see a specialist.
- The plan does not restrict you to only a certain group of providers.
- You can see any other Medicare-approved doctor, as long as the doctor is aware of your plan and agrees to accept the plan.
- If you seek treatment outside the network, you will have to pay more for your treatment.
- This plan cannot restrict you to network providers.
- They must cover costs you received from any Medicare-approved doctor who has agreed to treat you under the plan.
- The plan will have a copay, deductible, or coinsurance for services. You cannot use your Original Medicare for coverage.

Medicare Special Needs Plans (SNP) is a Medicare Advantage Plan that limits itself to individuals with specific diseases. This plan streamlines your care to meet your specific needs for your providers and medication formularies.

- This plan limits its enrollment to specific groups:
    - Individuals in a nursing home, certain nursing home institutions, or receiving nursing care at home. (Make sure that the plan's providers serve the institution you are residing in.)
    - Individuals who are eligible for Medicare and Medicaid.
    - Individuals who have a specific chronic condition or disability including but not limited to:
        - Individuals who have diabetes

        - Individuals who have end-stage renal disease (ESRD)
        - Individuals who have HIV/AIDS
        - Individuals who have chronic heart failure
        - Individuals who have dementia
    - This plan may have other limitations on enrollment.
    - This plan allows individuals to join at any time.
- You must get your care and services from doctors, facilities, and hospitals in the Medicare SNP network.
- In case of an emergency, when you need immediate care, you can go to any of the following facilities:
    - Emergency room
    - Urgent care
    - Out-of-area dialysis for individuals with end-stage renal disease (ESRD)
- This plan may require you to have a primary-care doctor or a care coordinator to help coordinate your care.
- You must have a referral to see a specialist. This plan generally has specialists available for the specific diseases or conditions that affect their members.
- The Medicare prescription plan coverage is part of this plan.
- This plan should coordinate your services and provide you the help you need.
- If you have Medicare and Medicaid, this plan will make sure that all the plan doctors, health care providers, and facilities accept Medicaid.

Medicare Medical Savings Account (MSA) plans are a consumer-directed plan. This plan gives you the flexibility to choose your providers or health care services.

- This plan has a high deductible and offers a medical savings account. You can use this savings account to pay for your medical costs. You will have to meet the high deductible before the plan will cover any costs.
- These plans have a medical savings account (MSA), which is a type of savings account. The funds in this account are deposited by this plan, so you are able to use this money to assist in paying your medical costs while you are trying to meet the deductible.
- These plans do not have a prescription plan. You would have to enroll in a plan through your Medicare Plan D prescription plan.
- This type of plan offers additional benefits at an added cost. These benefits are dental, vision, and long-term care that is not covered by Original Medicare.

What questions should I ask before enrolling in Medicare Part C plan?

- What is the cost of the premium for this Medicare Advantage plan? Remember, you are still responsible for your Part B premiums and/or Part A premium only if you do not have premium-free Part A. Please consider your income level if you fall under the IRMAA surcharge based on your income, which is listed in **chapter 4** to calculate your total monthly premium cost for your Medicare Part B and Part D.
- What are the copayment, deductible, or coinsurance for a primary-care doctor, specialist, labs and/or X-rays?

- Since these plans follow Medicare guidelines, check If a services would be denied by Medicare, will this plan consider payment?
- What does it cost to see an out-of-network doctor and go to a hospital or facility?
- Are there higher copays or costs for specialized care such as hospitalizations, home health, or specific care?
- How are specialized high-cost injections or infusions administered in my doctor's office covered?
    - Are they covered under my Part B benefits with the plan, or are those special medications covered under the prescription Part D coverage?
        - Under the prescription coverage, is there a deductible or cost on my part?
        - If the medication is covered under the prescription services (called Part D), does the medication fall under a different cost tier, and what is my cost?
        - If the medication for the injection or infusion is under the prescription services, does it need to be obtained from a mail-order pharmacy and mailed to the provider? Remember, you have to pay up front for this medication. Your provider can still bill your insurance for the administration and supplies used for your services but not the medication.
- How much is my out-of-pocket for in-network and out-of-network providers and/or facilities and hospitals?

- Are my doctors and facilities automatically in the plan's network? If they are not in the network, how will my visits be covered if I still want to see them?
- Which hospitals, home health care agencies, skilled nursing facilities, free standing X-ray and lab companies are in the network with this plan?
- If it is an HMO plan, who are the primary-care doctors on the plan in network that I can choose from?
- Does my doctor need to get prior authorization for me to:
    a. Be admitted into the hospital?
    b. Get high-cost injections related to my medical condition?
    c. Get infusions, an MRI, or high-cost diagnostic imaging?
- Do I need a referral from my primary-care doctor to see a specialist?
- Does this plan provide extra benefits for vision care, hearing, and dental services? What are the restrictions or limitations on this coverage for those benefits?
- Does this plan have coverage for outpatient prescription drugs?
    a. Review the list of prescription drugs you are currently on, and see if they are covered under the plan.
    b. Check to see if any of these medications require a prior authorization before this plan will cover your medication.
    c. Check if they impose any restrictions or limitations on your prescriptions like requiring you to use a generic drug before allowing you to use your brand-name medication.

- Does the plan limit you on the quantity of your medications?
- Does the plan require you to use a mail-order pharmacy instead of your pharmacy for coverage?
- Which mail-order pharmacy do I have to use?
- Does the mail-order pharmacy allow you to get a three-month supply, and is it cost-effective?

- How much will I have to pay for a brand-name medication or generic medication?
- Does my prescription plan require me to pay a deductible before the plan will cover my medication? If yes, what is the cost if the deductible is not met or is met?
- What is the coverage from this plan for my medication during the coverage gap (donut hole), and what will be my cost?
- Will this plan cover my prescriptions when I'm out of the area and traveling?
- What service area does this plan cover?
- If I have current insurance coverage, how does this plan work with this insurance plan? If I join, would this affect my current retiree or employer health insurance coverage, and can I lose this coverage?[28]

---

[28] "Types of Medicare Health Plans," Medicare Advantage Plans, https://www.medicare.gov/sign-up-change-plans/medicare-health-plans/medicare-advantage-plans/medicare-advantage-plans.html.

CHAPTER 10

Medicare Part D and Coverage

Medicare Part D is an optional benefit for an additional cost offered with Original Medicare or a Medicare Advantage Plan (Medicare Part C). Medicare Part D is a benefit for prescription drugs only. Insurance companies or other private companies only approved by Medicare will offer this additional coverage. There is an additional monthly premium cost to you if you choose to enroll for this coverage.

Medicare Part D Plan Enrollment Period:

Medicare Part D prescription-services enrollment can occur when you are first eligible for Medicare at the age of sixty-five, or at any age with a disability. This is called your **initial enrollment**.

- You can enroll three months prior to the month of your sixty-fifth birthday, during the month of your birthday, and during the three months after your birthday month.
    - If you have a **disability** and are under sixty-five years of age, you are eligible to sign up for Original Medicare after twenty-four months from the date your disability benefits started. You have until the twenty-eighth month after you get disability benefits to sign up for Original Medicare, Medicare Part C Advantage Plan, and/or Medicare Part D prescription plan.

- After your initial enrollment, if you choose not to enroll in Medicare Part D and do not have a creditable prescription plan for sixty-three days in a row, you may have a late-enrollment penalty. This penalty will be added to your monthly premium and will remain as long as you have Medicare Part D prescription plan.
- During the open enrollment period of October 15 through December 7 of each year. The following applies and will be effective January 1 of the next year:
    - You can switch from Original Medicare to a Medicare Advantage plan or conversely from a Medicare Advantage plan to Original Medicare.
    - You can switch from your Medicare Advantage plan to another Medicare Advantage plan.
    - You can switch from a Medicare Advantage plan that does not offer a prescription plan to a Medicare Advantage plan that does offer a prescription plan coverage.
    - You can switch a Medicare Advantage plan that does offer a prescription plan to a Medicare Advantage plan that does not offer a prescription plan coverage.
    - You can join a Medicare prescription plan.
    - You can switch from a Medicare prescription plan to another Medicare prescription plan coverage.
    - You can drop your current Medicare prescription plan coverage completely.

Medicare Advantage Disenrollment Period:

The Medicare Advantage disenrollment period is January 1 through February 14; this is a period when you can only switch from a Medicare Advantage plan to Original Medicare, and you have until February 14 to enroll in a Medicare Part D prescription plan. Your effective date on your coverage will begin on the first day of the month after your enrollment form is received.

What you should know about Medicare Part D (Prescription Plan)

- Medicare contracts with different insurance companies to provide prescription services to you.
- The key to the cost of your premium is based on the coverage of the plan, which includes copays, more coverage during the prescription gaps known as the donut hole. The better the coverage, the higher the premium.

The 2018 Medicare Part D plan's coverage is as follows:

- **The Initial Deductible** – For 2018, the initial deductible is $405. Some plans may or may not have a deductible associated with the plan. You will need to review plans that are available by state and check to see what benefits are offered and what the deductible is.

- **The Coverage** – The plan coverage for the Medicare Part D or Medicare Advantage Part D prescriptions generally offers a coinsurance or copay for medication.
    - There are different tier levels for certain medications, with varying levels of coverage. First check which medications you need and compare plans to see what the coverage is for each medication.
    - For 2018, the total retail cost of your medications is $3,750 for the **initial coverage limit** before you reach the coverage gap or donut hole. A donut hole is a coverage gap that requires you to pay a larger portion of the cost before you reach the **true out-of-pocket,** also known as **catastrophic coverage**.
    - For 2018, the true **out-of-pocket catastrophic coverage** is $5,000. Once you meet this catastrophic coverage, you will again have help with the coverage of your medication.
        - Some plans may have a lower initial coverage limit. Please make sure you review this to avoid ending up in the "donut hole" sooner and have to pay a higher out-of-pocket cost during this gap before you meet the true out-of-pocket coverage of $5,000.
- **The Coverage Gap or Donut Hole** – This stage is when you have met your **initial coverage limit** of $3,750; this amount differs depending on your Part D plan.

- During this gap called the donut hole, you will pay a higher portion of the retail cost of your medication until you meet your **true out-of-pocket** of $5,000.
  - For 2018, while you are in the donut hole, you now qualify for assistance called the Donut Hole Discount on your prescriptions.
  - **For generic medication**, Medicare Part D will pay 56 percent of the cost, leaving you 44 percent of the cost for your medications. The remaining 44 percent cost will be counted toward your true out-of-pocket costs.
  - **For brand-name medications**, Medicare Part D will pay 15 percent of the cost, along with the manufacturer discount payment of 50 percent, leaving you with 35 percent of the cost of your medication. Both the 35 percent of the cost that you paid and the 50 percent manufacturer discount payment will go toward your true out-of-pocket costs.

- **Catastrophic Coverage** – This is the stage that you meet when you have spent more than $5,000 out of pocket. Once this has been done, you can receive your medication at a substantially reduced rate.
  - For generic medications, the set rate for **2018 is $3.35**. You will be charged whichever is higher, the **5 percent** or the set price.

    - For brand-name medications, the set rate for **2018 is $8.35**. You will be charged whichever is higher, the **5 percent** or the set price.

Are all the prescription plans' coverages the same as the Medicare guidelines? What should we look for?

Not all of the prescription plans have to follow Medicare guidelines on coverage.

- Some plans may offer extra coverage during the donut hole gap. For example, they may offer a copayment for your generic and brand-name prescriptions, along with coverage for other higher tier-level medications.
- Just remember, the better the coverage, the higher the premiums.
- The best way to determine which cost fits what you need is to go to PDP-Planner.com and utilize the Donut Hole Calculator.
    - This will help you determine where you may fall in the donut hole during the year, depending on the medications you take.
    - The Donut Hole Calculator can help you determine if paying more on your premium with a better coverage during the donut hole will be more cost-effective on an annual basis. This can be compared to a basic plan with a lower premium and less coverage during the donut hole.

- It is absolutely important to review the initial coverage limit in the prescription plans that will put you in the donut hole sooner than later. This is vital to you because when you do fall into the donut hole gap, you will be paying most of your medication costs.
- Each plan differs by state on what is offered. Review the plans available in your state.
- Always review each plan's formulary to search for your medications and see how each one is covered.
    - Don't forget, some medications fall under a different tier level. The higher the tier level, the lower the coverage is and the more it will cost you for that medication.[29]

[29] "How to Get Drug Coverage," https://www.medicare.gov/sign-up-change-plans/get-drug-coverage/get-drug-coverage.html.

CHAPTER 11

Medigap Plans and Insurance Supplements

Medigap is an extra insurance that is offered by private health insurance companies to provide coverage to your Original Medicare to help cover the Medicare deductible, coinsurance, copayments, and excess charges. It can cover health care when you travel outside of the United States.

- Some Medigap plans extend your hospital coverage stay up to 365 days.
- Some plans offer **excess charges**. Excess charges are services performed for which the cost is above or beyond the Medicare-approved amount for that service. If you have this coverage, your Medigap will review and consider paying that additional cost, instead of you paying it.
- Medigap plans do not cover long-term care, dental care, vision care, hearing aids, eyeglasses, private-duty nursing, and prescriptions.
- If you move or relocate to another state as a Medigap enrollee, you do not need to reenroll. This plan's coverage crosses over state lines.
- If you want to switch to a different Medigap insurance, you will have to fill out an application, a medical questionnaire, and may be turned down based on preexisting conditions.
    - A preexisting condition was waived when you first applied during your initial enrollment, and you could not be turned down or charged more than a healthy person.

- Since this is outside the initial enrollment, some state plans may reevaluate new applications and preexisting conditions. They may deny coverage and/or elect to charge more for your premium.
- It is recommended, if you want to switch to another plan, to go ahead and apply for that plan. If you are approved, you have a thirty-day free-look period that starts when your new policy starts.
    - If you can, don't cancel the other policy until you are sure you like the new policy. The only issue is that you will have to pay both premiums. You can at least go back to your old policy if you find out within the thirty days that this new plan is not what you want.

- Medigap Select is a plan that limits you to a network of doctors, hospitals, and facilities.
    - Doctors, hospitals, and facilities can stop working with this plan at any time. If you have a Medigap Select plan, you will have to continually monitor and verify if they are current in your network.
    - This plan will not cover the cost if you go out of the network. You will be responsible for the cost that Medicare does not pay.
    - The plan may cover you on an emergency basis, but the emergency has to be approved and determined if it qualifies as an emergency. The premium cost may be low, but you are limited only to that network.

Medigap Plans:

There are ten types of federally regulated standardized plans available. Each provides a letter that outlines the type of coverage offered.

- All the policies offered in the majority of the states have the same basic benefits; there are some that offer additional benefits.
- Medigap plans in the states of Massachusetts, Minnesota, and Wisconsin may differ from standardized plans.
- For those who have purchased Plan E, H, and I before June 1, 2010, you may keep those plans, but those plans are no longer available for purchase.

2018 Medigap/Supplement Plans										
Medigap/ Supplement Plans	**A**	**B**	**C**	**D**	**F ***	**G**	**K**	**L**	**M**	**N**
Medicare Part A coinsurance covers hospital costs up to an additional 365 days after Medicare benefits are exhausted	X	X	X	X	X	X	X	X	X	X
Medicare Part B copayment or 20 percent coinsurance coverage	X	X	X	X	X	X	50%	75%	X	X ** Office visits $20 copay. ER $50 copay
First three pints of blood provided	X	X	X	X	X	X	50%	75%	X	X
Part A hospice care copayment and/or copayment	X	X	X	X	X	X	50%	75%	X	X
(SNF) Skilled nursing facility care coinsurance			X	X	X	X	50%	75%	X	X
Deductible Medicare Part A		X	X	X	X	X	50%	75%	50%	X
Deductible Medicare Part B			X		X					
Excess charges—Medicare Part B					X	X				
Travel outside US emergency coverage and plan limits			*** 80%	*** 80%	*** 80%	*** 80%			*** 80%	*** 80%
Medicare Part B preventive care coinsurance	X	X	X	X	X	X	X	X	X	X
Out-of-pocket (once out-of-pocket is met) including the Medicare Part B deductible for Medicare-approved services. These plans cover 100 percent until the end of the year.							$5,240 ****	$2,620 ****		

* Plan F also offers a plan with a deductible of $2,240 requiring out-of-pocket payment before the Medigap plan covers the balance Medicare leaves.

** Plan N—Medicare Part B covers 100 percent but leaves you a $20 copay for office visits and a $50 copay for emergency room visits, only if the visit does not result in you being admitted into the hospital after emergency room visit.

*** Plans C, D, F, G, M, and N cover foreign travel outside the United States, have a $250 deductible, and require out-of-pocket payment before insurance pays 80 percent costs, leaving you with 20 percent costs.

**** Plans K and L have out-of-pocket costs. Once you pay the Medicare deductible and meet out-of-pocket costs, the plans cover 100 percent of costs for the remainder of the calendar year.

Medigap Coverage outside the United States:

Please check with your Medigap plan on how the plan covers outside the United States before your travel.

- Your plan may offer additional coverage for health care services or supplies outside the United States.
- Medigap plans that offer foreign travel will cover an emergency during the first sixty days of your trip. If Medicare does not cover the costs, the following applies:

  - The plan will pay 80 percent of the cost billed, if it is considered medically necessary and after a $250 deductible has been met.
  - You will have to pay the $250 deductible before the insurance will pay 80 percent of the cost, still leaving you to pay the 20 percent balance. There is a lifetime limit of $50,000 for emergency coverage for foreign travel.

Medigap Enrollment Period:

Open Enrollment for Medigap is when you are first eligible for Medicare Part B at sixty-five years of age.

- Once you have turned sixty-five years of age and enrolled in Medicare Part B, you can purchase and enroll in a Medigap plan up to six months from the first day of the month you turned sixty-five and enrolled in Medicare Part B.
  - Federal law does not require Medigap plans to be offered before you turn sixty-five years of age. If your state does offer this plan, it may cost you more.
- If you enrolled during the initial open enrollment, you can purchase a Medigap plan sold in your state. During this initial enrollment, the Medigap plans cannot deny you coverage due to health problems or charge you more than someone who has no health problems.

- It is important to know if you have group health coverage through your employer, spouse's employer, or union and are actively employed. You may want to wait on enrolling in your Medicare Part B due to your age eligibility.
  - The reason for this is that there is no penalty if you have a group plan during active employment.
  - You can enroll in Medicare Part B when your group plan terminates due to retirement. Then you will not have the 10 percent Medicare Part B penalty, and you can enroll in the Medigap plan up to six months from the date you enrolled in Medicare Part B.
  - If you enroll in Medicare Part B when you are age eligible and still have a group health plan through your employer, then you would have to enroll in the Medigap plan then. Otherwise, if you wait to enroll when you retire and your group plan ends, you will be subject to the Medigap insurance reviewing your medical history and preexisting medical problems. The plan can refuse coverage or charge a higher premium.

Outside Enrollment:
If you wait until you are outside the open enrollment period, then there is no guarantee that the Medigap insurance companies will sell you a policy, because of not meeting the underwriting requirements. The Medigap plans use those

requirements when considering your application based on your preexisting conditions.

- In some states, Medicare Select, which is known as **Medigap Select,** is a plan that limits you to certain doctors, facilities, or hospitals in the plan's network.
    - You have the option to switch to a regular Medigap plan within twelve months, if this plan does not fit your needs.
- It is important to remember that outside the open enrollment period, if a Medigap insurance company offers you coverage, they can use a waiting period.
- They can exclude coverage on preexisting conditions for the first six months of coverage, leaving you the Original Medicare Part B deductible and coinsurance until after the six-month waiting period ends to start covering these conditions.
- You have a guaranteed issue right called Medigap Protections, which essentially provides you with rights protection during certain conditions and covers the following:
    - If you met the guidelines of a guaranteed issue right, you are entitled to be sold a Medigap plan.
    - The plan must cover your preexisting medical conditions.
    - You cannot be charged more for your plan based on your medical conditions. You must be charged the same amount as someone who is healthy.

Trial Right:

A trial right allows you to try to enroll in a Medicare Advantage Plan for the first time by allowing you to drop your Medigap plan. If you change your mind within twelve months, you can enroll back into Original Medicare and reenroll into a Medigap plan.

- It is only a twelve-month trial period.
- If your Medigap plan is no longer available, you are able to select a different Medigap plan that is available in your state.

Guaranteed Issue Rights:

Guaranteed issue rights are protected by federal law, but your state may have additional Medigap rights. Below are the situations that would protect you under the guaranteed issue rights:

- **If your Medicare Advantage plan is leaving, no longer contracts with Medicare, and no longer offers coverage in your area.**
    - You can purchase a Medigap plan, categorized as Plan A, B, C, D, F, G, K, L, M, or N (see table page 155). This plan is sold in your area without penalty only if you switch back to Original Medicare and not a Medicare Advantage plan.
    - You must apply for a Medigap plan no later than the following restrictions.
        - You must apply at the earliest of sixty calendar days before your coverage ends or no later than sixty-three calendar days after your coverage terminates.

  - Just remember that your Medigap plan cannot start until your Medicare Advantage plan terminates.
- **If you move out of the Medicare Advantage plan area.**
  - You can purchase a plan through Medigap; these are categorized as Plans A, B, C, D, F, G, K, L, M, and N (see table page 155) if sold in your area without penalty only if you switch back to Original Medicare and not a Medicare Advantage plan.
  - You must apply for a Medigap plan no later than the following restrictions:
    - You must apply at the earliest of sixty calendar days before your coverage ends or no later than sixty-three calendar days after your coverage terminates.
    - Just remember that your Medigap plan cannot start until your Medicare Advantage plan terminates.
- **If your secondary insurance plan to Original Medicare ends for no fault of your own. This includes retiree plans, group health plan, COBRA coverage, or union coverage.**
  - You can purchase a plan through Medigap; these are categorized as Plans A, B, C, D, F, G, K, L, M, and N (see table page 155) if sold in your area without penalty only if you switch back to Original Medicare and not a Medicare Advantage plan.

- If you have COBRA coverage, you have the option to purchase a Medigap plan immediately or wait until the coverage ends.
- For any other supplement plans, you must apply for a Medigap plan no later than the following restrictions:
    - You have sixty-three calendar days to apply for a Medigap plan from the date the coverage ends.
    - If you receive a note that your coverage is ending, the sixty-three days start from the date of the notice.
    - If you didn't get a notice, the date on the claim that was denied by your secondary insurance plan would start the sixty-three days.

Other circumstances may apply to give you an extra twelve months on your rights regarding secondary insurances. Please contact Medicare at 1-800-633-4227 to see if your circumstance will extend to twelve months.

- **If you have a Medicare Select plan and move out of the service area.**
    - You can purchase a plan through Medigap if sold in the new area or state you are moving to. These are categorized as Plans A, B, C, D, F, G, K, L, M, and N (see table page 155).
    - You must apply at the earliest of sixty calendar days before the date your coverage ends or no later than sixty-three calendar days after your coverage terminates.

    - You can always contact your Medicare Select plan to see if there are more options.
- **If you have enrolled in a Medicare Advantage plan when you were first eligible for Medicare Part A and Medicare Part B by age sixty-five. You then decide within the first year of joining you want to switch back to Original Medicare.**
    - This falls under your trial rights.
    - You can purchase a plan through Medigap; these are categorized as Plans A, B, C, D, F, G, K, L, M, and N (see table page 155) if sold in your new area and state.
    - You must apply for a Medigap plan with the following restrictions:
        - You must apply at the earliest of sixty calendar days before the date your coverage ends or no later than sixty-three calendar days after your coverage terminates.
        - Other circumstances may apply to give you an extra twelve months on your rights regarding secondary insurances. Please contact Medicare at 1-800-633-4227 to see if your circumstance will extend to twelve months.
- **If you joined All-Inclusive Care for the Elderly (PACE), defined as a state assistance program, when you were first eligible for Medicare A and Medicare Part B at the age eligibility of sixty-five, you can decide to switch back to Original Medicare within the first year of joining PACE.**

- This falls under your trial rights.
- You can purchase a plan through Medigap; these are categorized as Plans A, B, C, D, F, G, K, L, M, and N (see table page 155) if sold in your new area or state. You must apply for a Medigap plan with the following restrictions:
  - You must apply at the earliest of sixty calendar days before the date your coverage ends or no later than sixty-three calendar days after your coverage terminates.
  - Other circumstances may apply to give you an extra twelve months regarding secondary insurances. Please contact Medicare at 1-800-633-4227 to see if your circumstance will extend to twelve months.

- **If you dropped a Medigap policy to enroll in a Medicare Advantage Plan or to switch to a Medigap Select policy for the first time within twelve months and want to switch back**.
  - This falls under your trial right.
  - You can purchase and enroll in the Medigap plan or Medigap Select plan that you previously had, if it is still available in your state.
    - If your previous Medigap or Medigap Select plan is no longer available, you can purchase a plan through Medigap; these are categorized as Plans A, B, C, D, F, G, K, L, M, and N (see table page 155) if sold in your new area or state.

    - You must apply at the earliest of sixty calendar days before the date your coverage ends or no later than sixty-three calendar days after your coverage terminates.
  - Other circumstances may apply to give you an extra twelve months regarding secondary insurances. Please contact Medicare at 1-800-633-4227 to see if your circumstance will extend to 12 months.
- **If your Medigap insurance company goes bankrupt or ends through no fault of your own.**
  - You can purchase a plan through Medigap; these are categorized as Plans A, B, C, D, F, G, K, L, M, and N (see table page 155) if sold in your new area or state.
  - You must apply for a Medigap policy within 63 calendar days from the date your coverage terminates, no later than 63 days.
- **If you are forced to leave a Medicare Advantage plan or drop a Medigap policy because the insurance company did not follow the rules of the plan or you were misled.**
  - You can purchase a plan through Medigap; these are categorized as Plans A, B, C, D, F, G, K, L, M, and N (see table page 155) if sold in your new area or state.
  - You must apply for a Medigap policy within 63 calendar days from the date your coverage terminates, no later than 63 days.

What should I do if one or more guaranteed issue rights applies?

Keep in mind, more than one of the above situations may apply to you. Select the best option of the guaranteed issue rights that fit your situation. Here is what you will need to justify your guaranteed issue right and attach with your application for a Medigap plan to insure a smooth transition.

- Attach a copy of any letters, emails, notices, and/or any claim denials that include your name and proof that your plan coverage has been terminated.
- Include a copy of the envelope that this paperwork arrived in as proof of the date it was mailed to you. Remember, if you are leaving a Medicare Advantage plan and are returning back to Original Medicare, please apply for your Medigap plan before your Medicare Advantage plan ends.
- Advise your new Medigap plan to make the effective date no later than the termination date of your Medicare Advantage plan. This way you will have continuous coverage through your insurance plans.

Reminders:

- Some plans follow Medicare guidelines; if Medicare denies, then your plan will deny. Check if this plan pays or will consider payment if Medicare denies.
- Check if your plan covers out-of-network doctors or facilities.
    - If no, you will be responsible for 100 percent of the cost of seeing an out-of-network provider or utilizing that facility.

    - If yes, then find out what the benefits and coverage are for an out-of-network provider or facility secondary to your Medicare, so you can determine your cost.
- Check if your plan covers anywhere outside the United States or just inside the United States.
    - Check what the coverage is for foreign travel secondary to Medicare.
        - In the United States, Medicare pays for coverage.
        - For foreign travel, it does not provide coverage, with a few exceptions stated in chapter 12.
- Check how your plan secondary to Medicare covers high-end-cost diagnostic testing, infusions, and injections that your care requires. Do they require a prior authorization secondary to Medicare?
        - Some plans waive their prior authorization, secondary to Medicare, but don't forget to double check.
        - Medicare does not require a prior authorization, but you could be delayed in treatment because your secondary insurance does.
- If you are getting infusions or high-end injections, check if the medication is under your medical coverage or Part D prescription services.
    - If covered under the Part D prescription services, how is it covered? Does it fall under a higher tier level, what is the coverage?

    - Do you have to obtain this through a mailorder pharmacy? Does it have to be shipped to the doctor's or facility's office? Remember, under your prescription services, you have to pay up front for these medications before they will be delivered for your care. You doctor will still bill your insurance but just for the administration and supplies used while performing the service.

Don't rely on your health care professional or facility to know and advise you of your coverage. You need to know your benefits and make an educated decision on your care and the cost.

- Be responsible for your own care, choices of plans, and don't rely totally on your health care providers for the information that ultimately will be your responsibility for the cost of your services.
- When they present you with an advance beneficiary notice, that is a sign that there is something on the test that is questionable that Medicare may deny. It is an alert.
    - It could be that the test is not covered under Medicare or the frequency is too soon to have the test. It does not mean that if you actually need the test, Medicare will deny it.
    - Talk with your doctor or ordering practitioner to see if this is necessary for your treatment and care. Your doctor can add extra codes to tell Medicare why it is necessary for the test or why it needs to be done sooner than Medicare requires.

- This is why it is also important to check with your Medigap plan on how they cover circumstances like this.

Medicare Supplements/Secondary Retiree Plans:

Your retiree group insurance may be offered from your former employer and would be secondary to your Medicare Part A and B plan.

- Medicare will always pay first, and then your retiree group plan is secondary.
- If your employer offers this at the time of retirement, you can enroll or elect to go with a Medigap plan.
- Your retirement plan will offer a prescription service, whereas a Medigap plan does not. You would have to enroll in Medicare Part D prescription plan if you go with a Medigap plan.

What to know about your secondary retiree plan:
The plan coverage may or may not change once you retire and Medicare is primary. Please contact your health care plan office to see what the coordination of benefits is with Medicare as your primary coverage.

- Keep in mind, these plans can change in benefits and premiums at the renewal time of your plan. They can also change to a Medicare Advantage plan, in which case you may have to weigh the benefits of either staying with this plan or keeping your Original Medicare and selecting a Medigap plan.

    - Just remember, Medigap plans do not have prescription drug coverage, which will result in you having to enroll in a Medicare Part D prescription plan.
- The retiree plan can cancel coverage at any time.
- The retiree plan may have limits on how much it will pay. It may provide a stop-loss coverage, which will start paying out of pocket after a maximum amount is met.
- The retired coverage may affect your spouse and dependents on the plan. Make sure they can still be covered under your retired plan if you decide to drop the plan.
- You will have a premium for this plan.
- Check when your retiree plan renews.
    - It is important to know when this plan renews.
        - Check if it is a plan year (for example September 1 to August 31) or fiscal year (October 1 to September 30) or a calendar year plan (January 1 to December 31).
        - This is important to know because if you have a deductible on your secondary plan, it may not match with your Medicare deductible, which renews yearly and has a deductible that restarts on January 1.
        - You could end up with your secondary insurance plan deductible restarting in the middle of the calendar year. Then you would be responsible for the cost that Medicare leaves as your balance until you meet your secondary insurance plan deductible.

- Your retiree plan may have a deductible to be met first before they will pick up a coinsurance (percentage) or all of the costs that Medicare does not cover as the primary insurance.
  - That means you will be responsible for the Medicare deductible as well as the secondary deductible before the plans will pay a portion of your medical services.
  - If the secondary deductible is higher than Medicare's deductible, you will have 100 percent portion of the balance Medicare does not cover, until you meet the secondary insurance deductible. If your secondary insurance only covers a percentage and not 100 percent of Medicare balances, you will still have a small balance to pay for your medical services.
- Your retiree plan may have nonduplication benefits.
  - What this means is if Medicare pays equal to or more than your retired secondary plan for the same service, then your retired secondary insurance will pay zero.
  - If Medicare pays less than what your secondary insurance will pay for the same service, then the secondary insurance will consider paying the difference between the two plans.
- Your retiree plan may offer prescription coverage.
  - Check how your medications are covered.
  - If you do not have prescription coverage or want to opt out, you can enroll in Medicare Part D. Understand that your income could put you in the IRMAA surcharge (chapter 4).

- Your retired plan may require you to enroll in Medicare Part B in order to have coverage through the retired plan.
    - In some instances, you will lose the benefit if you do not enroll in Medicare Part B.
        - Tricare is a good example. When you become eligible for Medicare Part B, you have to enroll in order to continue to have coverage with Tricare for medical coverage as well as prescription coverage.
        - Your Tricare prime or standard plan will change on your sixty-fifth birthday. Your Tricare will become Tricare for Life and secondary to Medicare. This plan follows Medicare guidelines—if Medicare denies, Tricare for Life will deny. Tricare for Life covers the Medicare deductible and coinsurance.
        - One exception to the rule: you don't need to sign up for Medicare Part B if you have Medicare Part A and are an active-duty service member or an active-duty family member. This applies if you have US Family Health Plan (USFHP) before October 1, 2012 or under the eligibility age and also have Medicare for disability.

    - Effective October 1, 2012 and after if you are enrolled in the US Family Health plan (USFHP) and are Medicare eligible, age sixty-five, you will transition to Tricare for Life. You can no longer stay enrolled in USFHP.

Before October 1, 2012, those enrollees could stay with that plan, but if there is a break in your coverage and you are of enrollment age, sixty-five, you will have to enroll in Medicare Part B to continue having coverage. If after your initial enrollment, you break your coverage in USFHP and enroll in Medicare Part B, you will have the 10 percent penalty applied to your Part B premium because of your late enrollment. It is recommended that you enroll in Medicare Part B when you are eligible by age.

- Your retiree plan may only follow Medicare guidelines, which means if Medicare denies your medical claim, so will your secondary plan. Below is a good example of a plan that may provide coverage even though Medicare denies.
    - BCBS Federal waives their copay, deductible, and coinsurance and will pay Medicare deductible and coinsurance. If Medicare denies, then the plan will consider the claim and pay at the original BCBS federal coverage benefits.
- Your former employer may file bankruptcy or go out of business.

- You may be protected by the federal COBRA rules. This applies to any other companies within the same corporation and still offers a group health plan to its employees. They can offer you COBRA coverage.
  - If that is not available, you can enroll or buy a Medigap plan, even after your Medigap open enrollment period. You would qualify for the guaranteed issue rights, described in this chapter under Medigap.[30]

Reminders:

Some plans follow Medicare guidelines; if Medicare denies, then your plan will deny. Check if this plan pays or will consider payment if Medicare denies.

- Check if your plan covers out-of-network doctors or facilities.
  - If not, you will be responsible for 100 percent of the cost of seeing an out-of-network provider or utilizing that facility.
  - If yes, then find out what the benefits and coverage are for an out-of-network provider or facility secondary to your Medicare, to determine your cost.
- Check if your plan covers anywhere outside the United States or just inside the United States.

---

30 . "What's Medicare Supplement Insurance (Medigap)?", https://www.medicare.gov/supplement-other-insurance/medigap/whats-medigap.html.

- Check what the coverage is for foreign travel secondary to Medicare.
    - In the United States, Medicare pays for coverage.
    - For foreign travel, it does not, with a few exceptions stated in chapter 12.
- Check how your secondary plan to Medicare covers high-end diagnostic testing, infusions, and injections that your care requires.
    - Do they require a prior authorization secondary to Medicare?
        - Some plans waive their prior authorization, secondary to Medicare, but make sure to double check.
        - Medicare does not require a prior authorization, but you could be delayed in treatment because your secondary insurance does.
- If you are getting infusions or high-end injections, check if the medication used is covered under your medical coverage or prescription services.
    - If medication is covered under prescription services, inquire about the type of coverage and if it falls under a higher tier level. This may increase your cost out of pocket.

- ○ Do you have to obtain this through a mail-order pharmacy? Does it have to be shipped to the doctor's or facility's office? For prescription service, you may have to pay up front for these medications before they will be delivered. Your doctor will still bill your insurance for the administration and supplies used while performing the service.

Don't rely on your health care professional or facility to know and advise you of your coverage. You need to know your benefits and make an informed decision on your care and costs.

- Be responsible for your own care and plan choices. Don't rely solely upon your health care providers for the information. Ultimately, it is your responsibility to be informed of your costs.
- When they present you with an advance beneficiary notice, that is an indicator that there is something on the test that is questionable and Medicare may deny. It is an alert.
    - ○ It could be the test is not covered under Medicare; the frequency is too soon to have the test. It does not mean that if you actually need the test, Medicare will deny it.

- Talk with your doctor or ordering practitioner to see if this is necessary for your treatment and care. Your doctor can add extra codes to tell Medicare why it is necessary for the test or why it needs to be done sooner than Medicare requires.
- Ultimately, it is important to check with your secondary/retiree plan on how they cover circumstances like this.

CHAPTER 12

Medicare and Travel Coverage

Travel within the United States:

Original Medicare covers you anywhere in the United States at any Medicare-contracted doctor, hospital, or facility that accepts assignment.

- This includes all fifty states, the District of Columbia, Puerto Rico, Virgin Islands, Guam, American Samoa, and Northern Mariana Islands and will follow your coverage for your Medicare plan.
- Medicare Advantage plan (Part C) is limited on the coverage outside the area or your network.
    - Before you travel, first check with your health care plan travel benefits coverage.
    - These plans usually will cover emergency room visits and urgent care visits.
    - These plans may have rules that require a prior authorization. Contact your health plan prior to travel to find out what your coverage is, so you are aware of what your potential costs are.

Travel outside the United States/Foreign Country:

Original Medicare usually will not cover medical services outside the United States unless the care meets the following exceptions:

- Original Medicare will pay for emergency services in Canada only if you are traveling in a direct route without an unreasonable delay.
    - It has to be between Alaska and another state and the closest hospital is in Canada that can treat you.

- Original Medicare will cover medical care on a cruise ship if your ship is in United States territorial waters.
    - The ship has to be in a US port, within six hours of arriving to a US port or a departure from a US port.
- Original Medicare may cover nonemergency inpatient services, doctors, and ambulance cost in a foreign hospital only if that facility is closer, available, and equipped to treat your medical condition than the nearest US hospital. For example, if you live on the border of Mexico or Canada, this could happen.
- Medicare Advantage plan (Part C) may cover emergency care when you are traveling outside the United States. Check with your plan prior to traveling to check the coverage.
    - If it does provide coverage, verify specific steps needed to ensure the insurance covers this visit.
- Medigap plans C, D, F, G, M, and N do offer coverage in a foreign country for emergency care.
    - These plans have a $250 deductible that you have to pay first before the insurance will cover 80 percent of the cost and leave you the remaining 20 percent to pay. There is a lifetime limit of $50,000 for this benefit.[31]

---

[31] . "Your Medicare Coverage," https://www.medicare.gov/coverage/travel-need-health-care-outside-us.html.

Printed in the United States
By Bookmasters